Terrific Themes for Year-Round Fun

Creative Activities for All Curriculum Areas

by
Danielle Schultz

Carson-Dellosa Publishing Company, Inc.
Greensboro, North Carolina

Credits
Project Director: Sherrill B. Flora
Editors: Donna Walkush, Jennifer Weaver-Spencer
Layout Design: Betsy Peninger
Cover Design: Peggy Jackson
Contributing Writer: Lynn Ruppard
Cover Illustration: Ray Lambert
Inside Illustrations: Courtney Bunn
                        Jane Burns
                        Sabrina Burroughs
                        Mike Duggins
                        Melinda Fabian
                        Edward Fields
                        Erik Huffine
                        Julie Kinlaw
                        George Ling
                        Margeaux Lucas
                        Teresa Owens
                        J. J. Rudisill
                        Pam Thayer

Table of Contents

Metric Conversions

1 cup = 240 ml
2 cups = 475 ml
1/4 cup = 60 ml
1/3 cup = 80 ml
1/2 cup = 120 ml
2/3 cup = 160 ml
3/4 cup = 180 ml
1/4 teaspoon = 1.25 ml
1/2 teaspoon = 2.5 ml
1 teaspoon = 5 ml
1 tablespoon = 15 ml
1 fluid ounce = 30 ml

1/2 inch = 1.25 cm
1 inch = 2.5 cm
1 foot = 30.48 cm
13 x 9-inch baking pan =
32 x 23 cm baking tin

350°F = 150°C
400°F = 200°C

Welcome to School

Contents

What's Missing?

This activity may be completed as a group or individually. Copy and cut out the What's Missing? Cards (pages 6-9) and display them one at a time in front of the children. Have children study each picture and then ask if they can name what part of the object is missing. Have older students write descriptions of the missing parts. Ask them to describe what they think might happen if someone tried to use the object with the part missing.

Classmate Guess Who

Explain to children that you will describe a student in the class. As you describe the child, have students listen and try to guess who you are describing. When a student thinks that she knows who you are describing, have her raise her hand so that you can call on her to make a guess. Continue describing the child until someone guesses correctly. Repeat with other children. Begin your descriptions with a general trait such as hair or eye color. As you describe, become more specific so children can guess who you are describing.

Apple Tracing

Copy an Apple pattern (page 151) onto tagboard for each child onto tagboard. Give him a crayon or pencil, and his choice of red, green, or yellow construction paper. Show children how to hold the apples steady while tracing around them. Also show them how to line the patterns up if they move. Allow children to trace the patterns as many times as they like.

Our School Rules

Before the activity, create a target list of rules you would like to have in your classroom, but do not discuss them with students. Begin a discussion about the purpose of school rules. Ask children to describe what they think would happen if there were no rules to follow. The children should realize (with your help) that, without rules, children may not learn anything at school and may be in danger of getting hurt. Ask children to dictate what they think the rules should be and the consequences of breaking them. As children dictate, write their comments on chart paper or poster board. If they overlook an important rule, bring up a scenario that will help them think of an appropriate rule. Allow children's dictated rules to be your class rules.

Welcome to School Patterns
What's Missing? Cards

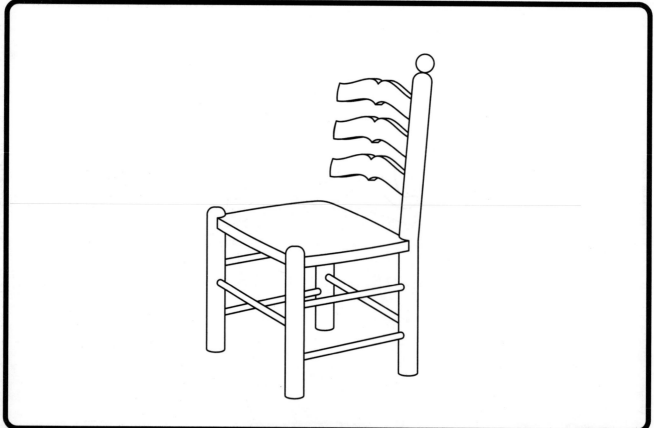

6

Welcome to School Patterns

What's Missing? Cards

CD-0817 *Terrific Themes for Year-Round Fun*

Welcome to School Patterns
What's Missing? Cards

CD-0817 *Terrific Themes for Year-Round Fun*

Welcome to School Patterns

What's Missing? Cards

9 CD-0817 *Terrific Themes for Year-Round Fun*

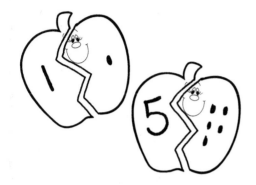

Apple Counting

Copy 10 Apple patterns (page 151) onto tagboard. Cut a wavy or zigzag vertical line through the center of each apple. On the left half of each apple, write a numeral from 1 to 10. On the right half of each apple, draw the corresponding number of seeds. Show children the apple halves and have them name the numerals and count the seeds on each half. Explain that they should count the number of seeds on the right half and match it to the left half that has the corresponding numeral. Place the apple halves at a math center for students to match during center time.

First vs. Last

Copy and cut out the First vs. Last cards (pages 11-12). Show a small group of children the cards. Ask them to explain what the word "first" means. Ask them the point out on the cards which object is first. Repeat with objects that are last. Then, ask children whether specific objects on the card are first or last. Continue this activity with small groups until each student has had a turn. Allow children to use the cards during center time.

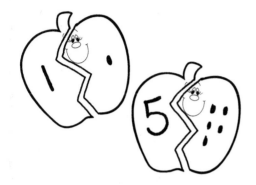

Shape Find

Begin by reviewing shapes (circle, square, triangle, rectangle, diamond, hexagon, star, etc.) with the class. Ask children to find different shapes around the room. Copy the Shape Find Bus pattern (page 13) and distribute the copies to students. Ask them to find and name as many shapes in the picture as they can. Then, have children color the pictures. Encourage them to take their pictures home and review the shapes in the picture with their parents.

Where Is the Pencil?

Using a pencil and a box, show students how the pencil can be in the following positions in relation to the box: inside, outside, beside, on top, under, over, in front, behind, left, right, etc. Hold the pencil in each position and have children use positional words to name the pencil's location. Then, call on students to place the pencil in specific positions.

Welcome to School Patterns
First vs. Last Cards

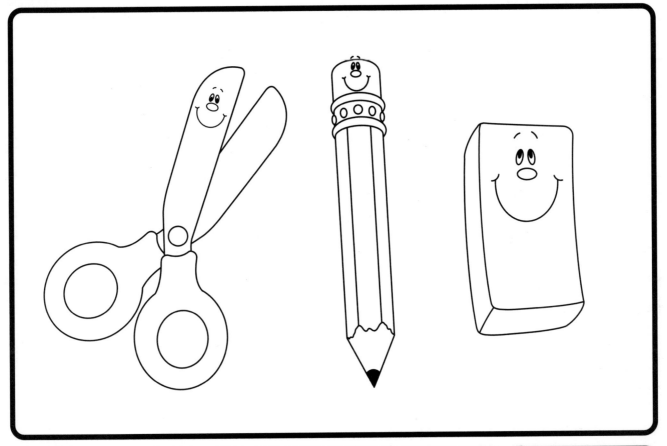

CD-0817 *Terrific Themes for Year-Round Fun*

Welcome to School Patterns

First vs. Last Cards

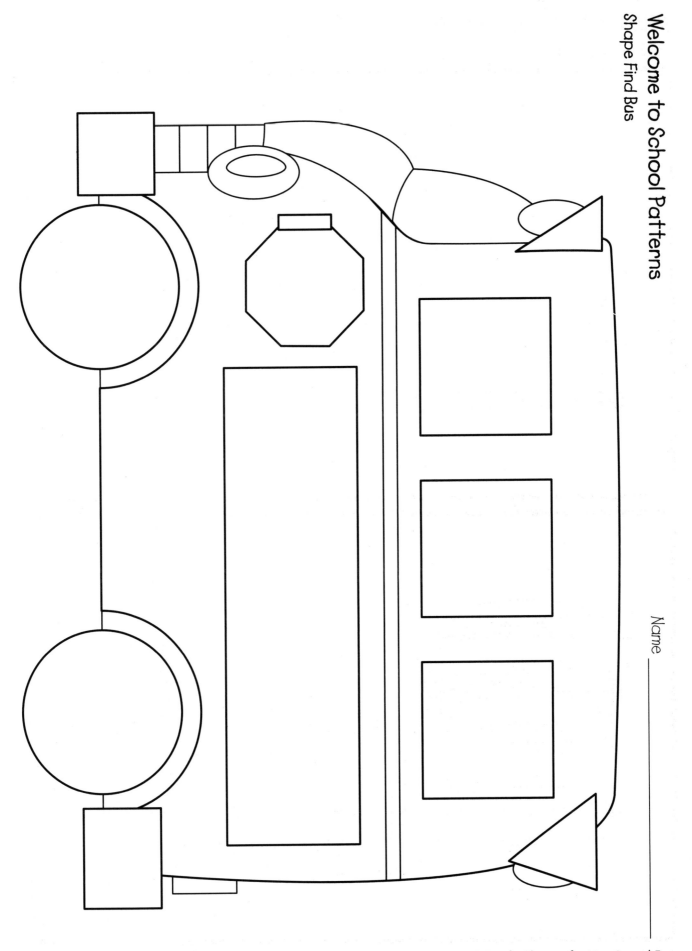

Name _____

Crayon Color Matching

Copy, color, and cut out the *Crayon Color Matching* patterns (page 15). The number of copies you need to make depends on the number of colors you want to teach or review. For each color, you should have a colored crayon pattern and matching circle. If desired, laminate these or glue them onto tagboard. Hold up each crayon and ask children to name its color. Repeat with each circle. Place tape on the back of each circle and ask children to attach each to a piece of poster board as they name its color. Repeat with the crayons, but have children attach each crayon beside the circle of the same color. Remove the tape and allow children to use the pieces during center time. Note: If you have a flannel board, the pieces can be made from felt and used on the flannel board.

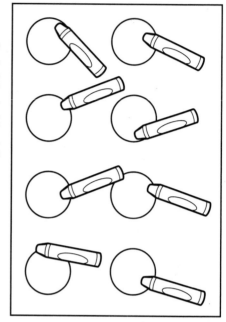

School Yard Friends

Ask children to think about the friends they see on the playground. Next, ask them what friends share their playground other than the children and adults. Explain that insects and other animals might also share the playground. Ask children to name the types of insects and other animals they have seen on the playground or at a park. Then, have the class go outside to see if they can spot any of the named animals. (Be sure to tell the children to follow a "Look, but don't touch!" rule as they look for animals and insects.) As a follow up, have children draw pictures of (and label) the creatures they found on the playground.

My Measurements

Copy the *My Measurements* pattern (page 16) for each child. Obtain a bathroom scale and measuring tape and invite a few children to measure themselves while the others are busy with center time tasks. Help them read the numbers on the scale. Encourage students to work with partners and help each other measure foot size, height, arm length, and waist size with the measuring tape. Assist children as they write down their measurements. Have each student draw himself in the space provided on the reproducible, or take an instant photograph of each child and tape it to his page. Repeat this activity at the end of the year and have each student compare his measurements between the two time periods.

Welcome to School Patterns
Crayon Color Matching

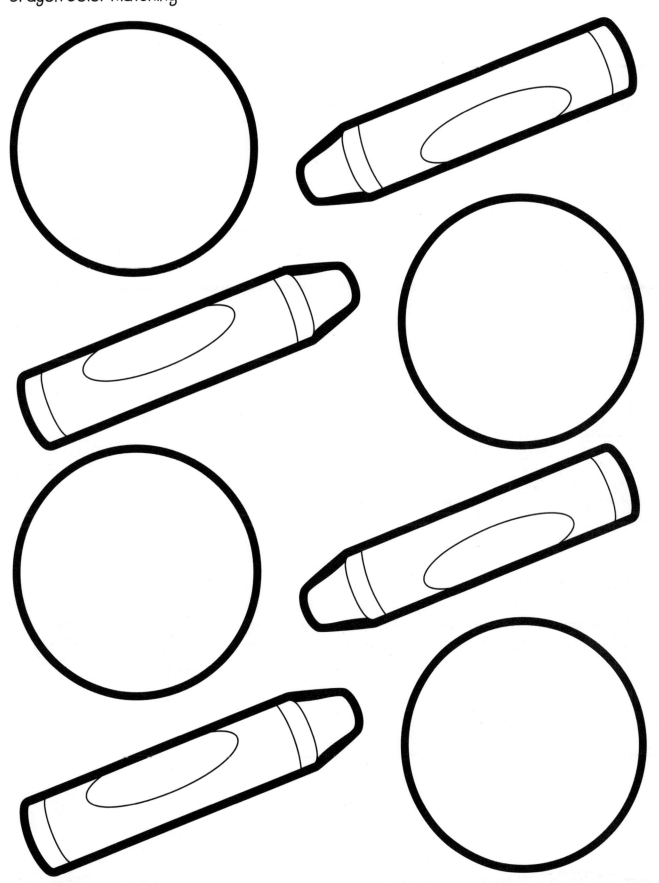

My Measurements

My name is _____ .

I am _____ tall.

My feet are _____ long.

My arms are _____ long.

My waist is _____ around.

I weigh _____ .

This is a picture of me.

Adapted Songs

This is the Way...
(to the tune of "Mulberry Bush")
This is the way we sit in a circle,
Sit in a circle, sit in a circle.
This is the way we sit in a circle,
Here at our school.

Other verses...
We read our books...here at our school.
We share with friends...here at our school.
We raise our hands...here at our school.
We build with blocks...here at our school.
We paint a picture...here at our school.
We eat our lunch...here at our school.
(Allow children to dramatize the actions as they sing.)

Where is Sally?
(to the tune of "Frere Jacques")
Class: "Where is Sally? Where is Sally?"
Sally: "Here I am. Here I am."
Class: "We're glad you came to learn,
        with us here at school."
Sally: "Thank you all. I am too."
(Repeat this song using each child's name.)

The Wheels on the Bus (Traditional)
The wheels on the bus go round and round,
Round and round, round and round.
The wheels on the bus go round and round,
All through the town.

Other verses...
The driver...says, "Move on back."
The horn...goes, "Beep, beep, beep."
The wipers...go, "Swish, swish, swish."
The money...goes, "Clink, clink, clink."
The people...go up and down.
The babies...go, "Waah, waah, waah."
The parents...go, "Shh, shh, shh."
(You may want to let children make up more verses.)

Little Schoolhouse
(to the tune of "I'm a Little Teapot")
I'm a little schoolhouse,
Happy all day;
The children inside me
Love to learn and play.

All the little children
Love their school.
They practice manners
And follow every rule.

Movement Activities

Marching in Line
Play a marching tune and have children practice marching in line. Choose a leader to lead the class around the room or on the playground.

Watching for Directions
Play music and instruct the class to watch you carefully. Move to the music in a variety of ways and instruct children to copy your movements. Allow children to take turns leading the group.

Schoolhouse Pasta Design

Copy the *Schoolhouse* pattern (page 19) onto red construction paper for each student. Place uncooked macaroni, small bowls of glue, and cotton swabs at an art table. Give each child a copy of the schoolhouse pattern and a cotton swab to apply glue, and instruct him to glue the uncooked macaroni onto the schoolhouse pattern. Allow students to make any design and use as many noodles as they wish. Children may opt to glue the noodles inside the schoolhouse, outside the schoolhouse, on the lines, or any combination of the three.

Community Mural

Cut an eight-foot length of white butcher paper and tape it to the floor in the classroom or on a sidewalk outside. Let children use crayons and/or markers to make a mural of their class and school. Explain that they may draw themselves, their classmates, their teacher, the classroom, the playground, etc. As each child finishes his part, ask him to title or describe what he has drawn. Write his title or description beside his section of the mural. Make sure students write their names beside their pictures (with your help, if necessary). When each child has had an opportunity to draw a part of the mural, display it in a prominent place under a caption that reads "Our Class Community."

School Bus Collage

Copy for each child a copy of the *School Bus Collage* pattern (page 20) onto white construction paper. Provide crayons for each student to color the bus, but not inside the bus windows. Allow children to look through magazines to find pictures of children's heads. Make sure students understand that they should choose pictures that are small enough to fit inside the bus windows. Have each child cut out four head shots and then glue each inside a bus window. Afterwards, use this art experience as the starting point for a discussion about bus safety rules and how students travel to school each day.

Welcome to School Patterns
Schoolhouse

Welcome to School Patterns
School Bus Collage

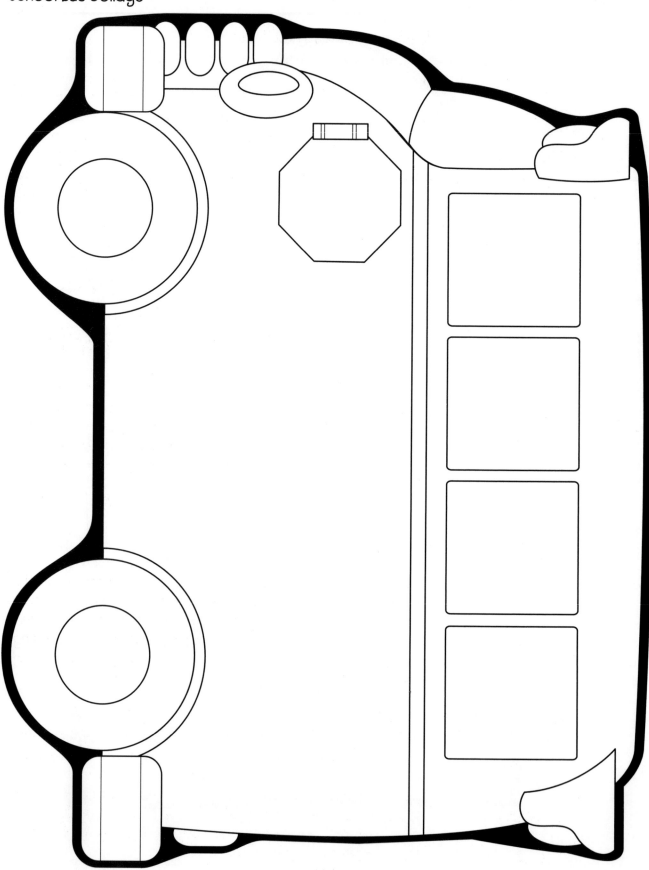

CD-0817 *Terrific Themes for Year-Round Fun*

Names Around the Circle

Have the children sit in a circle. Begin the activity by saying your name and have each student, in turn, say her name. Demonstrate how to walk around the circle touching each child on the head similar to Duck, Duck, Goose. Explain to children that as the walker touches each child's head, she should say that child's name. If the walker forgets a child's name, the child will say his name and then give the walker a task to complete. The task should be something short and simple such as "touch your toes," "do three jumping jacks," etc. Continue the game until everyone has had a turn being the walker.

Show Me

Explain to the children that the class is going to play a game of Show Me. Name an item in the classroom, such as a desk, pencil sharpener, window, door, etc., and select a child to find the item. Then, have him get up, touch (or point to) the item, and name it. Continue until each child has shown an item.

Name Game

Write each child's name on an index card. Show students the cards one at a time. Ask if anyone can identify the name on the card. If not, say the name and have children repeat it and spell it with you. Then, have the child whose name it is say and spell it for the class. Have students look for names that begin the same or have similar endings. Show the name cards periodically to allow students practice with reading their classmates' names.

Welcome to School!

Put a new spin on show-and-tell with this getting-to-know-you activity. Mail (or hand out at a before-school orientation) a letter to each student that welcomes him to your class, along with a personalized name tag for the student to wear on the first day of school. Greet students by name when they enter the classroom. On the first day of school, give each student a paper bag and tell him to place inside the bag a "mystery" object from home that tells something about him, and bring the bag to school the next day. Then, call on each student to come to the front of the class, introduce himself, and play 10 Questions by inviting the class to ask yes/no questions about the object in the bag. After the object has been guessed, have the student show the object and explain how it relates to him.

Outdoor Opposites

Gather children and say that they will be moving around the playground as instructed. Explain that two directions you will give together have words that are opposites. Then, give two-part directions such as "Jump rope forward two times, then jump rope backward two times" or "Walk slowly for five steps, then run quickly." Use other opposites such as over/under, top/bottom, up/down, loud/quiet, etc. You may want to give children opportunities to give directions.

All About Me

Contents

What Makes Us Special?

Gather children and explain that they should think about what makes each of them special and unique. Have them brainstorm these characteristics. As they come up with ideas, list them on a chalkboard or chart paper. Ideas may include the following: our bodies are all different, our personalities are all our own, everyone's home is unique, everyone's situation (family, possessions, school, etc.) is different, etc.

About Me Books

Copy each All About Me Book pattern (pages 24–29) for each child. Have the class work on one page of the book at a time, with each child drawing an illustration to match the topic of the page. As children work, ask them to dictate sentences about their pictures. Write the sentences above or below the pictures. When all pages are complete, give each child a piece of construction paper on which to illustrate a cover. When finished, gather all of the pages and staple them into a book. Allow children to share their books with the class, then send them home for parents' enjoyment.

About Me Poster

Gather a piece of poster board or chart paper for each child. Help each child make a poster about herself by gluing or writing any of the following items on the poster: a snapshot or drawn picture of herself, a favorite two-dimensional art project, handprints and footprints, height, weight, and other items that tell about the student. When the glue is dry, have her dictate sentences about herself and the items on the poster. Write these sentences on the poster. Display the posters and allow children to share them with their classmates.

"My Favorite Book" Day

Have each child bring in a favorite book from home. During circle time, give each child a turn to show his book to the class and briefly tell the story from memory. Have him tell why it is his favorite story, name his favorite part, and name his favorite character. If the child recalls, have him tell who gave the book to him. Use children's favorite books to read at story time over a period of several days.

Name _____

All About Me Book
A Picture of Me

Name _____

All About Me Book
A Picture of My Home

Name _____

All About Me Book
A Picture of My Family

CD-0817 *Terrific Themes for Year-Round Fun*

Name _____

All About Me Book
Pictures of My Favorites

My Favorite Food
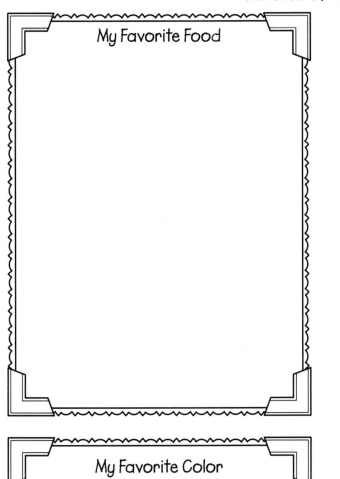

My Favorite Toy

My Favorite Color

My Favorite Book

Name _____

All About Me Book
A Picture of My Friends

Name _____

All About Me Book
What I Want to Be When I Grow Up

Measuring Center Information

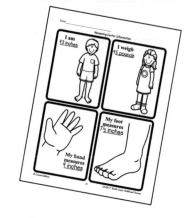

Make one copy of the Measuring Center Information pattern (page 31) for each child. Set up a measuring center with a scale and measuring tape. Let the children measure their heights, weights, and foot and hand lengths. Help them record the information on their Measuring Center Information sheets.

Mirror Ordering

Make a copy of the Mirror Ordering patterns (pages 32–33). Color and cut out the mirrors and laminate, if possible. Show the mirrors to children and have them describe what they see. They should notice that the mirrors are all different sizes. Explain that you would like them to place the mirrors in order from smallest to largest. Ask volunteers to find the smallest, the next largest, and so on, until the mirrors are in the correct order. Repeat so that each child has a turn. When finished, place the mirrors where children can work with them during center time.

More or Less Children

Make several copies of the More or Less Children patterns (pages 34–36). Color, cut apart, and laminate the cards. Have each child tell you the number of children in his family (including himself) and give him cards to match. For example, if a girl in the class has one brother, give her one boy card and one girl card. Then, have two children stand up and have the class decide which has more (or less) children in his family. They may use one-to-one correspondence to find out how many more children are in one family than another. You may also want to have two children count their cards and add the numbers together to see how many children there are in both families.

Which Are You?

Select one child to be the "counter." Have the "counter" count out five other children and line them up at the front of the classroom. Have the "counter" sit down with the class. Ask children in the line to count off from one to five. Have each child in the line tell you whether he is first, second, etc., in line. Then, ask the class who is at the beginning, middle, end, etc. Have children sit down, select a new "counter," and begin again. Continue until each child has been in the line.

Name _____

I am

_____

tall.

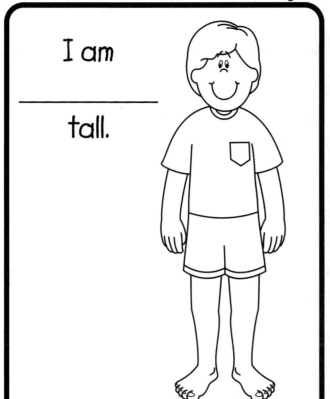

I weigh

_____ .

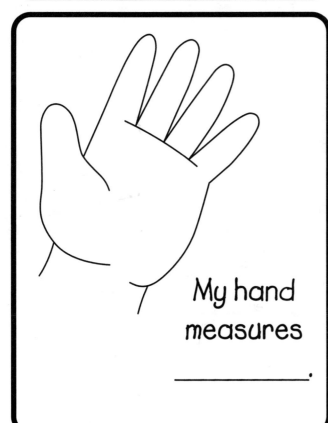

My hand

measures

_____ .

My foot

measures

_____ .

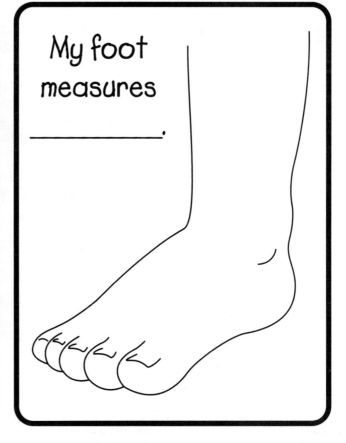

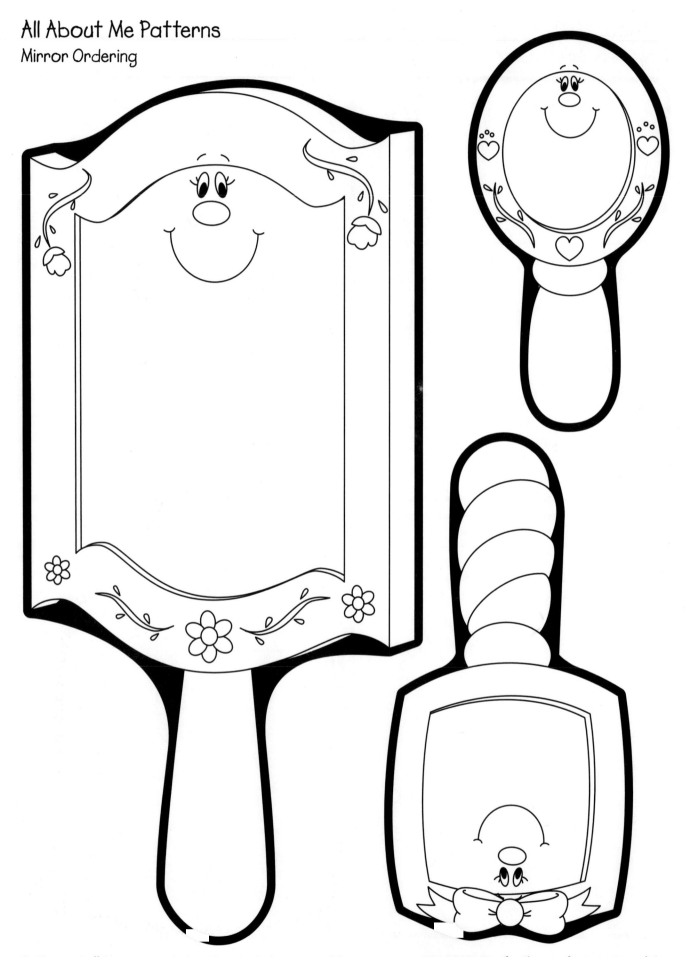

All About Me Patterns
Mirror Ordering

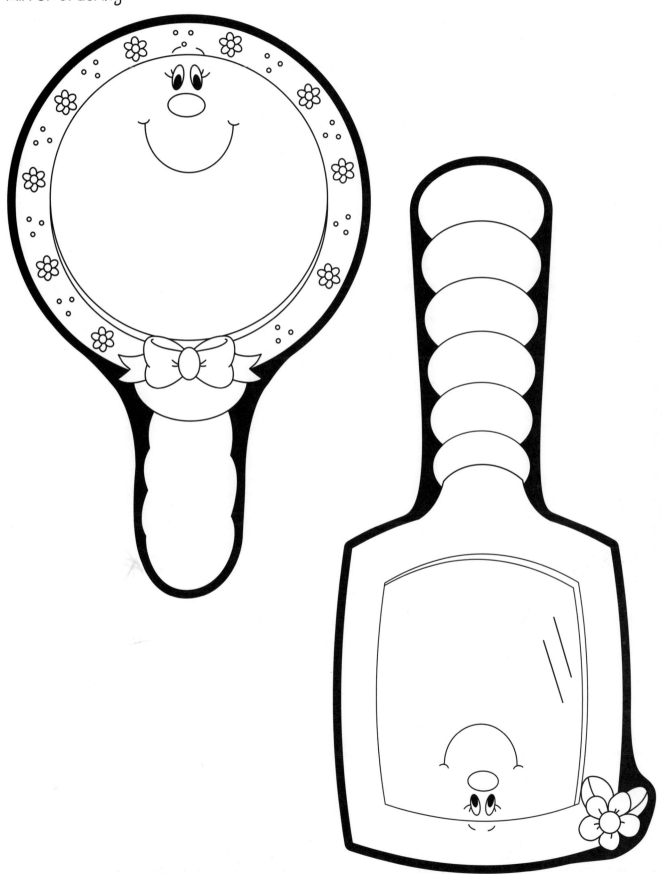

All About Me Patterns
More or Less Children

All About Me Patterns
More or Less Children

I Grow and Learn at My Own Pace

Make a copy of the Parent Information Letter (page 38) for each child to take home for his parents to complete. When the letters have been completed and returned, talk with children about how they have all grown and changed at different paces. Talk about how much they weighed and how long they were at birth. Make note of those that were smaller than others at birth, but are now bigger, and vice versa. To expand the activity, have students find out when they learned to walk, talk, etc. Point out that no matter when they began to walk (talk, etc.), each child learned to master the task at her own pace.

Using My Senses

Gather a variety of sensory exploration materials, such as a rose, small candies, sandpaper, a bell, etc., and place them out on a table. Invite students to use their senses to explore the items. Have them describe which senses they are using and how each item smells, looks, feels, and sounds. Have students identify items that can be experienced by taste, then allow each child to eat a piece of candy and describe how it tastes.

Magnifying Glass Play

Gather several magnifying glasses. Allow children to examine themselves under the magnifying glasses. Encourage them to look at their hands, fingerprints, fingernails, hairs on their arms, freckles, and so on. Have children make comparisons as to how their attributes look different with and without the magnifiers. Point out that we all have some similarities, but our unique attributes make us special individuals.

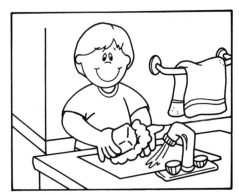

Keeping Myself Healthy

Gather children and ask them to name tasks that they do frequently or every day to keep themselves healthy and clean. As they list these tasks, have them identify the items they need in order to do them. Write the names of the items on a piece of chart paper and have children elaborate on how the items keep them healthy. Have them describe what might happen to them if they did not do these tasks or use these items. When the list is finished, allow each child to illustrate one task or item, then make a class book.

_____

Dear Parents,
Our class is completing a unit called "All About Me." During this unit, we will be discussing and comparing information about the children. Please fill out the questionnaire below regarding your child and return it by _____.

Thank you,

_____

Child's Full Name: _____

Address: _____

_____

Phone Number: _____

Birthday: _____

Birthplace: _____

Birth Weight and Height: _____

Age When First Word(s) Was Spoken: _____

First Word(s): _____

Age When First Steps Were Taken: _____

Parents' Names: _____

Siblings' Names and Ages: _____

_____

Grandparents' Names: _____

_____

Traditional Songs

"If You're Happy and You Know It"
"The More We Get Together"
"Head and Shoulders, Knees and Toes"
"The Hokey Pokey"
"Looby Loo"
"Punchinello"
"Mary Wore Her Red Dress"
"Put Your Fingers in the Air"
"Where is Thumbkin?"

Adapted Songs

Isabelle Is Here Today
(to the tune of "Farmer in the Dell")
Isabelle* is here today,
Isabelle is here today.
We're so happy, yes we are.
Isabelle is here today.

*Sing each child's name in turn. Invite the child to jump or dance in the circle while it is her turn. You may finish with, "The boys are here today...," "The girls are here today...," and "Everyone is here today...," and allow the appropriate children to jump or dance.

We Are Growing
(to the tune of "Where Is Thumbkin?")
We are growing, we are changing,
Everyday, everyday.
All of us are different, but each of us is special,
In our own way, in our own way.

Movement Activities

Music Interpretation
Play short excerpts of a variety of music types for children. Allow them to move any way they wish to express their feelings about the different types of music.

My Space
Talk with children about the need for personal space. Have children bring in towels from home or use nap mats and allow them to sit and play in their own spaces on the towels or mats.

All About Me

... Social Awareness

How Do You Feel Today?

Make a "How Do You Feel Today?" board on chart paper, a chalkboard, or a pocket chart, using the How Do You Feel Today? patterns (pages 41–42). Color, cut out, and laminate the patterns. Write each child's name on an index card. Gather children and explain that they should think about how they are feeling that day. Discuss the emotions and feelings shown on the cards. Place the index cards with children's names on a table or the floor. Tell children that when you call a name, you would like for that child to find her name (offer assistance if needed), then place her card next to the face showing how she is feeling that day.

How I Help at Home

Gather children and tell them that you would like them to think about all of the ways that they help their families. As each child takes a turn dictating his helpful deeds, list the deeds on a piece of chart paper along with the name of the child. When the list is finished, display it for parents to enjoy.

Feelings Puppets

Make feelings puppets from paper plates and Feeling Puppets patterns (pages 43–45). Color and cut out the patterns, then glue each to a paper plate. Glue a craft stick handle to the back of each plate. Give each child a turn with each puppet and allow him to name something that makes him feel like the face on the puppet. Let children use the puppets during center time to act out situations that cause different emotions.

How Would You Feel?

Make a copy of the How Would You Feel? worksheet (page 46) for each child. Ask children to look at and describe the pictures in both columns. Explain that each student should draw a line from each picture in the first column to the picture in the second column to show how she would feel in that situation. Let them know that there are no right or wrong answers and that they can have more than one line from some emotions and none from others. When the worksheets are complete, encourage children to explain their answers.

© Carson-Dellosa 40 CD-0817 *Terrific Themes for Year-Round Fun*

CD-0817 *Terrific Themes for Year-Round Fun*

All About Me Patterns
How Do You Feel Today?

CD-0817 *Terrific Themes for Year-Round Fun*

All About Me Patterns
Feelings Puppets

CD-0817 *Terrific Themes for Year-Round Fun*

All About Me Patterns
Feelings Puppets

CD-0817 *Terrific Themes for Year-Round Fun*

All About Me Patterns
Feelings Puppets

How Would You Feel?

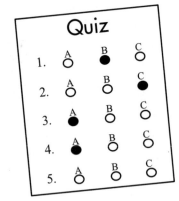

All About Me

My Glittery Hand

Help each child trace his hand onto a round piece of construction paper or a paper plate. Have the child fill inside the hand lines with glue and sprinkle with glitter. When dry, shake off excess glitter and write "My Hand," the child's name, and the date on the back. Punch a hole in the top and attach a ribbon hanger to make a keepsake.

My Silhouette

Make a silhouette of each child's profile from the neck up. Use an overhead projector to cast light onto a wall or screen. Have one child at a time stand between the light and the wall so that her shadow appears. Tape a piece of construction paper where the shadow of the child's head is. Trace around the edge of the shadow onto the construction paper. Allow children to decorate their silhouettes, then hang their finished pieces around the room.

My Name

Option 1: Write each child's name in block letters on a piece of construction paper. Allow children to decorate their names using crayons, markers, glue and glitter, stickers, pasta shapes, etc. Have children name the letters as they decorate them.
Option 2: Cut out the letters of each child's name. Allow children to come up and pick out the letters they need to form their names. Each child can decorate the letters with crayons, markers, stamps, stickers, or glitter and then glue the letters in the correct order onto construction paper.

Self-Portrait Puzzles

Give each child an 8 1/2" x 11" piece of tagboard and crayons. Explain that you would like him to fill the page with a picture of his face. Tell children that they will be using scissors to cut the pictures into puzzles. As each child cuts his picture, have him write his name or initials on the back of each piece, with your assistance if necessary. Label one sandwich bag with each child's name and have students place the completed pieces in their bags. When the puzzles are finished, allow children to trade self-portraits puzzles and put them together.

Emotions Die Roll

Make a copy of the Emotions Die pattern (page 49) and glue it to tagboard. When dry, cut and assemble into a die as directed. The completed project is a tagboard die showing an emotion face on each side. Have students sit in a circle. Show the die and have them name the emotion shown on each side of the die. Allow a variety of answers for each; one child might read a face as angry while another child reads it as frustrated. Tell children that they will each have a turn rolling the die. When a child has rolled the die, she should name the emotion shown on the face of the child. She should then name a few things that might make her feel that way. Last, have her describe a time when she felt that emotion. Continue until each child has had a turn to roll the die.

Just Like Me

Tell children that you will play a game in which they look for similarities between themselves and other children. Have the class sit in a circle and use a similarity between yourself and a child to demonstrate. For example, find a child with hair the same color as yours. Stand up and say, "I have (red) hair. Kayla has (red) hair just like me." Explain that you will go around the circle giving each child a turn. Let children know that they may choose any attribute to name as a similarity between themselves and another child. They may use physical similarities, likes and dislikes, types of clothing, etc.

I Believe You

Select a child to come to the front of the group and cover her eyes. Next, point to another child and have him say, "My name is _____," in a funny voice (not necessarily his own name). The first child then tells whether or not she believes the named classmate is the one who really spoke. Give each child a turn to guess and speak in a funny voice.

"I Am Special" Parade

Have children make ribbons using the "I Am Special" Ribbons patterns (page 50). Make one copy of the pattern for each child, then have him decorate it and cut it out. Let students wear their ribbons as they march in an "I Am Special" parade around the playground or school. Encourage children to work together to march in a line and wave at their schoolmates as they go by. At the end of the parade, gather children and, as each enters the classroom, have her name one reason why she is special.

All About Me Patterns
Emotions Die

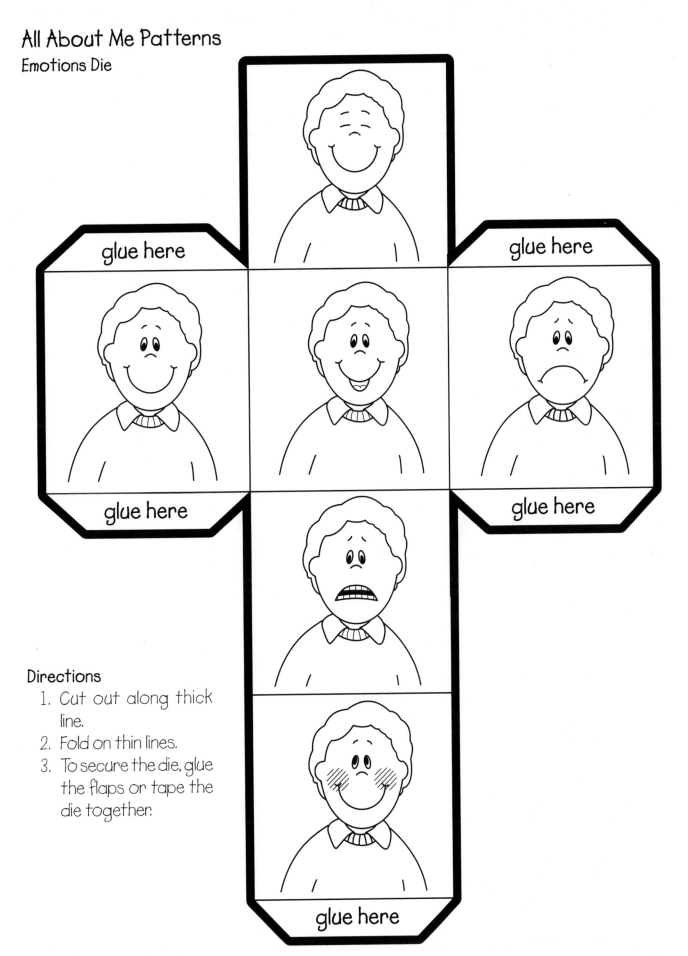

glue here

glue here

glue here

glue here

glue here

Directions
1. Cut out along thick line.
2. Fold on thin lines.
3. To secure the die, glue the flaps or tape the die together.

49

All About Me Patterns
"I Am Special" Ribbons

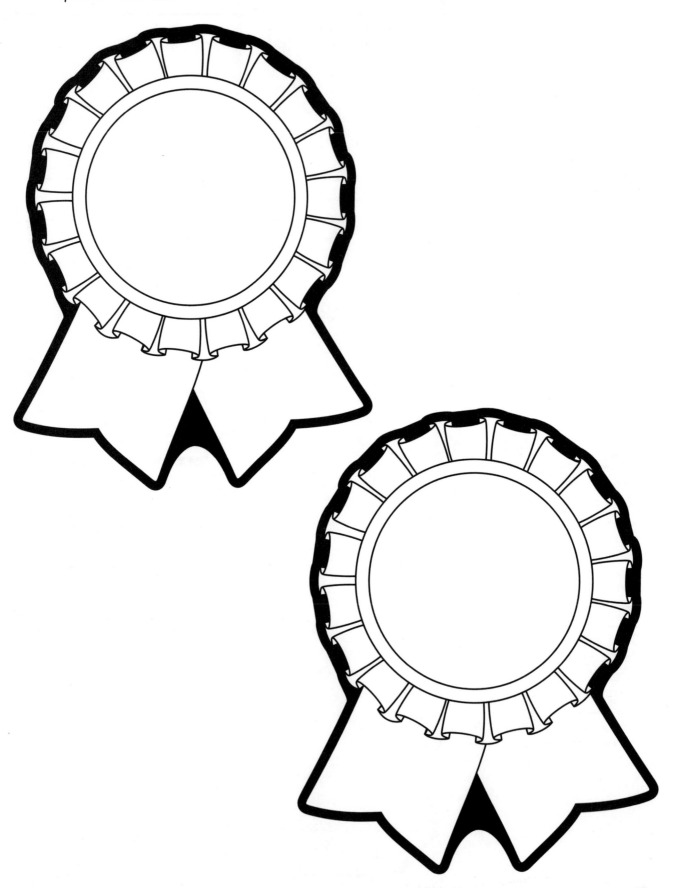

CD-0817 *Terrific Themes for Year-Round Fun*

Alphabet

Contents

Sandpaper Alligators

Curriculum Area: Art

Make a few tagboard alligator stencils from the Alligator pattern (below). Place the patterns, along with scissors, a few sheets of sandpaper, crayons, glue, and construction paper on an art table. Allow each child to trace the Alligator pattern onto the sandpaper, then cut out. Next, suggest that the child color the alligator body with the crayon of her choice. Then, have her glue the alligator body to a piece of construction paper and add background scenery.

Animal Cracker Sort

Curriculum Areas: Language Arts, Math

Purchase a package or two of animal-shaped cookies or crackers. Gather one small bowl for each type of animal in the package. Trace one of each animal onto construction paper, cut out, and tape to a bowl. Allow children to take turns sorting the animal crackers into bowls with the matching pictures taped to them.

Anteater Hunt

Curriculum Areas: Games, Math

Copy, color, and cut out the Ant pattern (below). You will need about five ants per child. While children are with another teacher, hide the ants on the playground. Take the group outside and allow them to pretend to be anteaters and find the ants. Have each child stop hunting when she has found five ants. If children enjoy the game you may allow one or two children to hide the ants while the others close their eyes. When the ants have all been found again, allow two more children to hide them.

Songs and Rhymes

"The Ants Go Marching"
"Apples and Bananas"
"Alouette"
"Alphabet Song"

Traditional Activity

Paper Airplanes

Bone Prints

Curriculum Area: Art

Purchase a box of bone-shaped dog treats. Gather smocks for students, a few shallow bowls or pie tins, tempera paint, and construction paper. Pour a few colors of paint into the bowls or tins and place them on an art table along with the dog bones and construction paper. Allow children to press the bones into the paint and onto their papers to create designs. If the colors of paint mix on the paper, discuss the new colors children made.

Bumblebee Balloons

Curriculum Area: Art

Purchase a package of yellow balloons. Gather a few black permanent markers and smocks. Allow each child to blow up a balloon. After each child puts on a smock, let him use a black marker to create a bumblebee by drawing stripes and a face on the balloon. Add wings made from tissue paper or laminating film.

Butterfly Catching

Curriculum Area: Games

Gather several sheets of colored paper and a few wire food strainers. Cut the colored paper into butterfly shapes. Take the butterflies and strainers outside. Allow each child to take a few butterflies and a strainer. Tell them that they should toss the butterflies into the air, then try to catch them with the strainers. Have children take turns as necessary. You may also allow children to use small nets if strainers are unavailable.

Balloon Band

Curriculum Area: Music and Movement

Provide a balloon for each child and have her blow up her balloon. Then, show the children how to hold the mouth of a balloon while letting the air escape. The balloon will make different noises. Play a song and allow children to "play" their balloons along with the music.

Berry Basket Toss

Curriculum Area: Games

Gather several clean, plastic berry baskets and one small ball for every two baskets. While on the playground, pair children and allow them to toss the small ball from one basket to the other.

Songs and Rhymes

"Bingo"
"Boom, Boom, Ain't It Great to Be Crazy"
"Baa, Baa, Black Sheep"
"The Bear Went Over the Mountain"
"Baby Bumblebee"

Cookie Cutter Prints
Curriculum Area: Art

Gather several different sizes and shapes of cookie cutters, tempera paint, and paper. Place the materials on an art table. Allow children to take turns making cookie cutter prints by dipping the cookie cutters into shallow bowls of tempera paint and pressing the cookie cutters onto paper.

Caterpillars
Curriculum Area: Art

Option 1: Allow children to glue craft pom-poms onto craft sticks to form caterpillar bodies. Let them glue or twist on chenille craft sticks for antennae.

Option 2: Make one large leaf from construction paper for each child. Place glue, scissors, and a few different colored skeins of yarn on an art table. Allow children to cut the yarn into 1" to 4" pieces and glue the yarn to their leaves to make caterpillars.

Cotton Ball Toss
Curriculum Areas: Games, Math

Obtain a package of cotton balls and a bucket. Place the bucket on the floor and mark a line on the floor about two feet away from the bucket. Give each child three to five cotton balls. Allow them to take turns standing on the line and throwing cotton balls into the bucket. Each time, have children count how many cotton balls landed in the bucket.

Cookie Counting
Curriculum Area: Math

Copy the Cookie Counting patterns (below). Show the cookies to children and allow them to take turns telling you how many chocolate chips are on each cookie. If you have an advanced group, allow them to add or subtract to find the difference in the numbers of chips on two cookies.

Candle Count
Curriculum Areas: Math, Science

Purchase a few packages of birthday candles in assorted colors. Have children name the colors of the candles and sort them by color. Have the children count how many candles are in each category.

Song
"Camptown Ladies"

Alphabet

Dd

Designer Doughnuts

Curriculum Area: Art

Enlarge the Designer Doughnut pattern (right) and make a tagboard stencil from it. Using the stencil, make a few dough-nuts from brown and/or white construction paper for each child in the class. Gather a few empty squeeze bottles (dish washing detergent, hand lotion, shampoo, etc.) and fill them with thick tempera paint. Allow children to use the squeeze bottles of tempera, markers, crayons, or other materials to decorate their own designer doughnuts.

Doily Painting

Curriculum Area: Art

Purchase enough paper doilies for each child to have one. Gather small squeeze bottles of food coloring in assorted colors. Allow each child to have a turn using drops of food coloring to make colorful designs on his doily.

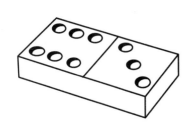

Domino Prints

Curriculum Areas: Art, Math

Gather a set of dominoes (with concave dots and flat edges), stamp pads of assorted colors, and paper. Allow each child to press the dominoes into the stamp pads and then press them onto paper to make designs. As children work, have them count the number of dots on each domino.

Dogs and Cats

Curriculum Area: Games

Gather children and select one child to be the dog. Explain that the dog's mission is to catch a cat. Explain that all of the other children are cats. They should meow as they run on the playground and try to stay away from the dog. When the dog catches a cat, the cat becomes the new dog and play begins again.

Songs and Rhymes

"Down by the Station"
"Hey Diddle Diddle"
"Deedle Deedle Dumpling"

Traditional Activities

Duck, Duck, Goose
Drop the Hankie
Doggie, Doggie, Where's Your Bone?

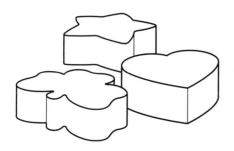

Eraser Prints

Curriculum Area: Art

Gather several fun-shaped erasers, tempera paint, small bowls, and paper. Pour a few colors of tempera paint into the small bowls. Place the bowls, along with the erasers and paper, on an art table. Allow each child to have a turn pressing the erasers into the paint, then onto paper to make creative print pictures.

Rolling Egg Painting

Curriculum Area: Art

Gather a few unpeeled hard-boiled eggs, tempera paint, a slotted spoon, paper, and a shoe box large enough for the paper to lie flat on the bottom. While children are busy with other tasks, allow one or two children to do this activity as you guide them. First have a child select a piece of paper and place it into the shoe box. Next, have her take an egg, immerse it in a cup of the paint, then use the slotted spoon to scoop the egg out of the paint and onto the paper. Have the child tilt the box so that the rolling egg will create a design. Allow her to continue using the same or different colors of paint until her design is complete.

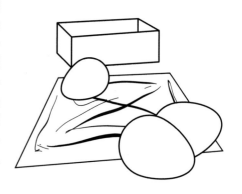

Eyedropper Painted E's

Curriculum Area: Art

Cut one large E from construction paper for each student. Place small bowls of tempera paint and eyedroppers on an art table. Allow children to use the eyedroppers and paint to create designs on their E's.

Elephant March

Curriculum Area: Games

Gather children while they are playing outside. Talk with them about elephants and explain that elephants often move in herds. Ask children what they think a herd of elephants looks and sounds like as it goes by. Allow them to take turns being the "lead" elephant as they move in a herd on the playground. You may also allow children to play a version of "Follow the Leader" by having them hold hands and walk in a line around the playground like circus elephants.

Fabric Collage
Curriculum Area: Art

Gather (or have parents bring in) fabric scraps. Place the scraps on an art table, along with scissors and glue. Allow each child to make a collage by cutting fabric she selects into various shapes and gluing them onto a piece of construction paper. If a child tells you something specific she made with her fabric scraps, note this at the bottom of the picture.

Footprint F's
Curriculum Areas: Art, Language Arts

Show children the letter F. Have them name as many words as they can that begin with the letter F. Allow each child to make a footprint F by stepping with a bare foot into a shallow tray of tempera paint, then stepping onto a large piece of construction paper to form the letter F.

Fishing for Balloons
Curriculum Area: Games

Gather a large bucket or small wading pool, a few wire strainers, and a package of small balloons. Fill the bucket half full with water. Blow up the balloons to about the size of an adult fist and place them in the pool. Allow children to take turns using the wire strainers to "fish" for the balloons.

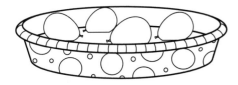

Graphing Favorites
Curriculum Areas: Math, Social Awareness

Select a favorite topic for children to use as a graph topic (such as favorite color, food, television program, etc.). Gather a large piece of poster board or use the chalkboard to create a graph. Allow each child to place a card with his name on it in the column showing his favorite. When each child's name has been placed, have children count the names and tell which item had the most. They may also count the differences between two columns, add two columns, etc.

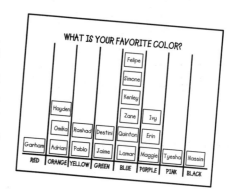

Songs and Rhymes

"Farmer in the Dell"
"Five Little Monkeys"
"Frere Jacques"
"Froggy Went A-Courtin'"

Traditional Activities

Flannel Board
Follow the Leader
Flying Disc (such as Frisbee® brand)

Giant "G" Drawing

Curriculum Areas: Art, Language Arts

Cut out a large G from butcher paper. Tape the G to the floor. Have children work together to draw uppercase and lowercase G's and items that start with the letter G on the butcher paper G. You may have children give special notice to those letters or pictures drawn with colors that begin with the letter G such as green, gray, gold, etc.

Gingerbread Cookie Lace-Up

Curriculum Areas: Art, Language Arts

Use the Gingerbread Cookie pattern (page 59) to make one gingerbread cookie on brown construction paper for each child. Give each child one pattern and let him decorate it. Next, allow the class to use a hole punch to punch holes around the edges of their cookies. Last, allow them to lace white yarn in and out of the holes to resemble frosting.

Golf Ball Painted G's

Curriculum Area: Art

Gather a few golf balls, shallow bowls of paint, construction paper cut into the shape of a G, and shoe boxes large enough for the construction paper G's to lie flat on the bottom. Allow each child to have a turn dipping a golf ball into the paint, then rolling it around on the G inside the box. Allow each child to continue until his design is complete.

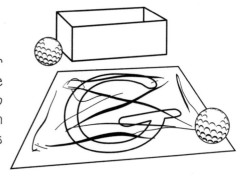

Gallop and Giggle Chase

Curriculum Area: Games

Gather the class and explain that you will play a silly version of tag. Tell them that you will select two children to be "it." Explain that everyone must gallop while playing the game. Tell children that there is one safe way to keep from being tagged: the students who are not "it" must stop and giggle. When a child is tagged, she joins the "its" and helps tag the others until everyone has been tagged.

Songs and Rhymes

"The Green Grass Grows All Around"
"Good Night, Ladies"
"Goosey, Goosey Gander"

CD-0817 *Terrific Themes for Year-Round Fun*

Alphabet Pattern
Gingerbread Cookie

CD-0817 *Terrific Themes for Year-Round Fun*

Alphabet

Huge Handprint H

Curriculum Area: Art

Obtain a piece of butcher paper and cut it into a large letter H. Pour different colors of tempera paint into pie tins or other shallow containers. Allow children to cover the H with their handprints. When the paint is dry, display the H for children and parents to enjoy.

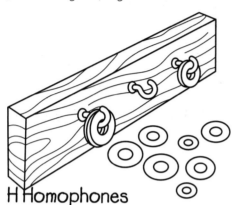

Hooks and Washers

Curriculum Areas: Language Arts, Math

Purchase a piece of finished wood approximately $1' \times 12' \times \frac{1}{2}"$ and one pack each of assorted sizes of cup hooks and washers at a hardware store. Screw the hooks securely into the wood. Allow children to hang the washers on the hooks. After they are familiar with the activity, encourage children to sort and hang the washers on the hooks by size.

H Homophones

Curriculum Area: Language Arts

Begin a discussion with children about homophones. Explain that homophones are two words that sound the same but have different meanings. Give children one of the words from the following sets to define: *hair* and *hare*, *hear* and *here*, *heel* and *heal.* Then, have them define each word's homophone. Allow children to brainstorm homophones beginning with other letters.

Hop Away

Curriculum Area: Games

Hop Away is similar to the traditional game of Duck, Duck, Goose. Have the class sit in a circle and select one child to be "it." "It" hops on one foot around the circle and tags a classmate, then continues to hop around the circle in the same direction. The tagged child hops in the opposite direction from "it." The child who reaches the tagged child's spot first sits down. The child left standing becomes or remains "it."

Songs and Rhymes

"Hickory, Dickory, Dock"
"Hokey Pokey"
"Happy Birthday"
"Hickety, Pickety"
"Home on the Range"

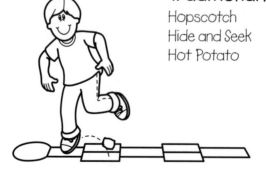

Traditional Activities

Hopscotch
Hide and Seek
Hot Potato

Alphabet

Initial Art

Curriculum Areas: Art, Language Arts

Cut out the initials of each child in the class from construction paper. Place the letters on a table in alphabetical order. Have each child pick out his initials. Then, allow children to decorate their initials in ways that tell others about them.

Ice Painting

Curriculum Areas: Art, Science

Gather powdered tempera paint, construction paper, craft sticks, and ice cubes. Sprinkle powdered tempera on each child's paper and have her to move a piece of ice through the powder with a craft stick. As the ice melts, it will mix with the powder, creating designs. Have children describe what is happening.

Inchworm Hunt

Curriculum Areas: Games, Math, Art

Make a stencil from the Inchworm pattern (right). Trace about five inchworms onto construction paper for each child. Cut them out and hide them on the playground or around the room. Allow children to hunt for the inchworms, counting as they go. Instruct them to stop hunting once they have found five inchworms. Finally, allow children to decorate the worms they have found, then glue them onto construction paper.

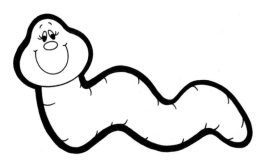

Allergy and Food Preference Note

Before completing any food activity, ask parental permission and inquire about children's food allergies. Common food allergies include peanuts and other nuts, dairy, eggs, berries, etc. Parents may have religious or other preferences that will prevent children from eating certain foods.

Ice Cream Island

Curriculum Areas: Snack, Science, Language Arts

Gather large, clear plastic cups, spoons, straws, vanilla ice cream, and fruit-flavored juice drink. Talk with the class about the word *island* and help them define and describe it. Then, allow each child to make an ice cream "island" by placing vanilla ice cream into a cup, and filling the cup with juice. While children enjoy their snacks, ask them to describe how their snacks are like islands.

Songs and Rhymes

"The Itsy Bitsy Spider"
"I'm a Little Teapot"
"If You're Happy and You Know It"
"I've Been Workin' on the Railroad"

Alphabet

Jazzy Jeans

Curriculum Area: Art

Make one copy of the Jazzy Jeans pattern (page 63) for each child. Explain that you will allow each to design a pair of jeans any way they wish. Allow children to use markers, crayons, sequins, glitter, etc., to make their Jazzy Jeans.

Jelly Bean Collage

Curriculum Area: Art

Create several jelly-bean shaped stencils (3" to 4" long) from tagboard. Place the patterns, along with colored construction paper, scissors, pencils, and glue, on an art table. Explain to children that they should trace the jelly bean patterns onto construction paper, then cut out the jelly beans. Tell them that they may do this several times. Then, let children glue their jelly beans to large pieces of construction paper to make collages.

Jigsaw Puzzle

Curriculum Areas: Art, Language Arts

Give each child a piece of tagboard. Explain that she should use crayons to draw a picture that covers the entire piece of tagboard. Let children know that when they are finished they cut their pictures into jigsaw puzzles. If necessary, assist each child with cutting and write each child's name or initials on the back of each piece of her puzzle. Place each puzzle in a resealable plastic bag, and allow children to trade and work each other's puzzles.

Jars and Lids Game

Curriculum Areas: Games, Math

Gather several different sizes of nonbreakable jars and their lids. Separate the jars from the lids and place them in different containers. During center time, allow a few children to work with the jars and lids and match each jar with its lid.

Jingle Bells

Curriculum Area: Music and Movement

Jingle bells are not just for the holidays! Allow children to shake bells while they sing this song (to the traditional tune): *Jingle bells, jingle bells, jingle all the way. Oh, what fun it is to jingle jingle bells all day!*

Songs and Rhymes

"Jack and Jill"
"Jack, Be Nimble"
"Jimmy Crack Corn"
"John Jacob Jingleheimer Schmidt"

Alphabet Pattern
Jazzy Jeans

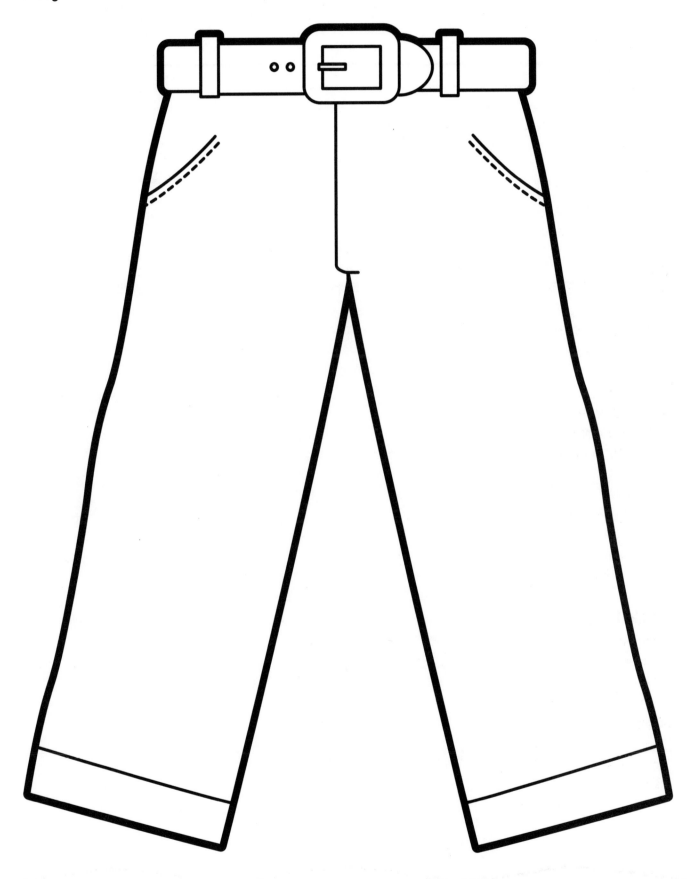

Alphabet

Kids' Collage

Curriculum Areas: Art, Social Awareness

Gather several old magazines containing pictures of children. Also gather scissors, glue, and construction paper and place them on an art table. Explain to children that they should look through the magazines and find pictures of children. They should then cut out the pictures and glue them to their papers to make collages. As students are working, have them describe the children they see in the pictures and the emotions the children might be feeling.

Kitchen Gadget Prints

Curriculum Area: Art

Gather several kitchen gadgets suitable for print-making such as spatulas, spoons, potato mashers, forks, etc. Place the gadgets, along with shallow bowls of tempera paint and construction paper, on an art table. Allow children to press the gadgets into the paint, then onto their papers to make prints.

Ketchup Bottle Painting

Curriculum Area: Art

Gather an empty squeezable ketchup container, red paint, paintbrushes, and white construction paper. Place the red paint into the ketchup container and allow each child to have a turn painting with the red paint "ketchup."

Key Matching

Curriculum Areas: Math

Gather 10-12 keys. (You may want to ask parents to bring in old keys.) Trace the keys onto a large piece of poster board. During center time, allow one or two children to match the keys with their outlines.

Kangaroo Races

Curriculum Area: Games

Gather children and explain that they will have a race. Show them a designated starting point and finish line. Tell children that the twist to this race is that it is a kangaroo race. Allow them to race while jumping like kangaroos.

Song

"Kookaburra"

Alphabet

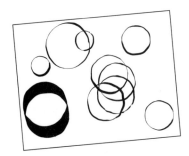

Lid Printing

Curriculum Area: Art

Gather the lids from different types of jars and plastic tubs. Place them on an art table along with shallow bowls of tempera paint and construction paper. Allow each child a turn at the table dipping the lids into paint and pressing them onto pieces of construction paper to make colorful designs.

Lace Collage

Curriculum Areas: Art, Social Awareness

Gather several different types and sizes of lace. (You may wish to ask parents to bring in scraps that they may have at home.) Place the lace on a table and allow each child to have a turn cutting the lace as desired and gluing it to a piece of construction paper to make a collage. As children work, have them name people they know who wear lace.

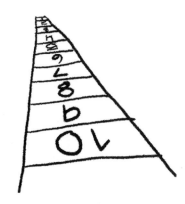

Ladder Climb

Curriculum Areas: Outdoor Games, Math

Draw a ten-rung ladder with chalk on a sidewalk or blacktop (similar to a hopscotch board). Divide children into groups of five and let each group play the game at a different time. Explain to children in the group that they will each take a turn rolling a die. Tell them that when they have rolled the die, they will count the number of dots and move that number of spaces. Let children know that the spaces will get crowded and they must try to find a spot and keep their balance to stay in the space. If they "fall off" the ladder, they must go back to the beginning. The first group to reach the tenth space wins.

Ladles

Curriculum Area: Language

Gather several ladles, large bowls, and either rice or cotton balls. Allow children to take turns moving the rice or cotton balls from one bowl to the other using the ladles. If you wish to make this an activity promoting left-to-right skills, you may have children use only two bowls. They are then to move the material from a full bowl on the left to an empty bowl on the right. When finished, they should swap the bowls and begin again.

Songs and Rhymes

"London Bridge"
"Looby Lou"
"Little Miss Muffet"
"Little Bunny Foo-Foo"

Alphabet

Macaroni Mosaics
Curriculum Area: Art

Purchase several boxes of different sizes of macaroni and other pasta. Place the macaroni on an art table along with paper and glue. Allow children to make pictures on construction paper by gluing the macaroni onto their papers. You may want to allow children to paint their creations with tempera paint after the glue has dried.

Magazine Maps
Curriculum Areas: Art, Social Awareness

Gather several used magazines and a few maps. Talk with children about maps. Explain that maps are pictures that help us find out where we are and how to get where we want to go. Have children describe the places they know in their area. Tell them that you would like them to find pictures in the magazines to help them make maps. Have them cut out and glue the pictures onto construction paper to make their neighborhoods, the school, etc. They may also use crayons or markers to draw or write in other details for their maps.

Marshmallow Mountains
Curriculum Area: Art

Gather a few bags of mini marshmallows, glue, and tagboard. Give each child a piece of tagboard and explain that she should use the marshmallows and glue to make a mountain on her piece of tagboard. When the glue is dry, you may wish to allow the children to paint their mountains with tempera paint.

Mirror, Mirror
Curriculum Area: Games

Gather children and have them form pairs. Explain that you want them to face each other. Tell them that they should pretend that they are looking in a mirror. One child should be the lead, with the other child mimicking every move the first child makes, just like a reflection in a mirror. After a few minutes, have children switch leads and continue.

Songs and Rhymes
"Miss Mary Mack"
"Muffin Man"
"Mary Had a Little Lamb"
"Mary, Mary, Quite Contrary"
"The Mulberry Bush"

Newspaper Collage

Curriculum Areas: Language Arts, Art, Math, Social Awareness

Have parents bring in a few days' worth of newspapers. Allow children to explore the newspapers to find items they want to cut out and use to make a collage. As children work with the newspapers, have them name letters and numbers they see. Have them describe the events they see in pictures. Also encourage children to try to cut out all of the letters of their names and glue them onto their papers.

Needlepoint Pictures

Curriculum Areas: Art

Obtain one piece of plastic needlepoint canvas (6" square or larger) for each child in the class. Also have available a few blunt plastic needlepoint needles and different colors of yarn. Show children the plastic canvas and explain that they can make designs on the canvas by pulling needles and yarn back and forth through it. Supervise children as they take turns making designs with the needles.

Numeral-to-Number Match

Curriculum Area: Math

Make Numeral-to-Number Match cards using stickers or stamps. Place one sticker or stamp on an index card, then write the numeral 1 on a different card. Continue until you have cards showing sticker or stamp sets up to 10, and numeral cards to 10. Gather children and explain that the word "numeral" refers to the symbols used when writing and reading numbers. Give an example by showing them one item and the numeral 1. Tell them that 1 is the numeral telling us how many items there are. Tell children to count the number of stickers or stamps on each card, then find the corresponding numeral card to place beside it.

Role-Play Opportunities

Nanny	NASA Astronaut
Newscaster	Newspaper Reporter
Nutritionist	Nursery Worker
Nurse	

Orange and Onion Prints
Curriculum Area: Art

Purchase several oranges and large onions. Gather construction paper and small bowls of tempera paint in assorted colors. Cut the oranges and onions in half. Allow children to dip the oranges and onions in the paint, then press them onto their papers to make designs. If the colors mix, talk about the new colors created. Ask the class if the prints look a little bit like a letter they know. You may want to have children use black crayons to draw the letter O around the edge of each print after their pictures have dried.

Ocean Finger Painting
Curriculum Area: Art

Purchase a can of shaving cream. Obtain a container of blue tempera paint (both liquid and powder will work). Tell children that they will be pretending to make ocean waves with shaving cream. Remind children that they should not put their hands near their faces while they have shaving cream on them. Give each child a squirt of the shaving cream and a few drops or a sprinkle of the blue tempera paint. Let children mix the paint and shaving cream together to make "foamy ocean waves." If you are concerned the blue paint will stain furniture, you may do this activity on trays or wax paper.

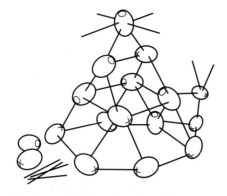

Olive Sculptures
Curriculum Areas: Art, Snack

Purchase a package of blunt toothpicks and a few cans of green and black pitted olives in assorted sizes. Allow children to use the toothpicks and olives to make sculptures. Encourage them to make free-form sculptures or those of animals, houses, etc.

Oatmeal Explorations
Curriculum Areas: Math, Science

Gather a large container of uncooked oatmeal, bowls, measuring cups, ladles, etc. Place the materials into a large dishpan and allow the children to explore by measuring and pouring the oatmeal.

Songs and Rhymes
"Once I Caught a Fish Alive"
"Open, Shut Them"
"Old MacDonald"
"Oats and Beans and Barley Grow"
"Over in the Meadow"

Traditional Activities
Obstacle Courses
Opposites

Pickle Prints

Curriculum Areas: Art, Science

Purchase a container of whole pickles in assorted sizes if possible. Rinse the pickles and cut them in half lengthwise. Place the pickles on an art table along with shallow bowls of paint and construction paper. Allow children to make pickle prints by pressing pickle halves into paint, then onto paper. While children are working, ask them if they know what vegetable is used to make pickles. If they do not know, explain that most pickles begin as cucumbers, and are placed in a special pickling liquid to make pickles. If possible, have a cucumber and a pickle to compare.

Peanut Butter Play Clay

Curriculum Areas: Art, Math, Science

Gather the following materials:

One large container of peanut butter
One large container of toasted wheat germ
One box of powdered milk
One bottle of honey
Several small bowls
Measuring spoons
Wax paper

Check with students about peanut butter and honey allergies before allowing students to participate in this activity. Have children wash their hands well, then allow each to measure the following into a small bowl: 1 tablespoon peanut butter, 1 tablespoon toasted wheat germ, 1 teaspoon powdered milk, and 1 teaspoon honey. Have children mix the ingredients well with their hands. When the dough is mixed, allow them to create letters with their peanut butter play clay on a sheet of wax paper. Write each child's name on the wax paper beside her dough letters. Allow the dough to chill and serve for a snack.

Pasta Necklace

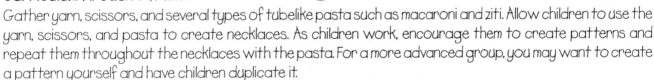

Curriculum Areas: Art, Math

Gather yarn, scissors, and several types of tubelike pasta such as macaroni and ziti. Allow children to use the yarn, scissors, and pasta to create necklaces. As children work, encourage them to create patterns and repeat them throughout the necklaces with the pasta. For a more advanced group, you may want to create a pattern yourself and have children duplicate it.

Songs and Rhymes

"Peter, Peter, Pumpkin Eater"
"Peanut Butter and Jelly"
"Pop Goes the Weasel"
"Punchinello"
"Polly Wolly Doodle"

Traditional Activities

Pin the Nose on the . . .
Pick-Up Sticks
Piñata
Puzzles
Puppets

Alphabet

Qq

Quarter Rubbings
Curriculum Areas: Art, Math

Gather several quarters, several sheets of newsprint paper, and crayons without wrappers. Explain to children that they can make rubbings of quarters by placing a quarter under newsprint paper and rubbing over it with the side of a crayon. Allow children to do this as many times as they wish. While they are working, talk about the fact that four quarters equal one dollar. When children have finished making as many rubbings as they wish, have them circle every four quarters. Tell them that if they count how many circles they have, they will know how many dollars' worth of rubbings they made.

Quilt Collage
Curriculum Areas: Art, Social Awareness

Gather several paper or fabric scraps, glue, and black crayons or markers. Talk with children about quilts and how they are made. Explain that in some cases quilts are inexpensive to make because they contain cloth scraps. Explain, however, that quilts are very time-consuming to make, so they may be expensive to buy. Show a quilt or photos of quilts from magazines to children. Allow them to cut or tear the scraps and glue them to larger pieces of construction paper to make quilts. Allow them to use the black crayons or markers to draw in the "stitches."

Quick Quartets
Curriculum Areas: Games, Math

Allow children to count and divide themselves into groups of four to make quartets. Give a ball to each group. Explain that they must quickly pass the ball around the group. Have children count in sequence from one to four as the ball moves around the circle. If a group drops the ball while it is being passed, the group sits down. The last team standing wins.

Quail Catch
Curriculum Areas: Games

Using the Net pattern (page 71), cut out paper nets from white construction paper and write each child's name on one. Have each child find her net, then have children sit in a semicircle in front of the board. Attach a construction paper Quail (page 71) to the board. Give each child a turn to try to "Catch the Quail." Blindfold the child (or have her close her eyes) and spin her around a few times. Give her the net with tape and her name on it and tell her to try to tape it on top of the quail. Continue until everyone has had a turn. The child whose net is closest to the quail wins.

Rhyme
"The Queen's Tarts"

Traditional Activity
Twenty Questions

Alphabet Patterns
Quail and Net

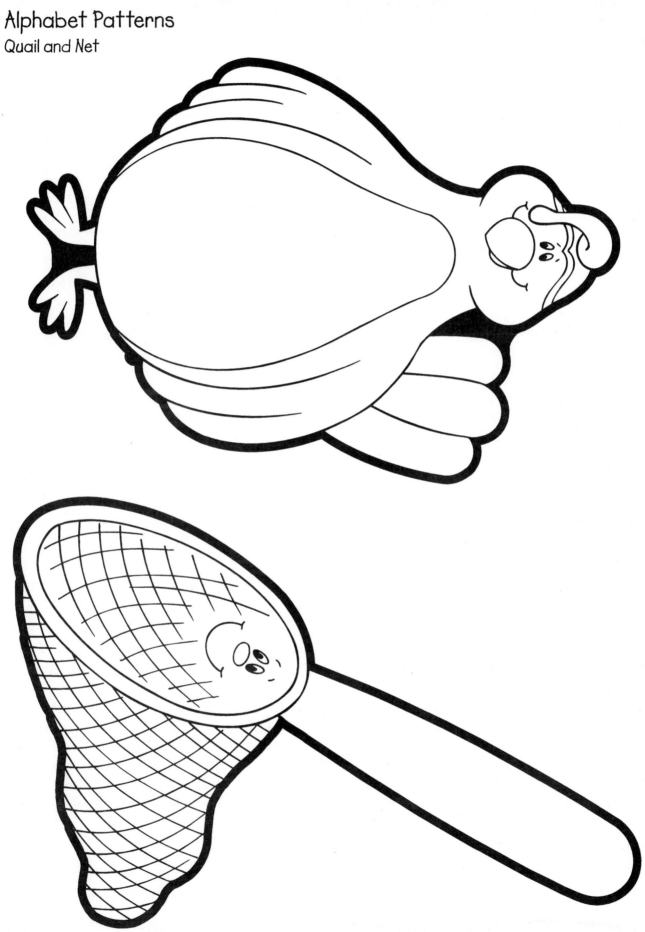

Rice Covered R's

Curriculum Areas: Art, Language Arts

Cut large pieces of red construction paper into R shapes. Give one to each child. Gather glue and a package of uncooked rice. Allow each child to have a turn gluing the rice to a red R. While children are working, encourage them to name words that begin with the R sound.

Rainbow Watercolor Resist

Curriculum Areas: Art, Science

Give each child a piece of white construction paper and crayons. Ask him to draw (by pressing hard with the crayons) a rainbow and any other details he wishes. When he has finished drawing, let him use blue watercolor paint to paint over his entire picture. He will end up with a beautiful rainbow in a blue sky. Have children tell you what they see happening and have them guess why the paint does not cover up the drawing. Explain to children that the wax of the crayons resists the water of the paint, so the paint will not adhere to it.

Ribbon Collage

Curriculum Area: Art

Gather several rolls of ribbon in assorted colors. Allow children to make collages by cutting lengths of ribbon and gluing them to paper. As children work, have them name the colors of the ribbons they are using.

Rhyming Riddles

Curriculum Area: Language Arts

Tell children that you will tell them some riddles. Explain that you will tell them a word that rhymes with the answer. Use the rhyming riddles below or make up some of your own. 1. It rhymes with cat. You wear it on your head. (hat) 2. This vehicle can take you far. It rhymes with tar. (car) 3. This helps you tell time. It rhymes with smock. (clock)

Songs and Rhymes

"Rain, Rain, Go Away"
"Row, Row, Row Your Boat"
"Rock-a-Bye Baby"

Traditional Activities

Ring Around the Rosie
Red Rover
Red Light, Green Light
Relay Races

Sandpaper Sand Crab Rubbings

Curriculum Area: Art

Gather a few sheets of sandpaper. Use the Sand Crab pattern (page 74) to trace several sand crabs onto the sandpaper. Cut out the sand crabs and place them at an art table for two or three students at a time to use. Have child place a sandpaper sand crab pattern beneath a piece of newsprint or other lightweight paper. Explain to children that by using the sides of crayons (without wrappers), they can make rubbings that show the sand crabs. After children have made their sand crab rubbings, encourage them to add details such as water, beach, palm trees, other crabs, etc.

Soup Fixin's Collage

Curriculum Areas: Art, Science, Snack

Make several tagboard stencils from the Soup Fixin's Soup Bowl pattern (page 74). Purchase a few packages of dried soup mix (the larger the variety of ingredients, the better). Show children the soup mix and ask them what they think it is. Explain that if you add water and cook the mix, it makes soup. Have each child trace the soup bowl pattern onto a piece of construction paper and cut it out. Then, allow children to draw soup ingredients in their bowls. As children work, heat the soup in a crock pot and discuss the smell. Serve the cooled soup in small cups for a snack.

Sock Tracing

Curriculum Areas: Art

Make tagboard stencils from the Sock Tracing patterns (page 75). Place the patterns on an art table along with pencils, crayons, colored construction paper, and scissors. Allow children to trace the socks onto construction paper and then decorate the socks with the crayons. They can also cut out the socks and glue them to another piece of construction paper to create a sock collage.

Songs and Rhymes

"Sing a Song of Sixpence"
"Skip to My Lou"
"Sara Sponda"
"Shoo Fly, Don't Bother Me"

Traditional Activities

Show and Tell
Statue
Soccer
Sandbox
Simon Says
Sack Races

Alphabet Patterns
Sand Crab and Soup Fixin's Soup Bowl

Alphabet Patterns
Sock Tracing

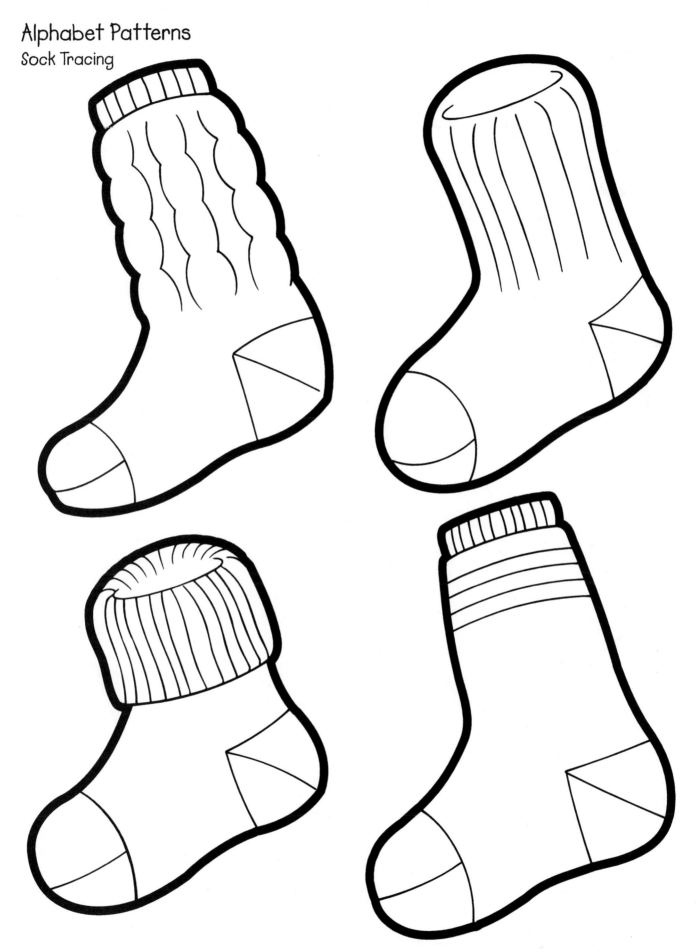

CD-0817 *Terrific Themes for Year-Round Fun*

Tape Resist Prints

Curriculum Area: Art

Gather a few rolls of transparent tape, watercolors, paintbrushes, and light-colored construction paper. Have children arrange pieces of the tape on their papers in any design they wish. When they are finished with the tape, have them paint over the papers with watercolors darker than their papers. The watercolor will absorb into the paper, but will not adhere to the tape, leaving interesting designs.

Tee Creations

Curriculum Area: Art

Gather a few packages of colored golf tees, several 1" or thicker pieces of plastic foam, and a few lightweight mallets or toy hammers. Allow children to tap the golf tees into the foam with the mallets to create designs.

Toothbrush Painted T's

Curriculum Area: Art, Language Arts

Cut a large letter T on plain, white paper for each child. Obtain one or two clean toothbrushes. Place several colors of tempera paint in shallow pans at the art easel. Allow one or two children at a time to paint their T's using the toothbrushes and tempera paint. As children work, encourage them to try to paint the letters T and t on their papers. Also encourage them to name as many words as they can that begin with the letter T.

Ticket Tearing

Curriculum Area: Math

Purchase a roll of tickets from a party or office supply store. Let children improve their fine-motor skills by tearing the tickets on the perforations. You may then want to have children count the tickets, sort them by color or sequence numbers, make patterns with different colored tickets, or tear them in half.

Songs and Rhymes

"Teddy Bear, Teddy Bear"
"This Old Man"
"Thumbkin"
"Twinkle, Twinkle, Little Star"
"Tisket-a-Tasket"

Traditional Activities

Telling Time
Tea Party
Tug of War
Teddy Bears
Tag

Unicorn Horns
Curriculum Area: Art

Gather one long cardboard tube for each child. Place the following materials on an art table: markers and crayons, stickers, stamps and stamp pads, a stapler, a hole punch, scissors, and yarn. Show children a picture of a unicorn and tell them they will be making unicorn horns. (Be sure children understand that unicorns are mythical creatures.) Give each child one long cardboard tube and instruct him to decorate it any way he wishes with the materials on the table. When the horn is decorated, help the child staple one end to create a point and punch two holes (opposite each other) on the other end. Help the child tie two pieces of yarn to the holes to make a chin-strap for his horn. Allow children to have a parade while wearing their unicorn horns. If desired, follow up with by reading a book or watching a movie about unicorns.

Universal T-Shirts
Curriculum Areas: Art, Science

Have parents send in one plain, white T-shirt for their child. Gather art sponges cut into the shapes of planets, rockets, stars, and any other universe-related shapes you wish. Place the sponges, along with fabric paints in shallow dishes, on an art table. (Be sure children are wearing smocks to protect clothing.) Allow each child to have a turn using the sponges to make a "universal" design on his shirt. Place a piece of newspaper or a T-shirt board inside the shirt to keep the paints from bleeding through. Allow the shirts to dry thoroughly before returning them to children.

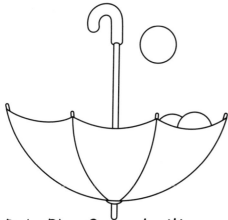

Umbrella Toss
Curriculum Areas: Games, Math

Gather a few umbrellas and beanbags, rolled up socks, or foam balls. Use string to hang the open umbrellas upside down at various lengths from the floor. Explain to children that they should toss the items into the umbrellas. Allow each child to have a turn tossing five items into an open umbrella. Encourage each child to count how many items landed in the umbrella. If you wish, you may have each child keep a record of how many times she was successful.

Role-Play Opportunities

Umpire
Unicorn

Violet and Vine Vests

Curriculum Area: Art

Gather the following materials: purple and green construction paper, glue, scissors, tagboard flower patterns for tracing, and one large paper grocery bag per child. To make a vest for each child, cut down the middle of a grocery bag and cut a hole in the bag's bottom for the child's neck. Cut two arm holes on the sides of the bag and then turn the bag inside out. Allow each child to have a turn tracing the flower patterns onto purple construction paper and cutting them out to make violets. Encourage them to use green construction paper to cut out vines. Let children glue their flowers and vines on the grocery bags to create violet and vine vests.

Vegetable Print Place Mats

Curriculum Areas: Art, Science

Gather the following vegetables and cut each in half: onions, bell peppers, potatoes, carrots, celery, etc. Allow children to dip the vegetables into shallow bowls of paint and press onto 12" x 18" sheets of white construction paper to make vegetable prints. When the prints are dry, laminate the papers to make creative place mats.

Violin Movement

Curriculum Area: Games

Play a recording of violin music and have children describe how the music makes them feel or what it makes them think about. Let students dance or pretend to play violins as the music plays.

Vanilla Play Clay

Curriculum Area: Art, Science

Allow children to help you prepare play clay by mixing 2 cups flour, 1 cup salt, 1 teaspoon cream of tartar, 2 tablespoons oil, 1 teaspoon food coloring, and 2 cups of water. Add $1/2$ tablespoon vanilla extract per cup of mixture. Give each child a scoop of the play clay mixture on wax paper. As children explore and manipulate the dough, ask them to describe how it smells and feels. (Remind students not to eat the mixture.) Have students name other items that have a vanilla smell.

Traditional Activities

Vacuuming
Valentines
Volleyball

Wet Chalk W's

Curriculum Areas: Art, Language Arts

Gather colored chalk, black construction paper cut into W's, and paper cups. Tell children that they will be drawing with chalk in a different way. Allow them to fill the paper cups with water. Explain that they should dip their chalk into the water before drawing with it. Ask them to guess what will happen when they draw. They should notice that the colors are brighter after they have dipped the chalk in the water. Encourage children to write the letter W with the wet chalk.

Water Relay

Curriculum Area: Games

Gather several large tubs or buckets and a few small pails (enough for two buckets or tubs and one pail per team). Divide the class into two or three teams. Explain that they will run a special relay race. Line up the teams at a starting point and place one bucket at the beginning of each line, and one tub for each team at the other end of the playground. Fill the buckets closest to the teams with water. The object is for one team to be the first to fill its tub at the end of the playground by transferring the water with the bucket.

Washcloth Prints

Curriculum Area: Art

Make a few washcloth printers. For each printer, wrap about six cotton balls inside a washcloth. Secure the washcloth around the cotton balls with a rubber band. Allow children to make washcloth prints by pressing washcloth printers into trays of tempera paint and then onto construction paper.

Wild Rumpus

Curriculum Areas: Language Arts, Games

Obtain a copy of *Where the Wild Things Are* by Maurice Sendak (Scholastic, Inc., 1983) and read it to the class. The next time you are outside, allow children to have a "Wild Rumpus."

Songs and Rhymes

"The Wheels on the Bus"
"Where, Oh Where Has My Little Dog Gone?"

Traditional Activities

Water Play
Wiggling
Wands
Wagons
Walking

Alphabet

Box Painting

Curriculum Area: Art, Social Awareness

Gather several large boxes, paintbrushes, and assorted colors of tempera paint. Place the boxes on the playground and allow children to paint the boxes any way they wish. They may create houses, cars, rocket ships, or anything else they imagine. Allow them to add details using crayons or markers if they desire.

X-Ray Drawings

Curriculum Areas: Art, Science

Give each child a sheet of black construction paper and a piece of white chalk. If possible, obtain a real x ray to show the class. Discuss the appearance of x rays, then allow children to draw x rays on the paper with the chalk. They may want to show human x rays or show how they imagine animals' skeletons look.

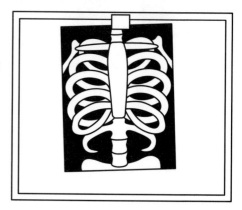

Wax Drawings

Curriculum Area: Art

Gather several assorted colors of wax candles. Place the candles and white construction paper on an art table. Allow children to experiment drawing with the wax candles on the construction paper. Point out that wax is also used to make crayons.

Excuse Me

Curriculum Area: Games

Gather children and explain that they will play a guessing game. Select one child to be "it." Explain that you will blindfold "it" or place her with her back to the group. You will then point to a child in the group. That child should say, "Excuse me," in a disguised voice. "It" has three chances to guess who said, "Excuse me." After three guesses, select a new "it" and continue.

Role-Play Opportunities

Saxophonist
Taxi Driver

Traditional Activities

Exercise
Experiments

Alphabet

Yarn Dying

Curriculum Area: Art

Gather white yarn, a box of food coloring in assorted colors, paper towels, small clear cups (one for each color of food coloring), scissors, glue, and construction paper. Pour the food coloring along with water into the clear cups. Allow children to cut pieces of the white yarn and dip it into their choice of the food coloring. Have each child place his yarn on a paper towel with his name written on it to dry. When the yarn is dry, let the children glue their dyed yarn onto construction paper to make pictures or designs.

Yardstick Experimentation

Curriculum Area: Math

Gather several yardsticks and allow children to experiment with measuring. Have children count how many yardsticks it takes to get across the room, how many yardsticks will fit between the swing and the slide, etc.

Yellow Collage

Curriculum Areas: Art, Science

Gather the following yellow materials: yarn, construction paper, crayons, markers, tissue paper, streamers, craft feathers, and any other yellow items. Also gather white construction paper, scissors, and glue. (Make the glue yellow by adding yellow liquid or powdered tempera paint.) Allow children to create collages with the yellow materials. While children are working with the yellow materials, encourage them to compare the similarities or differences between shades of yellow.

Allergy and Food Preference Note

Before completing any food activity, ask parental permission and inquire about children's food allergies. Common food allergies include peanuts and other nuts, dairy, eggs, berries, etc. Parents may have religious or other preferences that will prevent children from eating certain foods.

Your Yummy Yogurt

Curriculum Area: Snack

Check with parents about possible dairy or fruit allergies before completing this activity. Purchase a large container of vanilla yogurt and a variety of fruit toppings. Allow children to scoop a few spoonfuls of the yogurt into a cup or bowl. They may then add their choice of fruit topping(s) to the yogurt. Have children mix the fruit into the yogurt and taste the mixture. As they enjoy their snacks, encourage them to describe the taste of the food they are eating.

Songs and Rhymes

"Yankee Doodle"
"You Are My Sunshine"

Traditional Activities

Yo-Yo
Yolk Painting

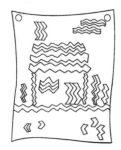

Zigzag Pictures
Curriculum Area: Art

Purchase several packages of rickrack in assorted colors and sizes from a craft or sewing store. Place the rickrack, along with scissors and glue, on an art table. Allow each child to create a picture or collage by gluing the zigzag rickrack to a piece of construction paper.

Zero Sponge Prints
Curriculum Areas: Art, Math

Gather several sponges cut into the shapes of zeros, shallow bowls of paint, and construction paper. Allow children to press the sponges into the paint and onto the construction paper. As they work, have them discuss the concept of zero. Encourage them to name the items of which they have zero (none). Also, have children discuss any new colors made by overlapping zero prints.

Zipper Board
Curriculum Area: Language Arts, Science

Purchase several zippers in a variety of sizes and colors. Use hot glue to attach the edges of the closed zippers to a board of any type in a lap-board size. (Heavy cardboard or sanded plywood works well.) Allow children to work with the zipper board by zipping and unzipping the zippers. Have children observe if any of the zippers are easier to operate than others. While they are working, have students name articles of clothing or other items they have with zippers, and discuss how zippers may make things easier.

Zoom Lens
Curriculum Areas: Science

Obtain several pairs of binoculars, hand-held magnifying lenses, and/or a camera with a zoom lens. Let students experiment with "zooming in" on various objects in the classroom and on the playground. Ask them to describe the details they see. You may want to have them draw "before and after" pictures, showing objects as seen with and without the lenses.

Zany Zone
Curriculum Area: Games

Create a "zany zone" in your classroom. Set aside an area with silly dress-up clothes, musical instruments, and other props. Discuss the meaning of the word *zany*. Allow students time to play in the zany zone and to be as zany and silly as they wish.

Traditional Activities
Zipping Zippers
Zoo Animal Role-Playing

Community Helpers

Contents

Career Pattern Pages

Each career has a page of pattern cards showing a community helper and items related to the career. These general pattern pages can be used in the following ways:

- Use the patterns to introduce students to different careers.
- Let students color enlarged copies of the patterns and use them to create a community helper bulletin board display.
- Create a matching activity in which each community helper is matched with the appropriate cards.
- Copy the patterns onto tagboard and attach a craft stick on the back of each to create Community Helper puppets.

Resource Visitors

During this unit, invite a variety of community helpers to come in to talk to students. Some organizations may have programs already prepared. Ask students' parents if any would like to talk to your class about their careers. Be sure to ask all visitors to bring in any work-related items that may be of interest to students.

Imagination Area Props

As you teach about each community helper, include an assortment of appropriate props in your imagination or housekeeping area. Each section includes a short list of suggested items. Encourage children to role-play the community helpers performing their duties.

Circle Time

Circle time is the perfect time to share information about community helpers and careers. You may choose to read a book about a variety of careers or one that is specific to the career you are studying. Show pictures of community helpers and ask the class to describe what the people are wearing, what they are doing, where they are, etc. Have children tell you if they might like to do a particular job when they grow up. You may also have children tell you what else they would like to do when they grow up.

Teach the following adapted song, as well as the traditional or adapted songs that are presented with each community helper. Allow children to sing and role play the songs throughout the Community Helpers unit.

Who Do You See?

(to the tune of "Look Through the Window")
Look through the window. (Hold hands up as if looking through a window.)
And who do you see? (Hold out hands questioningly.)
A mail carrier*, a mail carrier,
Bringing mail** just for me.

*Replace mail carrier with the name of each community helper as it is acted out.
**Replace bringing mail with a task that the community helper does for others.

Bread Cutting

Curriculum Areas: Language Arts, Social Awareness

Place several pieces of fresh bread in an airtight container. Have the bread and blunt plastic knives available for children. Have each child take a turn getting a piece of bread from the container and using one of the knives to cut the bread. Let students eat the bread they cut and add new pieces to the container as it is eaten.

Allergy and Food Preference Note

Before completing any food activity, ask parental permission and inquire about children's food allergies. Common food allergies include peanuts and other nuts, dairy, eggs, berries, etc. Parents may have religious or other preferences that will prevent children from eating certain foods.

Making Salad

Curriculum Areas: Language Arts, Snack, Math

Check with parents about possible food allergies before completing this activity. Gather tossed salad ingredients such as lettuce, mushrooms, cucumbers, tomatoes, sliced cheese, dressing, etc. Provide children with bowls, forks, and blunt knives and let them cut the ingredients to create their own salads. While children cut the ingredients, have them talk about the portions they will use, such as a half of a mushroom. Also have them talk about how many pieces they have. Allow each child to top his salad with his choice of dressing and enjoy for a snack or with lunch.

Ladling Water

Curriculum Areas: Language Arts

Place two large, deep bowls inside a large tub. Fill one bowl with water. Allow children to take turns using a ladle to move the water to the other bowl. Direct them to always begin with the full bowl on the left. This will help students get ready for the left-to-right movement of reading and writing.

Cookie Cutter Prints

Curriculum Area: Art

Gather a variety of cookie cutters, shallow bowls, tempera paint, and construction paper. Allow each child to take a turn using the materials to make cookie cutter prints. They should first press the cookie cutters in paint, then onto paper to make designs.

Traditional Songs

"Do You Know the Muffin Man?"
"Hot Cross Buns"
"Pat-a-Cake"

Adapted Nursery Rhyme

Rub-a-dub-dub,
Three workers in a tub,
Went sailing out to sea.
The chef, the baker, and the pasta maker,
Especially fine cooks all three.

Imagination Props

Provide the following for students to use during center time: baker and chef hats, cooking utensils, pots and pans, cookie sheets, cookie cutters, and rolling pins.

Community Helper Patterns
Baker/Chef Patterns

Community Helpers

Taxi/Bus Garages
Curriculum Area: Math

Make nine copies of the Bus/Taxi patterns (page 89). Cut out the cards and group them in pairs so that each pair has bus/taxi patterns. Place one dot on each pattern in the first pair; two dots on each pattern in the second pair; and so on. Laminate if possible. Gather nine clean, empty, quart-size paper milk cartons and cut the top off of each. Cover the milk cartons with construction paper and write a numeral on each beginning with 1. Instruct children to count the number of dots on the bus and taxi cards. Have them "park" each card in the milk-carton garage with the corresponding numeral.

Circle-Time Driving
Curriculum Areas: Language Arts, Games

While children are in circle time, explain that they will play a pretending game. Tell them that they will each pretend to drive a bus or taxi as you give directions. Give directions to the children as each "driver" gets in his vehicle, shuts the door, buckles his seat belt, adjusts the mirror, drives around (describe in detail), and parks. Allow children to make any sound effects they wish.

Appliance-Box Taxi and Bus
Curriculum Areas: Art, Math

Allow children to use markers, paint, construction paper, etc., to create buses and taxis out of appliance boxes or other sturdy material. Have children describe the shapes they are using to create the vehicles.

Steering Wheel Prints
Curriculum Area: Art

Gather several sponges and cut them into O shapes, with holes in the centers. If possible, use hot glue to attach a craft stick or spool to the back of each sponge for ease in printing. Provide children with tempera paint in shallow bowls and the O-shaped sponges. Let students use the sponges and paint to make steering wheel designs on construction paper.

Traditional Song
"The Wheels on the Bus"

Imagination Props
Provide the following for students to use during center time: taxi and bus driver hats, appliance-box taxis and buses (see activity above), toy buses and taxis, and steering wheels. You might also want to arrange some chairs to make an area of your classroom look like the inside of a bus or taxi.

Community Helper Patterns
Bus/Taxi Driver Patterns

Community Helper Patterns
Bus/Taxi Patterns

Woodworking Area

Curriculum Areas: Social Awareness, Math, Language Arts

Gather the following materials to create a woodworking area: wood pieces of differing shapes and sizes, nails, screws, hammers, sandpaper blocks, wood glue, carpenter hats and aprons, etc. Allow supervised children to carefully work with the tools to make creations. As children work, encourage them to name the shapes they are working with, count the number of times they hammer, etc.

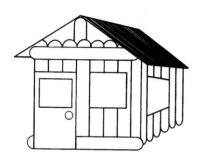

Ice Cream Stick Construction

Curriculum Area: Art

Place craft sticks, glue, construction paper, paint, and scissors on an art table. Allow children to use the craft sticks and glue to create structures of their choice. Encourage them to make buildings such as houses, dog houses, tree houses, etc. When children have finished, allow them to use the construction paper and paint to decorate their structures.

Nut and Bolt Printing

Curriculum Areas: Art, Math

Gather several real or play nuts and bolts. Place the nuts and bolts and shallow bowls of tempera paint and paper on an art table. Allow children to press the nuts and bolts in the paint and then on their papers to make designs. Encourage students to make patterns using different colors (yellow nut, green nut, yellow nut, green nut, etc.) or two shapes (nut, bolt, nut, bolt, etc.).

Finger Play
Johnny Hammers with One Hammer

Johnny hammers with one hammer,
One hammer, one hammer.
Johnny hammers with one hammer,
Now he hammers with two.

Repeat verses, adding one hammer each time until:

Johnny hammers with five hammers,
Five hammers, five hammers.
Johnny hammers with five hammers,
And now he goes to sleep.

Community Helper Patterns
Carpenter Patterns

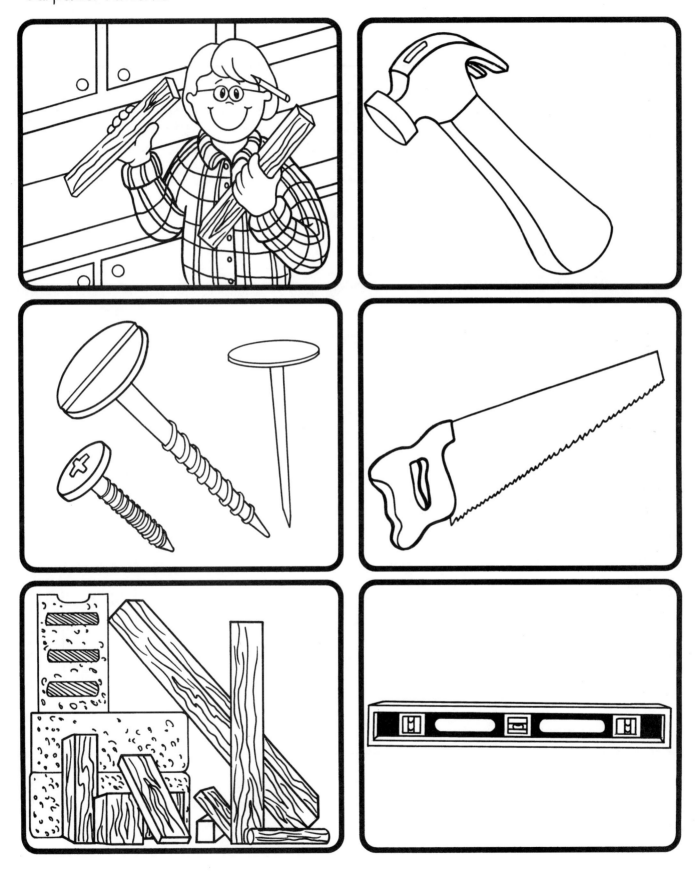

Bandage Match
Curriculum Area: Math

Make two photocopies of the Bandage Match patterns (page 94). Color, cut out, and laminate if possible. Gather children and tell them that they will play a matching game. Show the cards and explain that each bandage shape appears on two matching cards. Allow volunteers to make matches. When each child has had a turn, place the cards in a basket or plastic bag for use during center time.

Doctor's-Office Emotions
Curriculum Areas: Language Arts, Social Awareness

Give each child in the class one copy of the Doctor's Office patterns (page 95). Have students look at each scene and describe it. Allow a volunteer to describe how he would feel if he were the patient in the scene. Then, have a class discussion about the situation and how the other students would feel if they were the patient. Continue the review with the remaining scenes, allowing different students to volunteer their feelings about being in the situations pictured.

Listening to Heartbeats
Curriculum Areas: Science, Math

Obtain a real stethoscope and place it on a science table. While children rotate during center time, help pairs of children find their own and each other's heartbeats. Encourage children to count how many times their hearts beat in a set amount of time.

Doctor Collage
Curriculum Area: Art

Gather the following materials and place them on an art table: construction paper, glue, scissors, bandages, cotton balls, cotton swabs, tongue depressors, and gauze. Have each child use the materials to create a collage. As children work, encourage them to talk about what the items are and how they are used.

Adapted Song
I'm a Helpful Doctor (to the tune of "I'm a Little Teapot")

I'm a helpful doctor,
Dressed in white.
I help people feel better,
Day and night.
When you get hurt or sick,
Come see me.
I'll get you all fixed up,
Just as quick as can be.

Imagination Props
Provide the following for students to use during center time: play doctor's kit, white jackets, bandages, cotton balls, cotton swabs, gauze, tongue depressors, and dolls for doctoring.

Community Helper Patterns
Doctor/Nurse Patterns

Community Helper Patterns
Bandage Match Patterns

Community Helper Patterns
Doctor's Office Patterns

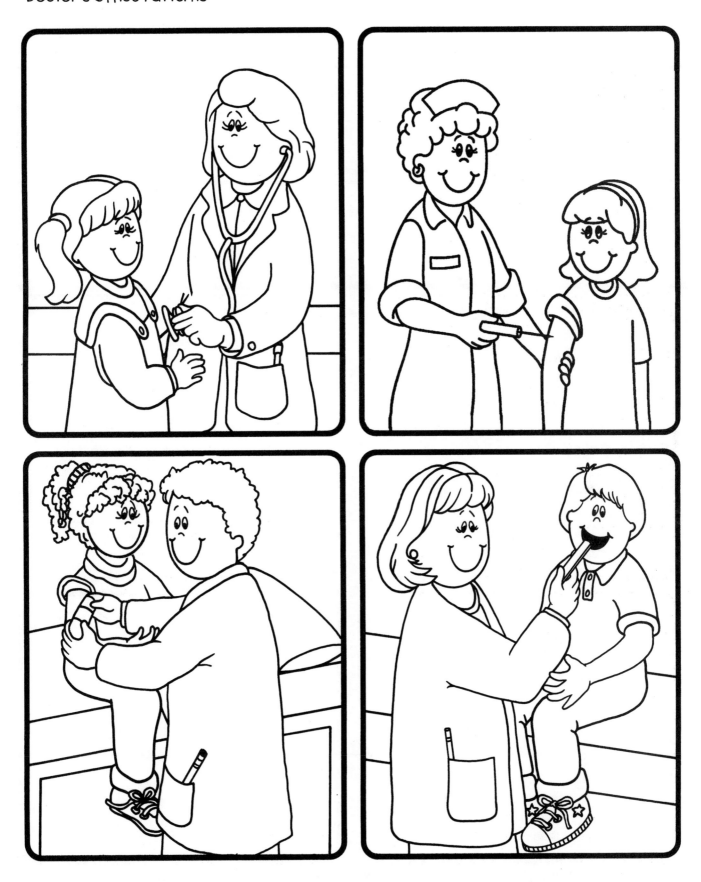

Bucket Brigade

Curriculum Area: Games

Divide class into two teams and have students on each team form a line. For each team, place one large bucket filled with water at one end of the line, and an empty bucket at the other end of the line. Give each team a large cup. Explain that, when playing the game, they cannot move from their positions in line. Members from each team have to work together and use the cup to pass the water from the full bucket to the empty one. The first team to move all of its water to the empty bucket wins.

Firefighter Helmet

Curriculum Area: Art

Gather a one-gallon bleach bottle for each child in the class. Be sure to wash the bottles out thoroughly before using. Cut each as shown in the illustration. Allow children to use red and black tempera paint to create their own personalized firefighter helmets.

Put Out the Fire

Curriculum Area: Games

Set up several targets outside on the playground. Use a red marker to draw pretend "fires" on white garbage bags and tape them to the fence or suspend them from trees with string. Allow children to practice "putting out the fires" by squirting the bags with water squirt bottles.

Shape Fire Engine

Curriculum Area: Art

Cut a variety of shapes of different sizes and colors from construction paper including several large rectangles from red construction paper. Place the construction paper shapes, large sheets of white construction paper, glue, and crayons on an art table. Allow each child to use one large red rectangle and other shapes to create a fire truck on the white construction paper. When the glue is dry, encourage children to draw details on their fire trucks using crayons.

Traditional Song

"Hurry, Hurry, Drive the Fire Truck"

Adapted Song

Brave Firefighters (to the tune of "Three Blind Mice")
Brave firefighters, brave firefighters,
See how they run, to put out the fire.
They leave the p when they get the call.
Putting out the fire won't take long at all.
They try to save buildings, big or small,
Brave firefighters.

Imagination Props

Provide the following for students to use during center time: firefighters' hats, boots, suspenders, telephones, flashlights, and hoses.

Community Helper Patterns
Firefighter Patterns

CD-0817 *Terrific Themes for Year-Round Fun*

Fry Letter Matching

Curriculum Area: Language Arts

Copy nine sets of the Fry Letter Matching patterns (page 100). Write uppercase letters on both the fries and the fry containers. Color, cut out, and laminate the patterns. Show children the cards and explain that each full fry container has a letter on it, and each empty container does also. Allow them to match the containers that show the same letters. Other options include using the patterns to match uppercase and lowercase letters, sequence the letters in ABC order, and match letters to objects that begin with the corresponding letters.

Taking Orders

Curriculum Area: Language Arts

Pair children and explain that they will take turns pretending to be food servers and customers in a restaurant. Give each "server" a piece of paper and a pencil or crayon. Have each "customer" tell her server what she would like for her meal. Allow the customer to request any items he desires, regardless of the actual time of day. If children can write, allow the server to write the order on the paper. Pre-writing children can draw pictures to show what the customer orders. Encourage each server to read the order back to the customer to check for accuracy. When everyone has finished, have the partners trade roles and play again.

Fork Printing

Curriculum Area: Art

Place plastic forks, shallow bowls of tempera paint, and finger paint paper or construction paper on a table. Allow children to take turns at the table using the forks to make designs on the paper. If the colors mix, encourage children to talk about the new colors they have made.

Adapted Song

The Customer Orders the Food (to the tune of "The Farmer in the Dell")

The customer orders the food,
The customer orders the food,
It happens at a restaurant,
The customer orders the food.

The server tells the cook . . .
The cook prepares the food . . .
The server brings it out . . .
The customer eats the food . . .
The customer pays the cashier . . .
The cashier takes the money . . .
The busser cleans the table . . .

Imagination Props

Provide containers from fast-food restaurants, plates and utensils, food server apron, note pads, trays, and play food for students to use during center time.

Community Helper Patterns
Food Server Patterns

Community Helper Patterns
Fry Letter Matching Patterns

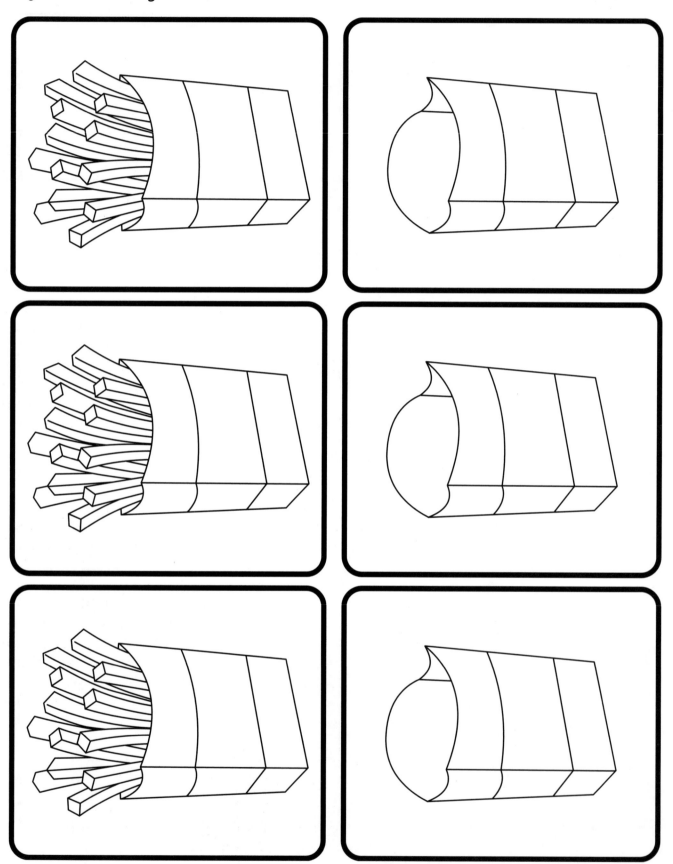

Department Sorting

Curriculum Areas: Language, Math, Science

Copy each Department Sorting pattern (pages 103–104). Cut out the cards and laminate. Show children the department cards (the long rectangular cards) and explain that each department has a different type of food. Show children the food cards (the small square cards) and allow volunteers each to select a food card and place it next to the appropriate department card. Allow children to work with the cards during center time. As an extension, talk with children about the recommended daily servings of the different types of food.

Box Sculptures

Curriculum Areas: Math, Art

Go to a local grocery store and pick up several empty boxes in a variety of sizes and shapes. (You may want to call first, as many stores recycle or crush their boxes once they are empty.) Allow children to take the boxes outside and let them work as a group to create box sculptures. Packing tape can be used to secure the boxes to each other. Students may make a sculpture of something real (such as a school bus or house), or they may make an abstract sculpture. As children work, have them describe the shapes and sizes of the boxes as well as the sculptures they create. You may want to allow children to use tempera paint, crayons, or markers to decorate their sculptures.

Food Box and Bag Collage

Curriculum Areas: Art, Language Arts

Ask parents to send in empty food boxes and bags and advertisements from newspapers and grocery store fliers. Allow children to cut the pictures and words from the boxes and bags. Have the children make a collage by gluing the clippings on construction paper. Encourage students to read the words on labels of food they recognize.

Adapted Song

Old Man Grocer Has a Store

(to the tune of "Old MacDonald")

Old Man Grocer has a store, yes siree, he does.
And in that store he has some carrots, yes siree, he does.
With a crunch, crunch here, and a crunch, crunch there.
Here a crunch, there a crunch, everywhere a crunch, crunch.
Old Man Grocer has a store, yes siree, he does.

Repeat with the following foods:
juice . . . gulp, gulp
popcorn . . . pop, pop
ice cream . . . lick, lick

Imagination Props

Provide produce department hats and aprons, empty food boxes, a play cash register, small grocery carts, plastic food, play money, and grocery bags for students to use during center time.

Community Helper Patterns
Grocery Store Worker Patterns

Community Helper Patterns
Department Sorting Patterns

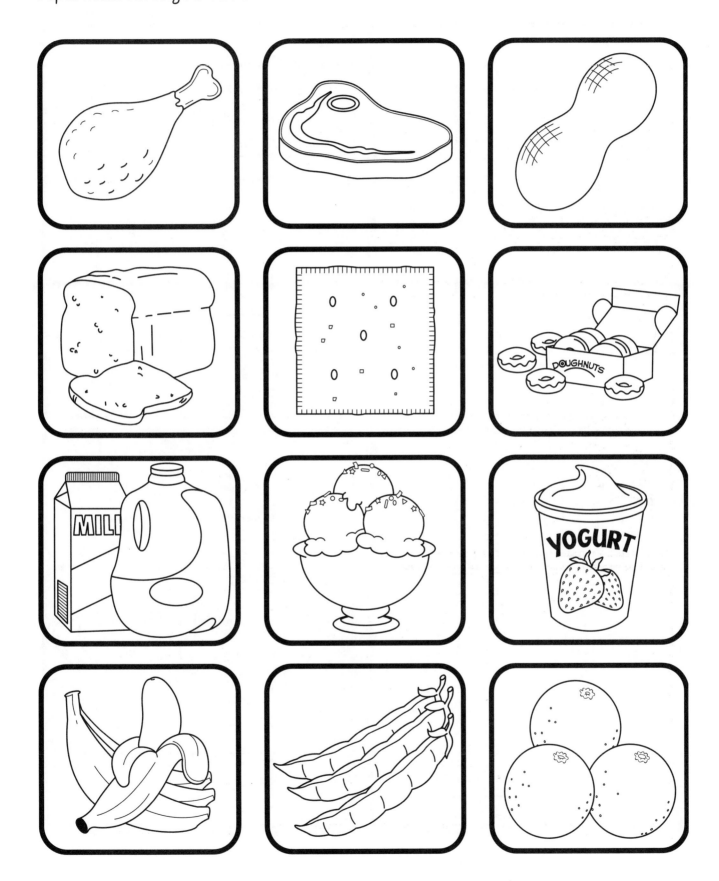

Community Helper Patterns
Department Sorting Patterns

FRESH PRODUCE

Community Helpers

Mail Carrier Meeting

Curriculum Area: Social Awareness

Find out what time the school's daily postal delivery comes. Call the post office to see if it is possible for children to ask questions of the mail carrier and look inside the mail truck. If so, arrange a time and have students plan what questions they will ask. If a short discussion with the mail carrier is not possible, allow children to watch the mail carrier deliver the mail one day.

Mailbox Matching

Curriculum Area: Language Arts

Create a mailbox for each child from a shoe box or paper bag. Write the child's name clearly on the mailbox. Then, write each child's name on an envelope. Allow children to take turns "delivering" the letters to the appropriate mailboxes by matching the names on the envelopes to the names on the mailboxes. Have each child name the classmate whose envelope he is matching.

As an extension, have students practice addressing envelopes. Provide them with blank envelopes and allow them to copy each other's names from the envelopes that you prepared. They may then deliver their handwritten envelopes to the correct mailboxes. This activity may also be completed with numbers (for addresses).

Cancelled-Stamp Collage

Curriculum Area: Art

Ask parents to save cancelled stamps from their mail for a few weeks. Place the stamps, along with glue and construction paper, on an art table. Allow children to use the stamps, construction paper, and glue to make collages.

Adapted Song

He'll* be Coming in His Mail Truck

(to the tune of "She'll be Comin' Round the Mountain")
He'll be coming in his mail truck when he comes,
He'll be coming in his mail truck when he comes,
He'll be coming in his mail truck,
He'll be coming in his mail truck,
He'll be coming in his mail truck when he comes.

Additional verses:
He'll be wearing his blue uniform . . .
He'll bring a package for me . . .
He'll bring mail for Mom and Dad . . .
He'll pick up letters from our mailbox . . .

*Substitute the words "she" for "he" and "her" for "his" depending on the gender of the school's mail carrier.

Imagination Props

Provide envelopes, stickers (for stamps), a cardboard mailbox, and a mail carrier uniform for students to use during center time.

Community Helper Patterns
Mail Carrier Patterns

Foil Badges
Curriculum Areas: Art

Cut a few badge-shaped patterns (page 108) from tagboard. Place these patterns, additional pieces of tagboard, tinfoil squares large enough to cover the badges, glue, pencils, and scissors in an art center. Allow each child to trace the badge pattern onto tagboard, then cut it out (you may pre-cut tagboard badges for very young children). Next, the child is to take a piece of the tinfoil and cover his badge. Let each child use the glue to secure the edges of the foil to the back of his piece of tagboard. Place a tape loop on the back of each badge so it can be worn.

Gradient Deputy Stars
Curriculum Area: Math

Cut five stars from yellow construction paper, each one larger than the last. Show children the stars and have them describe the differences in size. Explain that the goal of this activity is to place the stars in a line from smallest to largest. Allow volunteers to help you order the stars appropriately. When each child has had a turn, allow individuals or small groups to place the stars in order.

Directing Traffic
Curriculum Area: Games

While children are outdoors riding tricycles or other ride-on toys, allow them to take turns playing police officer. Draw roads on the pavement with chalk or masking tape and allow the police officer to direct the traffic. (If tricycles are not available, have children pretend to be cars.)

Deputy Star Sponge Prints
Curriculum Area: Art

Make several star stencils from tagboard by cutting a star shape in the middle of each. Place these cards, along with sponges, construction paper, and yellow, gold, or silver paint, on an art table. Show children how to place a stencil on a piece of paper, press a sponge into the paint, then press the sponge on the center of the stencil to make a star on the paper. Allow children to make as many stars as desired to create a design.

Adapted Song
What Do You Do When You Hear a Siren?
(to the tune of "Paw Paw Patch")
What do you do when you hear a siren?
What do you do when you hear a siren?
What do you do when you hear a siren?
You get out of the way.

Help is coming through when you hear a siren.
Help is coming through when you hear a siren.
Help is coming through when you hear a siren.
So, get out of the way.

Imagination Props
Provide police officer uniforms, play badges, appliance-box cars, and walkie-talkies for students to use during center time.

Community Helper Patterns
Police Officer Patterns

Teacher Feely Box

Curriculum Areas: Games, Science

Make a feely box by cutting a 3" x 3" hole in the side of a medium-sized box. Tape a piece of felt or fabric over the opening. Fill the feely box with items related to teaching: chalk, an unsharpened pencil, a pencil eraser, a chalk eraser, a plastic apple, blunt scissors, etc. Allow children to take turns reaching in the feely box to guess what the items are. Have children describe what their sense of touch allowed them to feel.

Walking on A, B, C's

Curriculum Areas: Language Arts, Gross Motor Skills

Use masking tape or chalk to make the letters of the alphabet on the pavement outside. Show the letters to the children and explain that they should walk on the letters. Before stepping on each letter, the child should say the name of the letter. After students are comfortable naming the letters, encourage each child to say words that begin with each letter as she steps on it.

Pencil Counting

Curriculum Area: Math

Gather several unsharpened pencils and clean, empty soup or vegetable cans. Cover the cans with construction or contact paper and place one dot on the first can, two on the second can, and so on. Allow children to count the number of dots on each can. Have a child say the number word that corresponds to the dots on a can, then place the matching number of pencils in it.

Construction Paper Chalkboard

Curriculum Area: Art

Place green or black construction paper and chalk on an art table. Allow children to take turns drawing on their "chalkboards." Encourage children to practice writing letters, numbers, their names, and various shapes.

Adapted Song

My Teacher Teaches Me

(to the tune of "Three Blind Mice")
My teacher teaches me, my teacher teaches me,
Lots of things, like the A, B, Cs.
She* helps me to count and to read and to play,
She reminds me to use my good manners each day.
She sings and plays games. I say "Hip, hip, hooray!"
Because she teaches me.

*Substitute "he" for "she" depending on the teacher's gender.

Imagination Props

Provide a small chalkboard and eraser, chalk, storybooks, chart paper, markers, a desk, and pencils for students to use during center time.

Community Helper Patterns
Teacher Patterns

Animal Tag

Curriculum Area: Games

Gather children and explain that they will play tag. Choose one child to be the veterinarian. Explain that all other children should pretend to be animals. Play begins with each child moving like the animal he is pretending to be and the veterinarian trying to "treat" the animals by tagging them. When a child is tagged, he must take a brief time-out to "visit the vet." Allow children to take turns being the veterinarian.

Animal Body Parts

Curriculum Area: Science

Enlarge the Bandaged Animals patterns (page 113). Show the cards to children and explain that each animal has a bandage on its body. Tell them that they should look for the bandage and name the bandaged body part. Complete this activity first with the whole class, then in small groups to assess understanding of animal body parts.

Puppy's Visit to the Vet

Curriculum Area: Social Awareness, Language Arts

Tell the following story about a puppy going to the vet for shots and have students describe the emotions the puppy may have felt.

> When the little puppy was born, he belonged to a person who didn't take good care of him. The puppy had stomachaches and seemed like he was always sick. His owner put him up for sale and a family that loved animals bought him. The family took him to a veterinarian's office. The vet checked the puppy, did tests, and gave the puppy shots. After his trip to the vet, the puppy began to feel better. His stomachache went away, he was no longer sick, and felt like playing.

As you tell the story, make up more details and allow children to share ideas about how the puppy might have felt. Another option would be to name an emotion and have children give a scenario at a veterinarian's office that might bring on that emotion in the puppy.

Finger Play

Tammie had a puppy that was sick, sick, sick. (Rub stomach as if sick.)
Her mom said, "Call the veterinarian, quick, quick, quick!" (Point and shake finger.)
Tammie called the vet as fast as she could, could, could. (Pretend to dial phone.)
In hopes the vet could make her puppy feel good, good, good. (Cross fingers hopefully.)
The nurse said, "It might be something your puppy ate, ate, ate." (Pretend to eat.)
She said, "Bring him in right this minute, don't wait, wait, wait." (Pretend to talk on phone.)
The vet saw Tammie's puppy and made him feel dandy, dandy, dandy. (Smile.)
He said, "Now keep your puppy away from that candy, candy, candy!" (Point and shake finger.)

Imagination Props

Provide a toy doctor's kit, a scale, stuffed animals, bandages, and an examination table for students to use during center time.

Community Helper Patterns
Veterinarian Patterns

Community Helper Patterns
Animal Body Parts Patterns

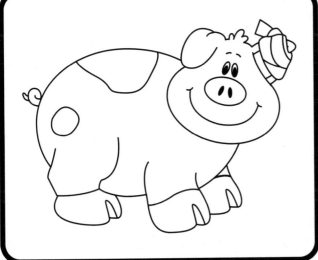

CD-0817 Terrific Themes for Year-Round Fun

Dinosaurs

Contents

Dinosaurs

What Wasn't Around?

Gather children and explain that dinosaurs lived long ago, even before humans. Talk about some things that existed during the times of the dinosaurs: mountains, oceans, trees, ferns, insects, etc. Then, ask children to think about some things that were not around when dinosaurs roamed the earth. If needed, help students by pointing out human inventions, such as telephones, radios, cars, etc. Write the list children brainstorm on chart paper or a chalkboard.

Dinosaur Directions Maze

Copy the Dinosaur Directions Maze Worksheet (page 116) for each child. Talk with children about the three dinosaurs on the worksheet, the Tyrannosaurus rex, the Apatosaurus, and the Saltopus. Give each child a worksheet and explain that it is a maze. Tell them that you will give them directions, and they should listen carefully. First, have them color each of the dinosaurs a different color. For example, say, "Color the Tyrannosaurus rex red." After children have colored the dinosaurs, tell them where to "take" each dinosaur. Give them directions such as, "Draw a trail from the Saltopus to the bone yard; draw a trail from the Apatosaurus to the forest," etc. As children work, walk around to observe their skills and assist as necessary.

Same or Different?

Copy the Same or Different? Cards (page 117). Explain to children that they should look closely at the dinosaurs. Tell them that some of the dinosaurs are just alike, while others have differences. Hold up one card at a time and allow volunteers to tell you whether the dinosaurs on the card are the same or different. If the child says they are different, have her tell how they are different.

Who Am I?

Copy the Dinosaur patterns (pages 118-126). Place several of the cards so that children can see the pictures. Give clues about each dinosaur and ask students to guess which dinosaur you are describing. Give clues such as number of legs walked on, meat-eater, plant-eater, nickname, etc. Have children point to the dinosaur they think you are describing.

Dinosaur Directions Maze Worksheet

CD-0817 *Terrific Themes for Year-Round Fun*

Dinosaur Patterns
Same or Different? Cards

Dinosaur Patterns

Allosaurus (al-o-SAW-rus)

Allosaurus was the biggest meat eater to live in North America.
Nickname: Different Lizard
Walked on two feet
Length: 36 feet
Weight: 2,000 to 4,000 pounds

Apatosaurus (a-PAT-o-SAW-rus)

Apatosaurus is no longer known as the Brontosaurus because it has been discovered that the two fossils are of the same species. The fossil given the name Apatosaurus was discovered first.
Nickname: Deceptive Lizard/Harmless Giant
Plant-Eater
Walked on four feet
Length: 65 feet
Weight: 50,000 pounds

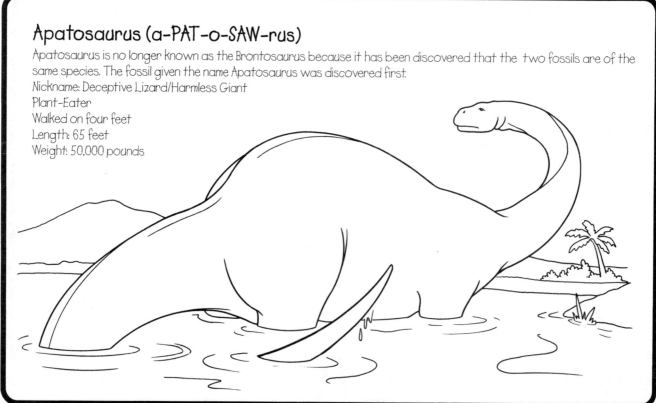

Dinosaur Patterns

Brachiosaurus (BRACK-ee-o-SAW-rus)

Brachiosaurus was one of the largest, longest, and heaviest dinosaurs ever.
Nickname: Arm Lizard
Plant-Eater
Walked on four feet
Length: 82 feet
Weight: 60,000 to 100,000 pounds

Coelophysis (SEE-lo-FISE-iss)

Coelophysis had light, hollow bones and dozens of small, serrated teeth.
Nickname: Hollow-Boned Beast
Meat-Eater
Walked on two feet
Length: 10 feet
Weight: 60 pounds

Dinosaur Patterns

Compsognathus (COMP-so-NAY-thus)

Compsognathus was about the size of a chicken. It was one of the smallest dinosaurs.
Nickname: Pretty/Elegant Jaw
Meat-Eater
Walked on two feet
Length: 2 feet
Weight: 5 to 7 pounds

Corythosaurus (cor-ITH-o-SAW-rus)

Corythosaurus' nostrils went up through a helmet-shaped, hollow, bony crest on top of its long head.
Nickname: Helmet Lizard/Duck-Billed Dinosaur
Plant-Eater
Walked on both two and four feet
Length: 33 feet
Weight: 7,000 to 8,000 pounds

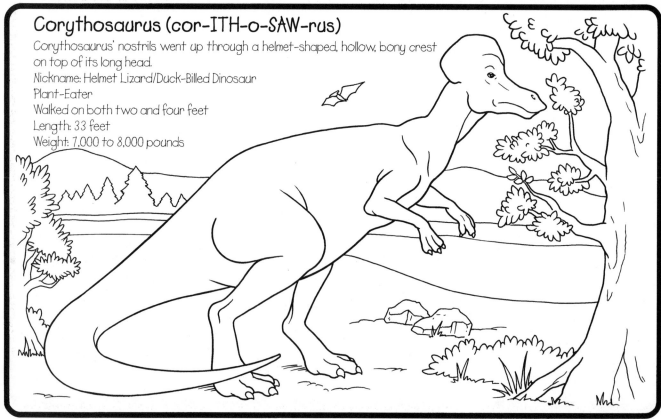

Dinosaur Patterns

Deinonychus (dine-o-NYK-us)

Deinonychus was a swift runner. It used large (5-inch long) sickle-shaped claws to attack its prey.

Nickname: Terrible Claw

Meat-Eater

Walked on two legs

Length: 9 feet

Weight: 150 to 175 pounds

Diplodocus (di-PLOD-o-cus)

Diplodocus had the smallest brain for body size. Its brain was the size of a small melon. Diplodocus also had nostrils on top of its head, almost between its eyes. It could lash its long tail against predators.

Nickname: Double-Beam

Plant-Eater

Walked on four legs

Length: 90 feet (35 feet for its neck alone!)

Weight: 24,000 pounds

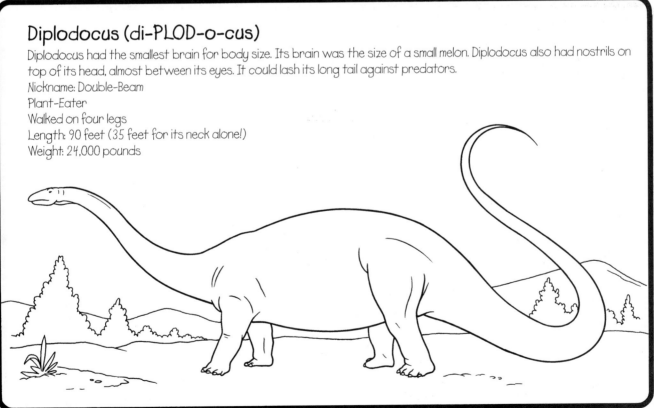

Dinosaur Patterns

Gallimimus (GAL-ih-MIME-us)

Gallimimus is believed to have been the fastest dinosaur. It had no teeth, but had a beak-like jaw.
Nickname: Chicken/Rooster Mimic
Meat-Eater and Plant-Eater
Walked on two feet
Length: 20 feet
Weight: 950 pounds

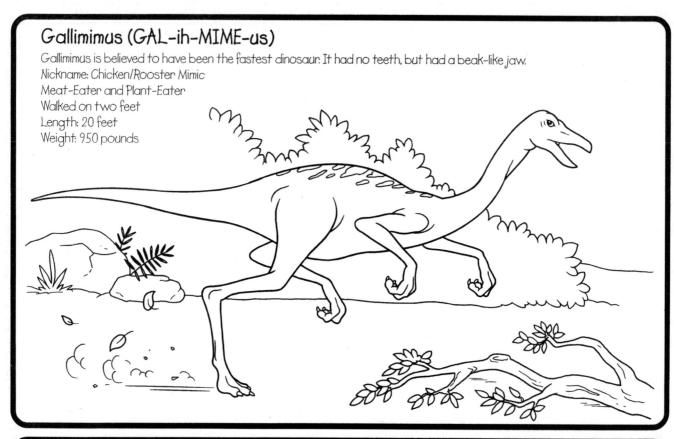

Iguanodon (ig-WAN-o-don)

Iguanodon had hoof-like claws and spiky thumbs used for protection.
Nickname: Iguana Tooth
Plant-Eater
Walked on two and four feet
Length: 30 feet
Weight: 8,000 to 9,000 pounds

Dinosaur Patterns

Oviraptor (OVE-ih-RAP-tor)

Oviraptor had a beak with two toothlike bones. It also had curved claws on its powerful forelimbs.

Nickname: Egg Thief
Meat-Eater
Walked on two feet
Length: 7 feet
Weight: 75 pounds

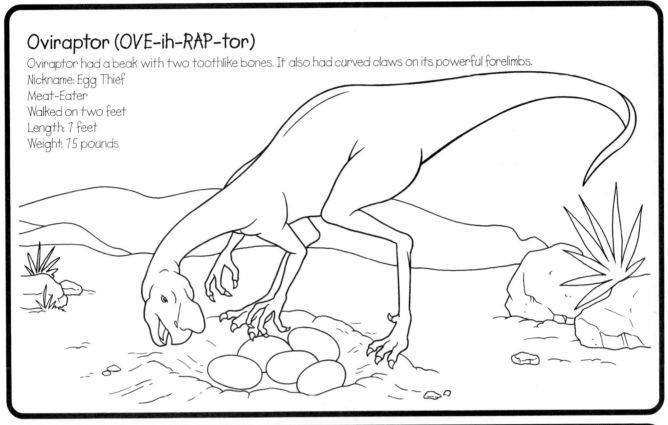

Pachycephalosaurus (PACK-ee-SEFF-a-lo-SAW-rus)

Pachycephalosaurus had bumpy knobs on its snout and along the rear of its thick skull.

Nickname: Thick-Headed Lizard
Plant-Eater
Walked on two feet
Length: 15 feet
Weight: 950 pounds

CD-0817 *Terrific Themes for Year-Round Fun*

Dinosaur Patterns

Parasaurolophus (para-SAWR-oh-LOAF-us)

Parasaurolophus had a tube as long as a baseball bat on top of its head.
Nickname: Crested Lizard
Plant-Eater
Walked on both two and four legs
Length: 33 feet
Weight: 4,000 pounds

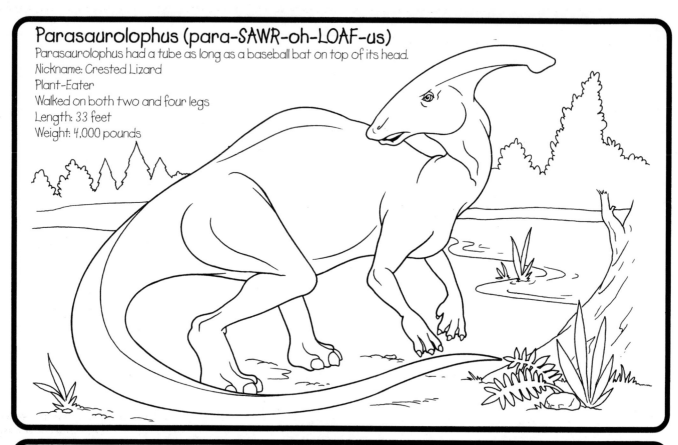

Saltopus (SAL-tuh-pus)

Saltopus was one of the smallest dinosaurs and was about the size of a house cat.
Nickname: Leaping Foot
Meat-Eater
Walked on two feet
Length: 2 feet
Weight: 3 to 4 pounds

Dinosaur Patterns

Seismosaurus (SIZE-mo-SAWR-us)

Seismosaurus is the largest dinosaur found yet. Its head was only the size of a horse's head.
Nickname: Earth-Shaking Lizard
Plant-Eater
Walked on four feet
Length: 130 feet
Weight: 60,000 to 90,000 pounds

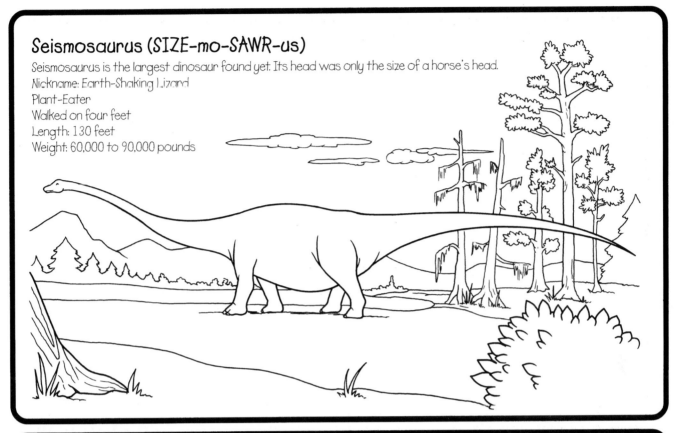

Stegosaurus (STEG-o-SAWR-us)

Stegosaurus is believed to have been the slowest dinosaur. It used the spikes on its tail for defense.
Nickname: Plate Lizard/Roof Lizard
Plant-Eater
Walked on four feet
Length: 30 feet
Weight: 6,000 pounds

Dinosaur Patterns

Triceratops (try-SERR-a-tops)

Triceratops had frills to protect its neck, horns for charging an enemy, and a parrot-like beak.
Nickname: Three-Horned Dinosaur
Plant-Eater
Walked on four feet
Length: 30 feet
Weight: 15,000 pounds

Tyrannosaurus rex (tie-RAN-o-SAW-rus REX)

Tyrannosaurus rex was one of the largest meat-eating dinosaurs.
Nickname: Tyrant Lizard King
Meat-Eater
Walked on two feet
Length: 40 feet
Weight: 12,600 pounds

Dinosaurs

Big vs. Little

Copy the Dinosaur patterns (pages 118-126). Ask children to sort the cards into two categories: dinosaurs that were big and dinosaurs that were small. When the group has finished, you might also allow children to sort the dinosaurs by other attributes: meat-eater/plant-eater; walked on two/four feet; fast/slow, etc.

Dinosaur Egg Size and Shape Sort

Copy the Dinosaur Egg Size and Shape Sort patterns (pages 128-129). Cut out the eggs. Talk with children about dinosaurs and the fact that most female dinosaurs laid eggs. Explain that different dinosaurs had different-shaped eggs. Some eggs were oval, some were round, and some were long and skinny. The smallest dinosaur eggs found were the size of chicken eggs. Some eggs have been found that were as large as a soccer ball. The largest dinosaur egg found is the size of a small watermelon and belongs to the 40 foot long Hypselosaurus. Show children the egg patterns and allow them to become familiar with the terminology of oval, round, and long. Have them sort the eggs by size and then by shape. Have children also practice matching skills by finding each egg's exact mate.

Two Tiny Dinosaurs

Copy the Dinosaur patterns (pages 120 and 124), showing the Compsognathus and the Saltopus. Tell children about the sizes of these two small dinosaurs. Both were about two feet long and weighed about five pounds. Explain that these two dinosaurs were about the size of a house cat or a chicken. Gather a bathroom scale and several items for weighing (both under and over 5 pounds). Let children estimate which items they think are heavier and which are lighter than the two tiny dinosaurs. You may also want to let them use a ruler to draw a line on the floor with chalk to show how long the two tiny dinosaurs were.

Apatosaurus Measure

Gather a roll of yarn and a measuring tape. Take children to the playground and ask them how long they think the large dinosaurs were. Have them estimate how far one might have to stretch the yarn from a mark on the playground to show the length of one of the large dinosaurs. Use the tape measure to help you place 70 feet of yarn on the ground. (You might want to tie the ends to a rock to secure the yarn.) Explain to children that the yarn shows the length of an Apatosaurus. See how many steps, body lengths, etc., it takes to get from one end of the Apatosaurus to the other.

Dinosaur Patterns
Dinosaur Egg Size and Shape Sort Patterns

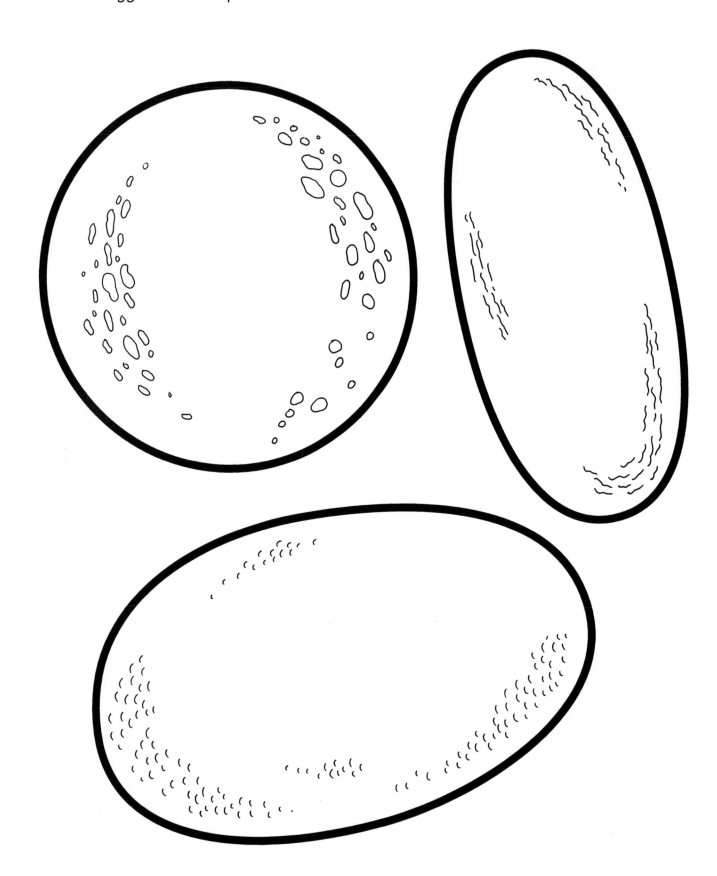

CD-0817 *Terrific Themes for Year-Round Fun*

Dinosaur Patterns
Dinosaur Egg Size and Shape Sort Patterns

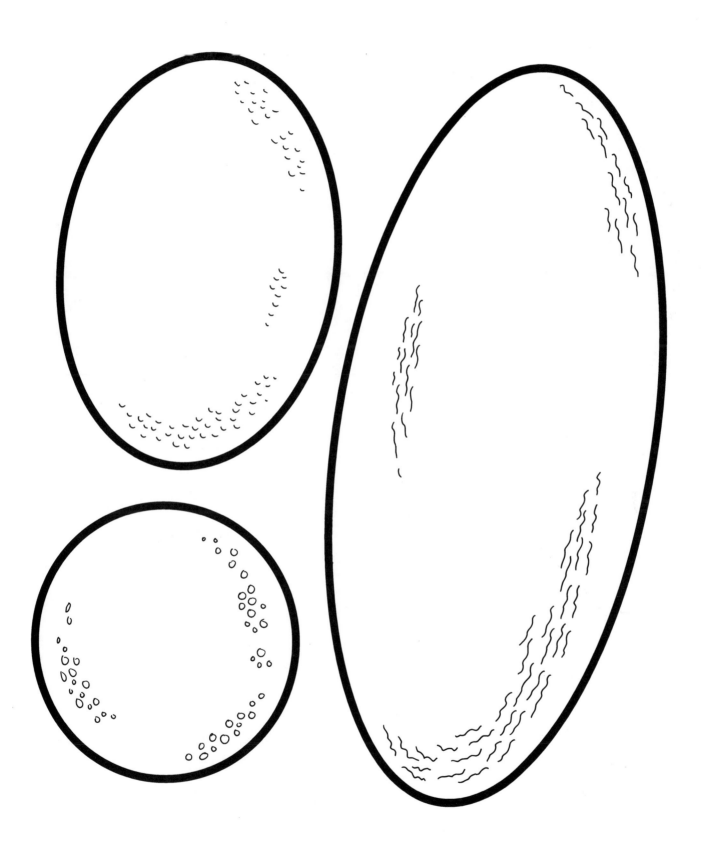

Fossil Match Worksheet

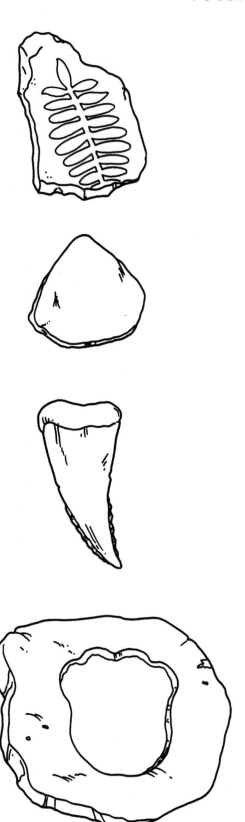

Dinosaurs

Fossil Match Worksheet

Copy one Fossil Match Worksheet (page 130) for each child. Talk about fossils and how they are made. Explain that some fossils are created when a plant or animal makes an imprint in sand or mud. When the item (such as a plant) rots away, the print is left behind in the rock. Other items such as bones and teeth turn to stone over a long period of time. Tell children that they will solve a puzzle. On the Fossil Match Worksheet there is one column of fossils and another of items that made the fossils. Allow children to match each fossil with its maker by drawing a line between the two.

Dinosaur Tooth Sort

Begin a discussion with children about the differences between meat-eaters and plant-eaters. Ask students what types of teeth each dinosaur needed. Explain that meat-eaters needed very sharp teeth to tear the meat from their prey. Most plant-eaters had flat teeth for grinding plants. Some plant-eaters had sharp beaks to tear limbs and other parts from plants. Make several copies of the Dinosaur Tooth Sort Cards (page 132) and have children sort them into meat-eater and plant-eater groups.

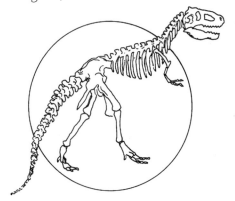

Bone Puzzle Worksheet

Copy the Bone Puzzle Worksheet (page 133) for each child. Discuss some of the special attributes of the dinosaurs on the worksheet. Explain that in one column of the worksheet there are pictures of bones from dinosaurs. In the other column are the pictures of dinosaurs to which the bones belong. Have children draw a line from each bone to the corresponding dinosaur.

Which Makes Footprints?

Gather dish pans or buckets half-filled with each of the following: mud, wet sand, dry sand, cotton balls, water, etc. Explain to children that fossilized dinosaur footprints helped paleontologists study the speed of dinosaurs and determine if the dinosaur that made the footprints walked on two or four legs. Show children the containers and have them predict in which materials a footprint can be made. Allow children to press their feet into different containers to see if their predictions are correct.

Dinosaur Patterns
Dinosaur Tooth Sort Cards

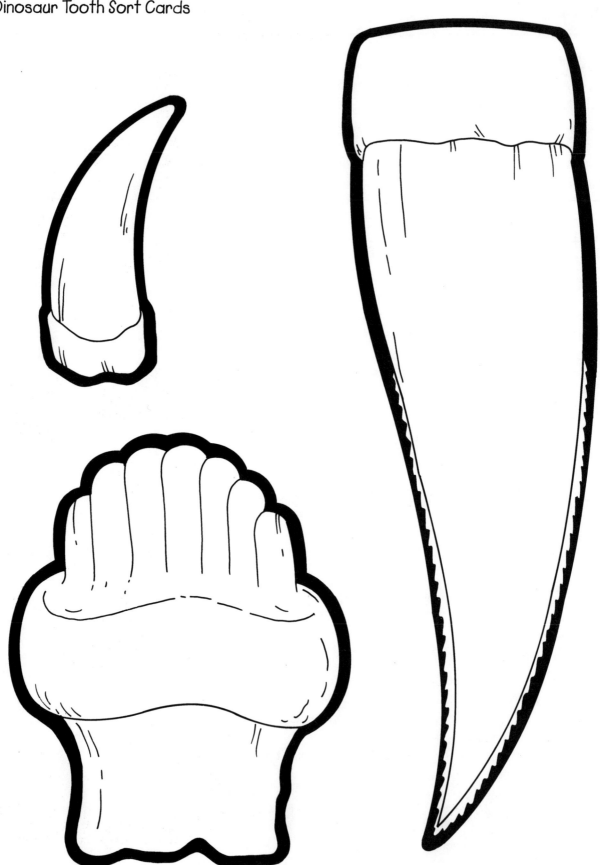

Bone Puzzle Worksheet

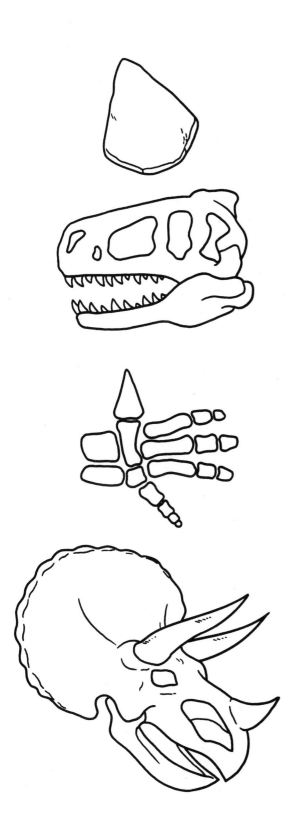

Adapted Songs

The Dinosaur Song

(to the tune of "The Wheels on the Bus")
The Tyrannosaurus rex had great big teeth,
Great big teeth, great big teeth.
The Tyrannosaurus rex had great big teeth,
When the dinosaurs roamed.

Additional verses:
The Apatosaurus had a very long tail…
The Diplodocus's nostrils were on top of its head…
The Saltopus was as small as a cat…

The Dinosaurs Go Marching

(to the tune of "The Ants Go Marching")
The dinosaurs go marching one by one, hurrah, hooray.
The dinosaurs go marching one by one, hurrah, hooray.
The dinosaurs go marching one by one, the little one
  stops to stand in the sun,
And they all go marching round and round and up and down.

Additional verses:
Three… to eat from a tree.   Two… to admire the view.
Five… to stay alive.   Four… to give a roar.
Seven… to look to heaven.   Six… to gather some sticks.
Nine… to scratch his spine. Eight… to roller-skate.
                             Ten… to feel the wind.

Dinosaurs, Dinosaurs

(to the tune of "Teddy Bear, Teddy Bear")
Dinosaurs, dinosaurs stomped around.
Dinosaurs, dinosaurs shook the ground.
Dinosaurs, dinosaurs far and near.
Dinosaurs, dinosaurs are no longer here.

I'd Like to Be a Dinosaur

(to the tune of "Mary had a Little Lamb")
I'd like to be a dinosaur, dinosaur, dinosaur.
And if I were a dinosaur, I would be
a _____.
(Allow each child to name the dinosaur she
would want to be.)

Movement Activities

Dinosaur Stomping

Explain to children that some dinosaurs moved slowly and some moved quickly. Have students match your stomping rhythm. Then, have them match your stomping patterns, such as slow, slow, fast, fast, fast.

Dinosaur Dancing

Allow children to make the dinosaur tails described on page 137. Play dancing music and let students dance like dinosaurs while wearing the dinosaur tails.

Who Are You?

Gather children and have them stand in a circle holding hands. Teach them the song that follows and then have them sing it while walking in a circle. At the end of the song, describe a dinosaur and have children guess which one you are describing. (To the tune of "Skip to My Lou") Who, who, who are you? Who, who, who are you? Who, who, who are you? Which dinosaur are you?

Dinosaur-Related Jobs

Begin a discussion with children about the people who work with dinosaur studies. Have them list as many jobs as they can think of that relate to dinosaurs. Write down the list. After students have named all of the jobs they can think of, discuss each in detail, including the ones listed below. Allow children to tell you which jobs they think they would enjoy.

Geologist—scientist who studies rocks and minerals. A geologist can tell how old the rocks are and where they came from.
Museum Director—oversees the setup and production of dinosaur exhibits
Paleontologist—scientist who studies ancient animals and plants

How Would You Feel?

Begin a discussion with children about feelings. Have them name a few feelings and what might make them feel that way. Explain that you will give them situations and you want them to tell you how they might feel if they were the dinosaur in the situation. Use the examples listed below and add your own. Remind children that there may be many correct answers to each example. You may also wish to have them make up a few examples of their own for the other children to answer.

How would you feel if...

1. You were a hungry Tyrannosaurus rex who just chased another dinosaur for a very long time and didn't catch it? (tired, hungry, frustrated, angry, etc.)
2. You were a baby Apatosaurus and you saw a Tyrannosaurus rex running toward you? (scared, curious, nervous, etc.)
3. You were a mother dinosaur watching her babies hatch? (happy, excited, nervous, etc.)

Taking Turns

Obtain a large plastic or stuffed dinosaur toy. Ask children to sit in a circle. Explain that they will pass the dinosaur around. Tell them that while they are holding the dinosaur, they should answer the question you ask at the beginning of the round. Each round, ask a question like, "What is your favorite dinosaur?" or "What do you like best about dinosaurs?" Focus children's attention on the importance of listening to others and waiting for their turns to speak.

Fossil Necklace

Allow each child to roll a piece of self-hardening clay into a medium-sized ball (about 2" in diameter). After the clay is in a ball shape, have each child use a roller to flatten her clay into a circle, about $\frac{1}{4}$" thick. Have each child use a straw to punch a hole in the top of her circle. Children should then make "fossil" impressions by pressing items in to the clay, taking care not to go through. Recommended items for pressing are toy dinosaur feet, leaves, shells, etc. Let the clay harden and attach yarn through the hole to make a necklace.

Dinosaur Skin Texture Rubbing

Talk with children about how dinosaurs' skin may have looked and felt. Have children make texture rubbings from objects around the room and on the playground. To make texture rubbings, have children place pieces of newsprint paper on top of textured areas such as bricks, trees, etc. Have them color small areas on the paper by rubbing with the sides of crayons. Explain that they should circle areas that show textures that were rough and bumpy like dinosaur skin might have been.

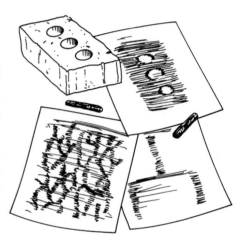

Mock Amber Fossils

Gather small bowls, a spoon, yellow food coloring, a container of clear-drying glue, small paper cups, and an assortment of small, inexpensive trinkets. Talk with children about amber fossils. Explain that in prehistoric times, insects or leaves sometimes got trapped in tree sap. If conditions were right, the sap fossilized into amber. If possible, show children pictures of amber fossils. Tell them that they will make pretend amber fossils. Allow children to squirt some glue and a few drops of the food coloring in a bowl and mix completely. Then, have each child arrange a few trinkets in the bottom of a paper cup. Next, have him pour some of the glue mixture over the trinkets. Have children carefully set their arrangements, now covered with glue, on an out-of-the-way counter or shelf. Let dry for a few days until clear-yellow. You may wish to allow children to check their creations periodically to watch the stages of the drying glue. When the glue is dry, children may tear off the paper cups so they can see through their fossils.

Fern Rubbings

Explain to children that the fern is a plant that has been around since dinosaur times. Gather several pieces of ferns, wrapper-less crayons, and newsprint paper. Place the materials on a table and allow children to place the ferns under pieces of newsprint and rub with the sides of crayons to make fern crayon rubbings.

Dinosaur Tails

Gather a few packages of paper cups and a skein of yarn. Show children how to punch a small hole in the bottom of a cup and thread yarn through the hole. Demonstrate how to tie knots in the yarn as they go so the cups will stay in place. Each child should thread his yarn through about eight paper cups. When finished, allow children to attach their creations to their clothes to make dinosaur tails. Have children tell you which dinosaur they are pretending to be.

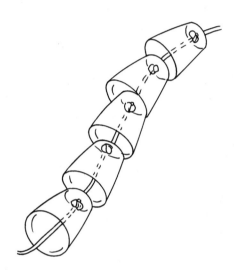

Dinosaur Door Stops

Have parents bring in clean, empty bleach bottles the week before you plan to do this activity. Gather the bleach bottles, a variety of colors of construction paper, scissors, glue, markers or crayons, a dishpan or bucket, a funnel, a ladle, and a bag of kitty litter. Trace the Dinosaur Door Stop patterns (pages 138-140) onto tagboard. Place the materials on an art table. Pour the kitty litter into the dishpan or bucket and place the ladle and funnel nearby. Allow children to use the patterns to create a dinosaur with the construction paper and markers. When they have cut out the pieces for their dinosaurs, have them first use the funnel and ladle to pour several scoops of kitty litter into the bleach bottles and tightly secure the lids. They are then to glue their dinosaur patterns onto the bleach bottles to create colorful door stops.

Dinosaur Patterns
Dinosaur Door Stops

CD-0817 *Terrific Themes for Year-Round Fun*

Dinosaur Patterns
Dinosaur Door Stops

CD-0817 *Terrific Themes for Year-Round Fun*

Dinosaur Patterns
Dinosaur Door Stops

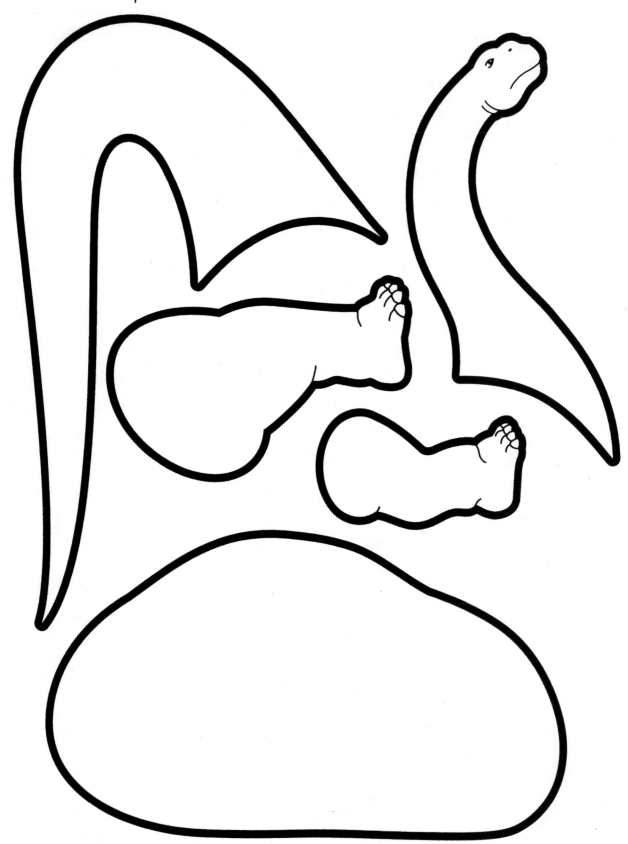

CD-0817 *Terrific Themes for Year-Round Fun*

Herd Walking

Tell children that there is evidence that some dinosaurs traveled in herds. Have them stand in a tight group and try to walk around or run in herds on the playground. This will most likely begin as chaos. Ask children how they can work together to move in a herd. Let them experiment with their ideas to see which ones work.

Dinosaur Bone Drop

Gather a package of clothespins (old-fashioned push style if possible) and a large coffee can or plastic fish bowl. Paint the clothespins white to represent dinosaur bones. Allow children to take turns standing over the coffee can or fish bowl and dropping the "dinosaur bones" into the target. Encourage them to improve their scores each time.

Dinosaur Race

Copy the Dinosaur Race Game Board pattern (pages 142-143), color it, and mount it in a file folder. Gather a die and several different-colored plastic toy dinosaurs small enough to fit in the game board spaces. Invite two to four children to each pick out a dinosaur for his game piece. Allow each child to have a turn rolling the die, counting the dots, then moving his dinosaur that number of spaces. The first child to reach the end of the board is the winner. If your students can read, add phrases in the spaces such as, "Move back two spaces," or, "Bonus: Move ahead to the red space," etc.

Dinosaur Toss

Gather a bouncy ball and draw a picture of a dinosaur on it. Round up children and have them stand in a circle. Select a child to be the "dinosaur catcher" and have her stand outside the circle. Children standing in the circle toss the "dinosaur" (ball) to each other. The dinosaur catcher tries to tag the child holding the "dinosaur." The other children try to toss the "dinosaur" to someone else before the person holding it is tagged. So children do not become frustrated, limit each round to a few minutes or have more than one dinosaur catcher at a time.

Dinosaur Patterns
Dinosaur Race Game Board

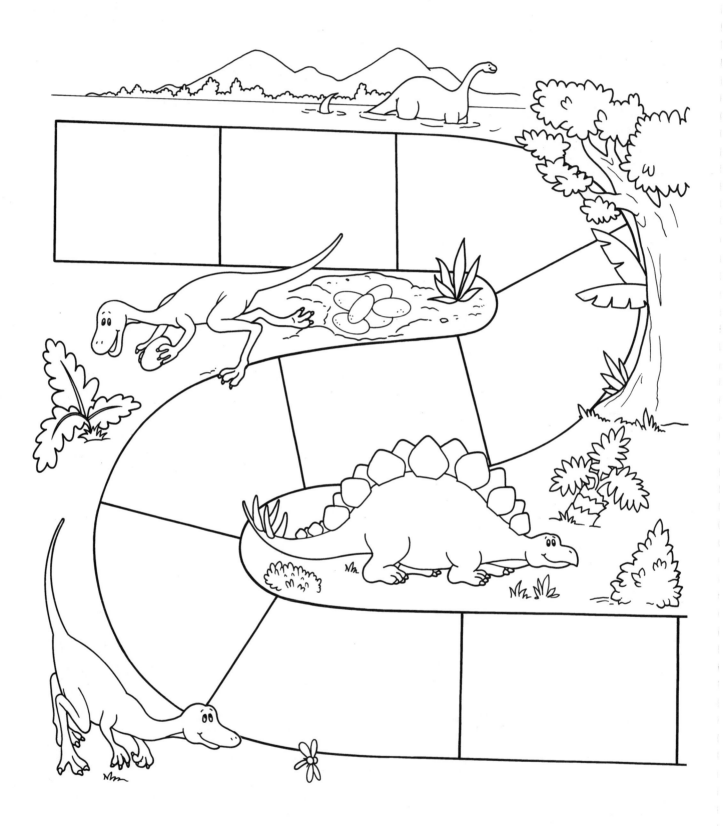

Dinosaur Patterns
Dinosaur Race Game Board

CD-0817 *Terrific Themes for Year-Round Fun*

Dinosaurs

Dinosaur Eggs

Allow children to help you with the following directions: Gather at least one hard-boiled egg for each child in the group. When cooled, gently crack the eggs but do not peel. Mix up a package of powdered juice drink and pour into a large bowl. Gently place the cracked eggs into the juice mix and refrigerate for two days. On the third day, allow children to peel and eat these colorful "dinosaur eggs."

Allergy and Food Preference Note

Before completing any food activity, ask parental permission and inquire about children's food allergies. Common food allergies include peanuts and other nuts, dairy, eggs, berries, etc. Parents may have religious or other preferences that will prevent children from eating certain foods.

Dinosaur Bone Biscuits

Purchase a few packages of canned biscuits. Have children wash their hands and give each an uncooked biscuit on a paper plate. Allow children to mold their biscuits into dinosaur bone shapes, then bake as directed and enjoy for a snack.

Dinosaur Dip

Gather a bottle of ranch dressing, green food coloring, small cups, plastic spoons, and an assortment of broccoli, cauliflower, carrots, or any other desired vegetables. Give each child a spoon and cup. Allow him to pour a small amount of ranch dressing into his cup, then add a few drops of the food coloring. Have each child stir his dressing until he has "green dinosaur dip," then enjoy with the vegetables.

Meat-Eaters' and Plant-Eaters' Delight

This is a good activity to substitute for the regular lunch menu if possible. Talk with children about how some dinosaurs were meat-eaters and some were plant-eaters. Place a variety of cold cuts along with fruits and vegetables for children to choose from. As children select their assortment of foods, have them tell which type of dinosaur would have enjoyed each food.

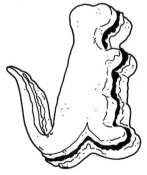

Dinosaur Sandwiches

Gather a loaf of bread, peanut butter, and jelly. Allow each child to make his own peanut butter and jelly sandwich. Then, to make a dinosaur sandwich, allow children to use dinosaur-shaped cookie cutters to cut their sandwiches. While children are enjoying their sandwiches, encourage them to talk about their favorite dinosaurs and what they ate.

Fall

Contents

Fall

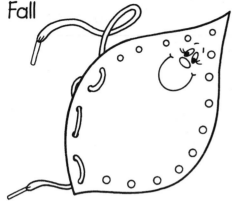

Lacing Leaves

Using the Leaf pattern (page 148), cut several leaf shapes from tagboard. Use a hole punch to place holes as indicated on the pattern. Allow children to lace the leaves using shoelaces or blunt plastic needles and yarn.

Berry Basket Weaving

Obtain several plastic berry baskets, yarn in fall colors, plastic needles, and tape. Attach a length of yarn to each needle by threading the needle and taping the short end of the yarn to the longer piece. Show children how to weave the yarn through the basket by moving the needle through the holes.

Fall Lotto

Copy the Fall Lotto Card pattern (page 149) for each student and, using a variety of fall stickers, place a sticker in each of the spaces. Give each child a card and have children use bingo chips to cover the fall shapes on their cards as you call them out. The first child to get three in a row is to call, "Lotto!"

Fall Characteristics

Take students for a walk outside and have them notice events or items related to the season. Discuss what they see. After the walk, ask students to individually dictate what they noticed about fall. You may want to do this during a time when children will not hear each other's answers. As a child dictates, write his words on the bottom of a piece of construction paper. Allow child to illustrate his words with crayons, markers, or chalk. Display the pictures where the parents can see them. As an extension to this activity, discuss what the outdoors was like during the summer and what has changed since then. Ask children to predict how they think it will be different in the winter.

Find the Missing Word

Tell children that you will say sentences about fall that have missing words and that they should guess what the missing words are. Explain that there may be more than one correct answer. Use the following sentences and then make up your own additional sentences.

Apples are red; pumpkins are _____.

Pumpkins grow on vines; acorns grow on _____.

Nuts are brown; corn is _____.

Acorn Tracing and Texture

Copy and cut out and trace the Acorn pattern (page 150) onto thick pieces of paper. Give each child a pattern, a brown crayon, and his choice of red, orange, or yellow construction paper. Show children how to hold the acorn pattern while tracing around it. After they have finished tracing their acorns, take them outside to a tree and show them how to make rubbings. Each student should hold his construction paper against a tree trunk with an interesting bark texture. She can then rub the side of a wrapper-less crayon on the construction paper to get the tree impression inside the acorn shape. Have each child write the the word acorn below her rubbing.

Rhyming Brainstorm

Ask children to define the word "rhyme." Encourage them to give examples of rhyming words. Tell children that you want them to think of words that rhyme with "fall." Give each child a chance to give you a word. As children dictate, write the words on the chalkboard or butcher paper and repeat together when completed. You can also use the words "leaf," "corn," "tree," and other words that pertain to the season.

Apple and Worm ABC Match

Using the Apple and Worm patterns (page 151), make 26 tagboard apples and 26 tagboard worms. Write an uppercase letter on each apple and a lowercase letter on each worm. Show the apple cards to the class and have students say the letters with you. When you have said the alphabet several times, ask for volunteers to name the letters. Repeat with the worm cards. Then, hold up three pairs of matching uppercase and lowercase cards and ask children to match the letters together. Gradually increase the number of letters offered at one time. Allow children to use the cards during center time.

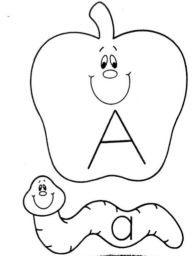

CD-0817 *Terrific Themes for Year-Round Fun*

Fall Patterns
Leaf

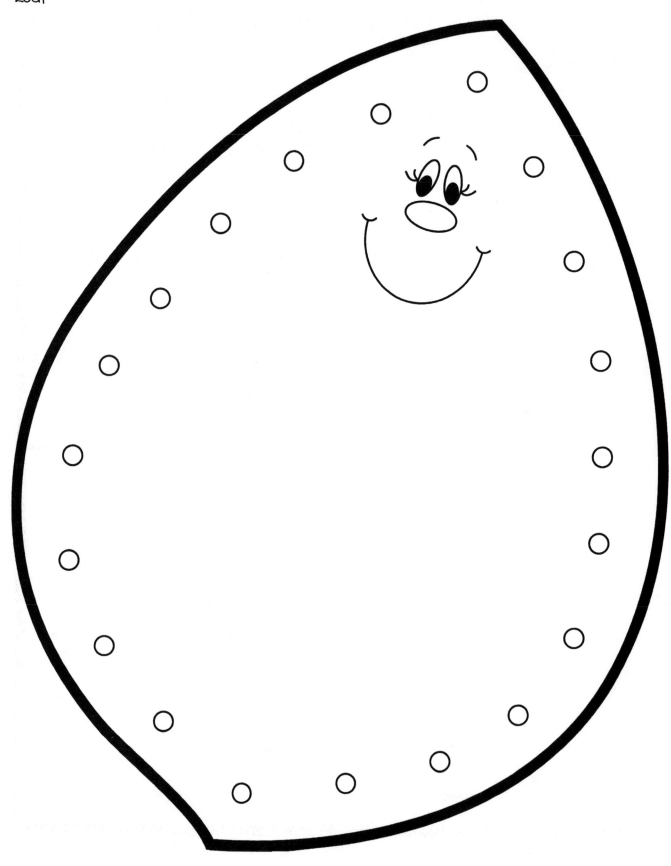

Fall Patterns
Lotto Card

Fall Patterns
Acorn

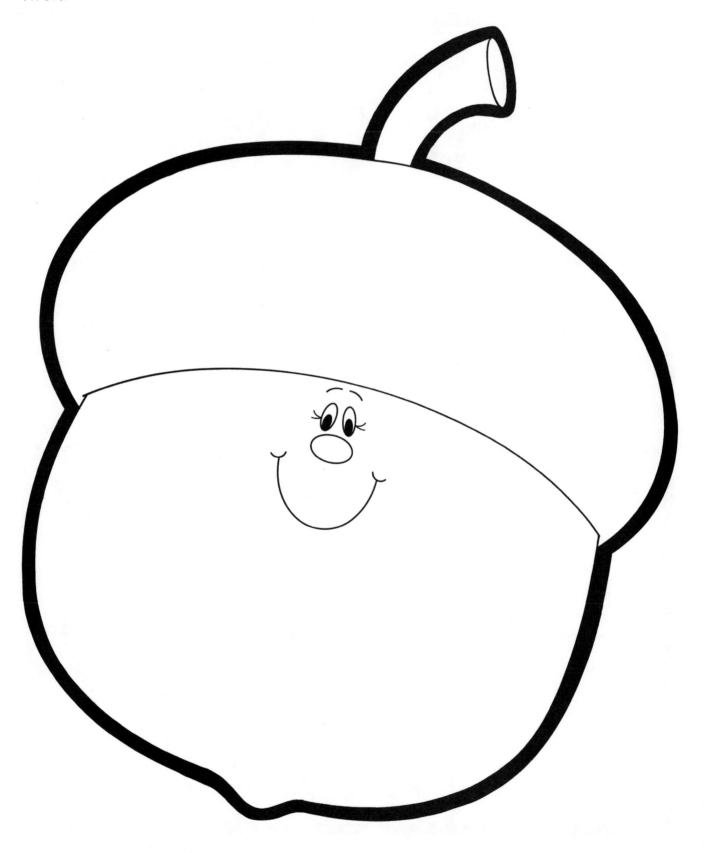

 CD-0817 *Terrific Themes for Year-Round Fun*

Fall Patterns
Apple and Worm

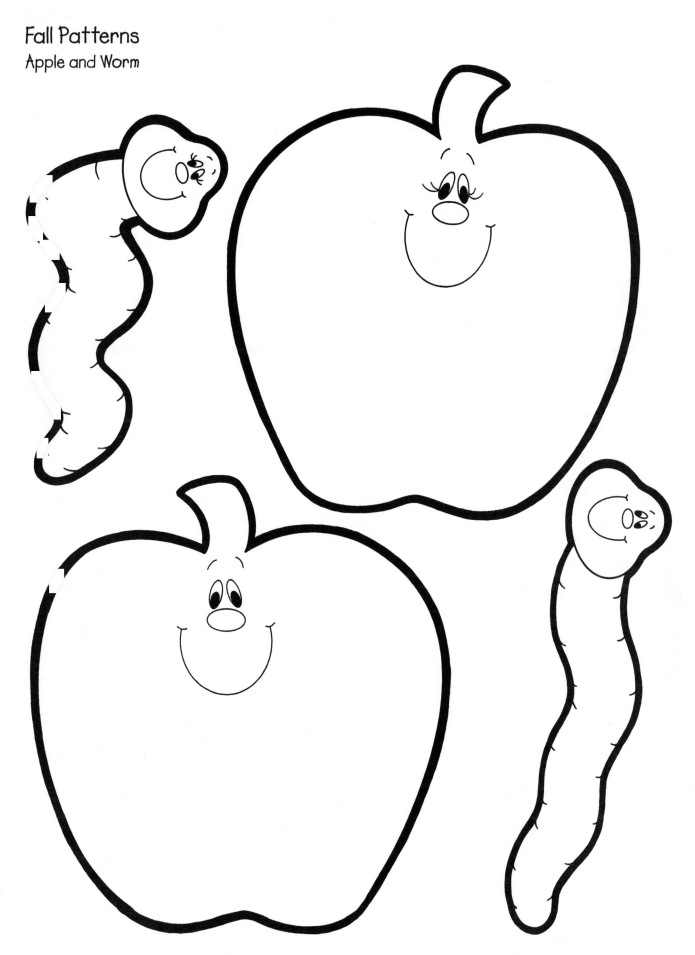

Nut Sorting

Gather an assortment of nuts (acorns, walnuts, pecans, etc.) and a muffin tin. While children rotate to centers, invite one or two children to join you at a table with the materials. Place one of each kind of nut in a separate section of the muffin tin. Have children sort the remaining nuts with their matches in the tin.

Smallest vs. Largest Acorns

Copy and cut out the assorted sizes of Acorns patterns (page 154). Gather a small group of children and have them review the different pattern sizes and show you a small acorn, then a large acorn. Explain that the words "smallest" and "largest" describe the ones that are smaller or larger than all the rest. Ask each child to show you either the smallest or the largest acorn. Then have students arrange the patterns from smallest to largest.

Sorting Leaves

Hold up real, silk, or colored-paper leaves (patterns on page 155) one at a time and have children describe them. Then, hold up two at a time and ask them to look for similar qualities. Explain that you can sort the leaves by color, size, shape, etc. Have children sort the leaves by these attributes.

Leaf Graphing

If you are able to collect fall leaves around your school, take students outside and ask them each to collect three leaves. This works best in early fall before leaves turn brown. If you cannot collect the leaves outside, use the patterns on page 155 and cut leaves from yellow, red, brown, and orange construction paper. Cut enough leaves so that each child has three. Make sure you cut a different number of each color leaf. Draw a graph on butcher paper, chart paper, or the chalkboard, listing the four colors at the top. Allow each child to use tape and place his leaves on the graph under the appropriate colors. After all of the leaves have been placed on the graph, ask children to tell you which color has the most, which has the least, how many more one color has than another, if any have the same amount, etc.

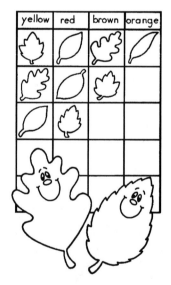

yellow	red	brown	orange

Apple Cutting

For this activity, you will need an apple, a kitchen knife for you, four to six dull plastic knives, and enough soft red modeling clay to give four to six children apple-sized pieces. Show a small group of children the apple. Ask them how you might make the apple into two pieces so you could share with a friend. The children should say that you can cut the apple in half. Cut the apple in half. Ask children how many pieces you have. Explain that when you cut something into two equal pieces, you have "halves," each being called a "half." Give each child a piece of red modeling clay and ask him to mold it into the shape of an apple. Allow students to use the dull knives to cut their "apples" in half. Encourage children to try to cut equal pieces.

Crayon Match

Using five enlarged Apple patterns (page 151), make a set of cards that have colored lines the length of crayons. The first apple should have one line, the second should have two lines, the third should have three lines, etc. Ask children to place crayons on the lines. Then, ask them to count the crayons. For an extra challenge, have children match the crayons' colors to the colors of the lines.

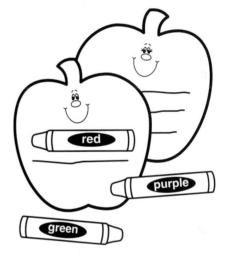

Fall Match-Ups

Gather several different objects related to fall. Tell children that you will describe a fall object and will ask them to find something with a similar trait. For example, you may tell a child, "This leaf is orange; please find something orange," or, "This nut is round; please find something round." After each child has found something, allow volunteers to make up problems for their classmates.

Tall vs. Short

Copy, color, and cut out the Tall vs. Short Flashcards (pages 156-157). Talk with children about the words "tall" and "short." Ask them to describe something using each word. Hold up the flashcards and ask children to tell you which objects are tall and which are short. Later, during center time, allow children to use the cards individually.

Fall Patterns
Assorted Sizes of Acorns

Fall Patterns
Leaf

CD-0817 *Terrific Themes for Year-Round Fun*

Fall Patterns
Tall vs. Short Flashcards

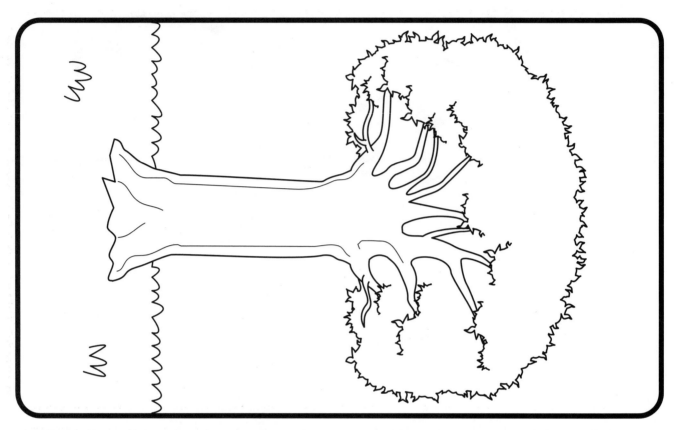

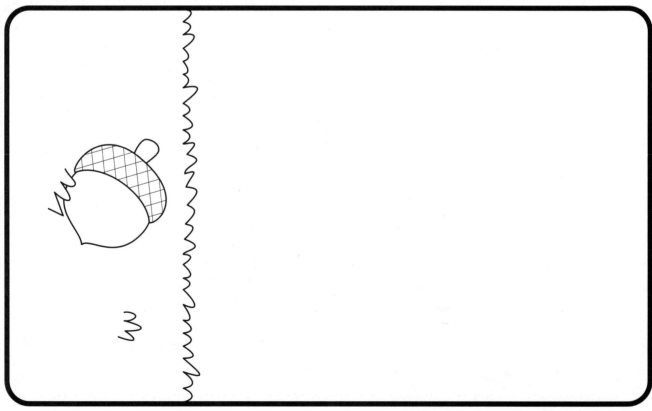

CD-0817 *Terrific Themes for Year-Round Fun*

Fall Patterns
Tall vs. Short Flashcards

Seeds We Eat vs. Seeds We Don't Eat

Gather seeds that can be eaten, such as assorted beans, peanuts, corn, peas, pumpkin seeds, pecans. Also gather seeds that are not eaten, such as acorns, watermelon seeds, peach pits, flower seeds. Make a poster from butcher paper or poster board with the caption "Seeds We Eat" on one half and "Seeds We Don't Eat" on the other. Show children each seed and ask them to identify it if they can; otherwise, identify it for them. Ask them if the seed is normally eaten by people. After children decide if it is eaten or not eaten, write the name of the seed on the appropriate side of the poster and allow a child to tape the seed beside the name.

Fall-Colored Celery

Show children a stalk of celery. Ask them to describe it to you. Explain that celery is a plant and, like people, plants need water to live. Allow them to watch as you cut the edge of the celery to expose a new edge. Cut the celery down the middle of the stalk and stop about two inches from the leaves on the end. Allow volunteers to help you fill one glass with water and red food coloring, and one glass with water and yellow food coloring. Place one half of the celery stalk into each glass. Ask children to guess what will happen to the celery and food coloring, and write down the guesses to review later. The next day, you will have a brightly colored piece of celery: red or yellow on the cut parts of the stalk, and orange where the colors join. Ask children to describe what they think happened, and why the celery is different colors. Review their guesses to see if anyone correctly guessed what would happen.

Allergy and Food Preference Note

Before completing any food activity, ask parental permission and inquire about children's food allergies. Common food allergies include peanuts and other nuts, dairy, eggs, berries, etc. Parents may have religious or other preferences that will prevent children from eating certain foods.

Corn Tasting Party

Obtain many types of corn (popcorn, corn on the cob, canned corn, frozen corn, and creamed corn) and prepare them for a tasting party. Encourage children to taste as many different types of corn as they desire. Ask them to describe the way each tastes and feels, and how it differs from the others. Ask children to describe how they think each type of corn was processed and how it is different from the others.

Adapted Songs

Little Apples
(to the tune of "Ten Little Indians")
One little, two little, three little apples,
Four little, five little, six little apples,
Seven little, eight little, nine little apples,
On my apple tree.
Munch little, munch little, munch little apples,
Crunch little, crunch little, crunch little apples,
A bunch of little, bunch of little, bunch of little apples,
Good for you and me.

Apple, Apple on the Tree
(to the tune of "Twinkle, Twinkle Little Star")
Apple, apple on the tree,
I know you are good for me.
You are fun to munch and crunch,
For a snack or in my lunch.
Apple, apple on the tree,
I know you are good for me.

Leaves, Leaves Everywhere
(to the tune of "Row, Row, Row Your Boat")
Leaves, leaves everywhere,
Falling off the trees,
Red and yellow, orange and brown,
A wonderful sight to see.

I'm a Little Squirrel
(to the tune of "I'm a Little Teapot")
I'm a little squirrel, fuzzy and gray.
When fall comes, I gather nuts all day,
So that when the winter comes, you see,
I'll have food for my family and me.

Movement Activities

Falling Leaves
Play music for children to listen to (waltzes work well for this activity). First have children lie down on the floor, close their eyes, and listen to the music. As they listen, tell them to picture in their minds a large tree. Have students describe the tree with its fall colors. Tell them to imagine feeling the breezes blow gently, then a harder wind that blows the leaves off the trees. Next, instruct them to slowly stand up and pretend to move like the leaves in the gentle breeze. Then, have them move as if a strong wind is blowing (making sure to watch out for classmates). Allow children to finish the dance as leaves falling to the ground.

Comin' Round the Mountain
Gather materials (such as water jugs, spoons, wash boards, etc.) for a "barn dance." Tell children that people all over the world celebrate harvest. Many people celebrate by throwing parties (hoedowns or barn dances). Allow students to dance and sing and use the materials to perform the song, "She'll be Comin' Round the Mountain."

Finger Play

The Apple Tree
Way up high in the apple tree. (Point up, then hold arms in circle overhead.)
Two little apples smiled at me. (Hold up two fingers, then point to cheeks and smile.)
I shook that tree as hard as I could. (Pretend to shake tree.)
Down came the apples. Mmm, they were good! (Point down, then rub tummy.)

Harvest Hoedown

Have children help you plan an old-fashioned hoedown and allow them to invite their families. Include hay rides, watermelon-rolling races, spoon-and-egg races, etc. Allow children cooking time to prepare treats such as pigs-in-a-blanket, sugar cookies, apple cider, homemade butter, etc. Enlist a parent volunteer to dress up as a scarecrow to read fall-related stories. Depending on your school, you may wish to hold the event during a school day or on a weekend. Allow children to create invitations for the event and posters to display throughout the school using a variety of art media. Encourage families to come dressed in farm attire. If your budget allows, offer a door prize for the best costume.

Field Trips

Several field trip destinations lend themselves to added experiences for fall. You may wish to take the group to an apple orchard to see the apples being readied for market. Visit a farm to see actual harvesting firsthand. A visit to a park to see the trees' changing leaves would be an ideal opportunity to have a last picnic before winter.

Weather Dresss

Copy, color, and cut out the Weather Dress patterns (pages 161-163). Glue them to tagboard for extra durability. If you wish to use the pieces with a flannel board, cut each pattern from an appropriate color of felt. If you do not have a flannel board, laminate all pieces or cover them with clear contact paper. Place the cutouts on the flannel board, or tape them to the chalkboard or wall. Hold up each article of clothing and ask for volunteers from the group to identify each and describe the type of weather in which they would wear it. Next ask the class to describe the weather outside. Place the clothing patterns on a table and ask children to choose clothing appropriate for fall. Allow them to place the clothing on the cutouts.

Fall Patterns
Weather Dress Patterns

CD-0817 *Terrific Themes for Year-Round Fun*

Fall Patterns
Weather Dress Patterns

Fall Patterns
Weather Dress Patterns

Apple Seed Apples

Save apple seeds from other activities and snacks. Using the Apple patterns (page 151), cut red, yellow, and green construction paper into the shapes of apples, or have children do so if their skills permit. Let each child choose the color he would like his apple to be. Allow children to use the apple seeds and glue to decorate the construction-paper apples.

Hand Tree Mural

Squeeze puddles of fall-colored tempera paints on several plates. Prepare a piece of butcher paper by drawing or painting a bare tree on it. Provide paint smocks for children to wear. Instruct each child to press his hand in a plate of paint and then onto the bare tree to make a leaf on the tree. Have him describe the leaf he made by naming the color or colors found in it. Allow each child to repeat using all of the colors. Do not have the children wash their hands between leaves because the mixing of colors will look like fall leaves and may bring up discussions about color mixing. Encourage children to remember fallen leaves they have seen at the bottoms of trees and to add a few at the bottom of the tree on the mural.

Apple Prints

Cut three apples in half. Prepare shallow dishes for red, yellow, and green paint and place two apple halves in each. Place the materials and white construction paper on an art table and allow two children to work at the station at a time. Instruct children to press the apples in the paint and then onto their papers to make apple prints. Tell them to create designs with their apple prints and allow them to use the paint to add details to their pictures.

Cardboard Tube Tree

Gather short and long cardboard tubes. Cut the long cardboard tubes in half. Have each child paint his tube with brown tempera paint and let it dry. Then, ask children to tear fall-colored tissue paper into three-inch strips. Have them glue the tissue paper to the inside and outside of the top edge of the tube to make a beautiful fall tree.

Fall Crayons

Give each child one brown crayon and two each of red, yellow, and orange. Instruct children to remove the crayons' paper wrappers and break the crayons into small pieces. Have children drop their crayons into a foil-lined muffin tin (one section per child). As they do this, make a chart to record the location of each child's crayons in the muffin tin. Place the muffin tin in an oven preheated to 300°F. Allow the crayons to stay in the oven for about six minutes, until the crayons are blended, not completely melted. Let children peek at the crayons if your oven has a window and safety measures allow. Remove the muffin tin from the oven and allow it to cool for 30-40 minutes. When it is cooled, remove the foil and pass out the colorful fall crayons. Allow students to create fall pictures with their new crayons.

Leaf Crayon Rubbings

Collect fallen leaves of many shapes. Place the leaves, newsprint paper, and fall-colored crayons without the paper wrappers on the art table. Instruct children to place the leaves under their papers one at a time and gently rub over them with the flat sides of the crayons. Encourage them to use many leaves and colors in their pictures.

Nature Painting

Take students outside and ask them to each find something "natural" with which they would like to paint. You may need to give them examples such as a blade of grass, leaf, pine needle, acorn, etc. Once children have found objects with which to paint, allow them to use the objects, 12" x 18" paper, and fall-colored tempera paints to make paintings. (You may want to do this outside if the weather permits.) Write each child's name and the object used on each paper. Then, give children opportunities to show their papers, describe the objects used, and explain how they worked. Discuss with the group why some objects worked well and some did not. Allow children to share objects or gather more to add to their paintings if they wish.

Hide and Seek Apples

Cut out construction-paper apples so there are two apples for each student (Apple pattern on page 151, if needed.) Hide the apples in the classroom before or after class, or ask children to cover their eyes while you place the apples around the room for the them to find. Instruct children to begin looking for the apples. After a child has found two apples, he should return to his seat with his apples. Then, permit children, a few at a time, to take turns hiding the apples for their classmates. The apples can be decorated and displayed in the room after the games are complete.

Johnny Appleseed Says

Begin by teaching the rules to the game Simon Says, but for a fall twist on the game, call this activity "Johnny Appleseed Says." If you are playing with young children, do not have them sit out if they make a mistake. Instead, have them correct their actions. Give each child an apple or paper apple cutout. The teacher should be Johnny Appleseed for the first game to be sure children understand the rules. Give directions in reference to the apple. For example: "Johnny Appleseed say . . . hold your apple over your head, shake your apple in front of you, etc." Allow children to take turns being Johnny Appleseed and giving directions in reference to the apple.

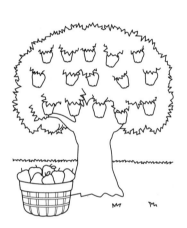

Fall Color Beanbag Toss

Gather four shoe boxes and cover them with red, brown, yellow, and orange construction or contact paper. Make beanbags from coordinating material and beans. Have children take turns picking up a beanbag, naming its color, and trying to toss it into the matching box.

Fall Concentration

Copy each Fall Concentration Cards page (pages 167-168) twice. Color, laminate, and cut out the cards. Show a small group of children the cards and explain that there are two of each card. Explain that you will place the cards facedown and they are to take turns turning over two cards to see if the pictures on the cards match. When a student finds a match, he should take the two cards and put them in his pile. If two cards turned over do not match, the cards should be turned facedown again. When all of the cards have been gathered, each child should count the number of pairs in his pile. The child with the most pairs is the winner.

Fall Patterns
Fall Concentration Cards

Fall Patterns
Fall Concentration Cards

Farm Animals

Contents

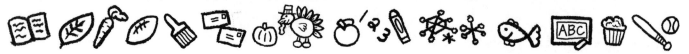

Lacing Ducks

Enlarge the duck pattern (page 173) to about 8" x 10". Make several copies, cut them out, glue them to tagboard, and laminate. Use a hole punch to make holes about one inch apart and one-half inch from the edge around the border of each duck body. Have students lace the ducks with shoelaces.

Pigs and Piglets ABC Match

Make 26 tagboard pigs and 26 tagboard piglets from the pattern (page 177). Write a different uppercase letter on each pig and a different lowercase letter on each piglet. Laminate the cards. Show the pigs and piglets to the class, one set at a time, and have children recite the letters with you. After they have gone through the letters several times, ask for volunteers to name the letters. Hold up three pairs of matching uppercase and lowercase cards and ask children to match the letters together. Gradually increase the number of letters offered at one time. Place cards at a language center for children to work with during center time.

Story Time

Read nursery rhymes or stories that have farm animals as characters (*The Three Little Pigs, The Ugly Duckling, Little Bo-Peep, Hey Diddle, Diddle,* etc.). Follow up by asking children questions about the stories. Ask them to tell you who their favorite character is and why, and discuss the reasons the characters acted as they did. Also, have children sequence the events from the stories by telling what happened first, next, last, etc.

Farm Picture Storytelling

Gather pictures from magazines that show scenes from farms (a cow being milked, a field being plowed, a pig eating, ducks swimming in a pond, etc.). You can also use the cards on pages 183-184. Cut out, glue to tagboard, and laminate. Give each student one picture. Ask students to study their pictures and make up stories about what they see. Encourage students to describe what people or animals in the pictures are doing, what their names might be, what the weather is like, etc. Give each student the opportunity to tell the class his story. As a student tells his story, write it down. At art time, have students illustrate their stories. Display the stories in the reading center.

Farm Animal Patterns
Hen, Rooster, Chicks

CD-0817 *Terrific Themes for Year-Round Fun*

Farm Animal Patterns
Cow, Bull, Calf

CD-0817 *Terrific Themes for Year-Round Fun*

Farm Animal Patterns
Duck, Duckling

Farm Animal Patterns
Horse, Foal, Donkey

CD-0817 *Terrific Themes for Year-Round Fun*

Farm Animal Patterns
Goat, Kid

175

Farm Animal Patterns
Goose, Gosling

Farm Animal Patterns
Pig, Piglet

CD-0817 *Terrific Themes for Year-Round Fun*

Farm Animal Patterns
Sheep, Lamb

Farm Animal Patterns
Turkey, Poult

CD-0817 *Terrific Themes for Year-Round Fun*

Farm Animal Patterns
Rabbit, Bunny

Farm Animal Pattern
Cat, Kitten

CD-0817 *Terrific Themes for Year-Round Fun*

Farm Animal Patterns
Dog, Puppy

CD-0817 *Terrific Themes for Year-Round Fun*

Farm Animal Patterns
Storytelling Cards

CD-0817 *Terrific Themes for Year-Round Fun*

Farm Animal Patterns
Storytelling Cards

CD-0817 *Terrific Themes for Year-Round Fun*

Cow Count

Enlarge and copy 10 Cow patterns (page 172). Color and cut a wavy vertical line through the center of each cow to make a two-piece puzzle. On the front half of each cow, write one numeral from 1 to 10. On the back half of the cow, draw the corresponding number of spots. Laminate the patterns. Show students the cow shapes. Have them name the numerals and count the spots as a group. Mix up the cards and ask students to match the sets of dots with the numerals. Allow a few students to demonstrate for the group.

Sorting Animals

Gather children together and hold up plastic toy farm animals or animal pictures (from magazines or the patterns on pages 171-182) one at a time. Have children describe each animal. Then, hold up two animals at a time and ask them to look for similar qualities. Explain that you can sort the animals by number of legs, type of covering, type of feet, etc. Have children sort the animals by these attributes.

Favorite Farm Animal Graph

chicken	●	●	●	
pig	●	●		
cow	●	●		
horse	●	●	●	●
goat	●			
turkey	●	●		
sheep	●			

Draw a graph on a chalkboard or chart paper with the name or a picture of each farm animal (from magazines or the patterns on pages 171-182) down the left side of the graph. Make as many squares across the chart as you have students. For each student, cut out a construction-paper circle to fit in a square of the graph. Tell students that each should decide which farm animal is her favorite. Give each student a circle and allow her to tape her circle in the row designated for her favorite animal. After all students have placed their circles, have the class count how many votes each animal received. Ask students to tell you which animal got the most, the least, and which, if any, got zero votes. Ask students to compare two side-by-side rows and tell you how many more votes one received than the other.

Bo-Peep Match

Copy and cut out several Sheep patterns (page 178). Make construction-paper tails for the sheep. Draw a different shape (circle, square, rectangle, triangle, diamond, star, oval, etc.) on each sheep and the same shape on its matching tail. Laminate the tails and sheep. As a group, have students name the shape on a sheep and find the tail that has the matching shape. Allow students to complete the activity in small groups or individually.

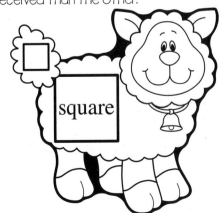

square

Farm Animals

Life Cycles

Copy and cut out the Life Cycle Flashcards (pages 187-188). Discuss with students how small they were when they were born. Ask them what a brand-new person is called (a baby or infant.) Explain that animals (including humans) go through changes even before they are born and until they are full-grown. Tell students that this process is called a life cycle. Show students the Life Cycle Flashcards as you tell them the name of each animal and the stages of its life cycle (explain the order). After you have gone through this process several times, ask for volunteers to name one of the animals shown on the cards and describe its life cycle stages. Next, show the life cycle stages out of order and allow students to put them in the correct order.

Home Matching

Copy and cut out the Farm Animal Homes patterns (pages 189-190) and corresponding animal patterns (pages 171-182). Discuss where farm animals sleep. Show the home patterns and see how many homes students already know. Have students name the farm animals and then tell which type of home each lives in (barn - horse, cow, goat; pen - pig; pond - duck, goose; coop - chicken, etc.) Place the home patterns on a table and give an animal pattern to a student to place on the correct home pattern.

Egg Hatching

Locate a local agency that has a chicken egg hatching program for classrooms. (Often chicken hatcheries, 4-H Clubs, and agricultural agencies and universities have school programs in place.) After you have secured fertilized chicken eggs, an incubator, and instructions on caring for the eggs during the incubation period, show students the eggs and explain that the baby chicks are inside waiting to be born. Describe what will happen when the chicks are ready to hatch. Discuss the special care that the eggs must receive to grow and hatch. Allow students to examine the eggs daily and to watch closely as the chicks hatch. As a math extension, show a calendar of the estimated due date of the chicks. Each day, allow students to count how many more days there are until the chicks are expected to arrive. When the chicks arrive, assist students in figuring out how close the due date was to the actual hatching date. Note: Arrange for a farm or the agency that you received the eggs from to provide a home for the chicks after they are born.

Farm Animal Job Match

Copy, color, cut out, and laminate the Farm Animal Job Cards (pages 191-194). Discuss the various roles or jobs of farm animals. Ask children to tell you what job(s) each animal performs (cows give milk, etc.). Teach children the farm animal jobs they do not know using the Farm Animal Job cards. Have children say the animal jobs with you. For a matching activity, you could mix up cards made from the farm animal patterns (pages 171-182) with the job cards and have children match the animals and their jobs.

Farm Animal Patterns
Life Cycle Flashcards

Farm Animal Patterns
Life Cycle Flashcards

Farm Animal Patterns
Farm Animal Homes

Farm Animal Patterns
Farm Animal Homes

CD-0817 *Terrific Themes for Year-Round Fun*

Farm Animal Patterns

Farm Animal Job Cards

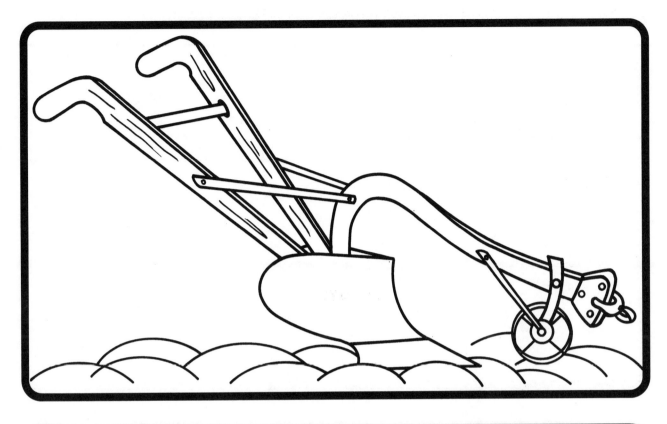

CD-0817 *Terrific Themes for Year-Round Fun*

Farm Animal Patterns
Farm Animal Job Cards

Farm Animal Patterns
Farm Animal Job Cards

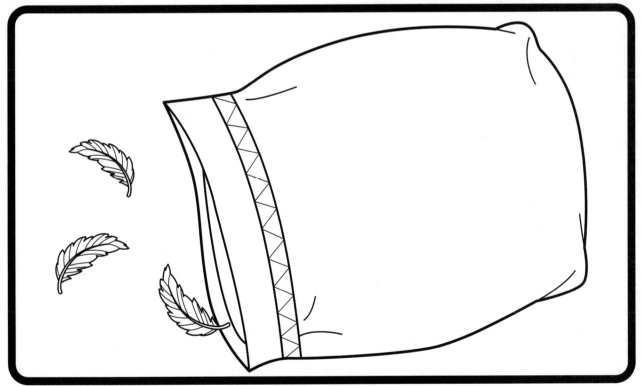

Farm Animal Patterns
Farm Animal Job Cards

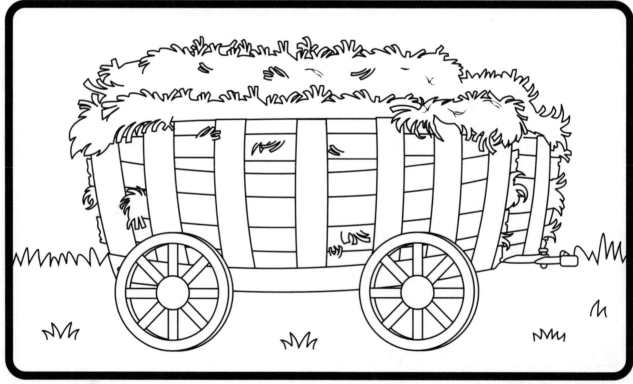

194

Adapted Songs

Can You....?
(to the tune of "Do Your Ears Hang Low?")
Can you baa like a sheep?
Can you moo like a cow?
Can you neigh like a horse?
Can you oink like a sow?
Can you cluck like a hen
who is pecking in her pen?
Can you make that sound?

Milk, Milk, Milk the Cow
(to the tune of "Row, Row, Row Your Boat")
Milk, milk, milk the cow,
While sitting on a stool,
Pulling, squirting,
Pulling, squirting,
Until the bucket's full.

Movement Activities

Chicken Dance
Locate the music for the "Chicken Dance"
and teach students the movements.

Finger Plays

This Little Cow
This little cow eats grass, (Point to thumb.)
This little cow eats hay, (Point to index finger.)
This little cow drinks water, (Point to middle finger.)
This little cow runs away, (Point to ring finger.)
This little cow does nothing, (Point to pinky.)
But sleep in the sun all day! (Place hands under head like pillow.)

Traditional Songs
"Old MacDonald"
"B-I-N-G-O"
"Five Little Ducks"
"Baa, Baa, Black Sheep"
"Mary had a Little Lamb"

Two Mother Pigs
Two mother pigs lived in a pen, (Show thumbs.)
Each had four babies, and that made ten. (Show 10 fingers.)
These four babies were black as night, (Hold up 4 fingers on one hand.)
These four babies were black and white. (Hold up 4 fingers on other hand.)
But all eight babies loved to play,
And they rolled and rolled in the mud all day. (Roll hands over each other.)
At night, with their mothers, they curled up in a heap, (Make fists, palms up.)
And squealed and squealed until they went to sleep.

Farm Family Chores

Have the students brainstorm a list of chores they or others in their families complete at home. Then, have them think about the chores that members of a farm family do. If you have students who live on farms, invite them to describe the chores that their families complete often or every day. Discuss how members of farm families sometimes get up very early to complete their chores before going to school or work. Explain that many farm chores involve taking care of animals. Have children think about what might happen if someone ignored these chores. Ask children to tell you why it is important for every member of a family that lives on a farm to do "his fair share." Then, ask students to describe how the people in their own families complete household chores and if they do their fair share.

Farm Construction

Allow students to build with wooden blocks or other construction toys. Encourage students to build farms and allow them to use plastic farm animals or pictures of farm animals to imitate life on a farm. As students construct their farm structures, have them tell you the names of the structures, their purposes, and what types of animals might be found in the structures.

Field Trips

Set up field trips to places like produce farms, dairy farms, horse stables, petting zoos, etc. Talk with students ahead of time about what they may see. Have them predict what they will see and what may happen. When you return from the field trip, encourage students to discuss what they enjoyed about the trip, what surprised them, what they learned, etc. Have students dictate sentences about the trip to you as you write it on construction paper. Encourage students to illustrate their sentences. Display these for others to see and then compile the pages into a class book for your book shelf. Also, let the children illustrate or write thank-you notes to tour guides or others who assisted with the field trip.

Resource Visitors

Invite farmers, dairy council representatives, feed store employees, farm equipment suppliers, etc., to come in and discuss their jobs with students. Prior to the visit, discuss manners and politeness. Have students think about questions they may have for the visitor. After the visitor has left, allow each student to draw a picture of something he or she learned. Have each student dictate a sentence. Send the sentences and pictures along with a thank-you note to the visitor.

Media Resources

Bring in stories or articles about farm animals from magazines or the newspaper. Children's magazines such as *Ranger Rick* or *Your Big Backyard* have many related articles. Your local librarian can recommend good children's books related to your topic. Many children's videos, such as *Charlotte's Web*, *The Ugly Duckling*, and *The Three Little Pigs*, are available. Notify parents of the theme and encourage them to send in any farm-related materials for their child to share with the class.

Paper Plate Pig

Cut different sizes and styles of pig eyes, noses, and ears from pink construction paper. Give each student a paper plate and allow her to color or paint the plate pink. Allow each student to draw eyes, ears, and a nose to her pink plates to create a face for her paper plate pig.

Wooly Sheep

Copy and cut out one Sheep pattern (page 178) for each student, glue it to tagboard, and cut around the shape. Pass out black, brown, and gray crayons and allow each student to choose a color to color the sheep's features. Provide cotton balls and allow students to glue or paste them onto their sheep. If desired, make a class display by tacking up a barn and fence and allowing students to put their sheep inside the fence.

Palm Print Animals

Paint each student's palm the color of any of the following animals: rabbit, turkey, pig, cat, pony, cow, or horse. Have each student press his palm on a piece of construction paper. When the print is dry, allow him to use crayons, markers, paint, or construction-paper shapes to add the animal's face, tail, markings, etc. Encourage student to draw a background showing the animal's environment (where it sleeps, what it eats, etc.).

Tissue Paper Ducks

Use the Duck pattern (page 173) to cut duck shapes from white construction paper. Give each student a sheet of yellow tissue paper. Instruct students to tear their tissue paper into small pieces. When they are finished tearing the tissue paper, allow them to glue it onto their ducks. If desired, use blue bulletin board paper to create a large duck pond. Allow students to place their ducks in or around the pond.

Farm Animal Collage

Allow students to look through old magazines to find pictures of farm animals. Have students cut or tear out the animal pictures they see in the magazines. When they have finished gathering farm animal pictures, instruct them to glue or paste the pictures on construction paper. When finished, have each student show the class his collage and name the farm animals he found.

Chicken, Chicken, Who Has Your Egg?

Choose one student to be the chicken. Have him sit with his back to the class with a plastic egg behind him. Tell students that you will tap one person on the shoulder. That person should quietly sneak up behind the "chicken," take the egg, then return to his seat and hide the egg in his lap. Encourage students to hide their hands as if they have the egg. After students are ready, the class asks, "Chicken, chicken, who has your egg?" The "chicken" turns around, surveys the class, and guesses who has the egg. He is allowed three guesses. If he does not guess correctly, the student with the egg becomes the next chicken. If he does guess correctly, he gets another turn.

Animal Switch

Copy and cut out two sets of the farm animal patterns (pages 171–182). Make sure you have enough animal patterns for each student to have one. Have students sit in a circle. Give each student an animal pattern, making sure that the same animal pattern is given to two different students. Tell students to listen for the names of their animals or the sounds their animals make. When you say an animal name or imitate an animal's sounds, the two students who are holding the cards of that animal should switch places in the circle. For extra fun, encourage students to make the animal noises as they switch places.

Ball Butting

Discuss how goats butt objects with their heads. Explain that male goats do this as a game when they are young to show who is the strongest, and as a mating tactic when they are older. Tell students that they will pretend to be goats by butting balls with their heads. Use big beach balls or other lightweight balls for this activity. Split the class into groups of two to four (depending on the number of balls you have) and allow one student to gently pitch the ball in the direction of the others and have the others butt it back. Be sure to tell students that the balls are the only things they are allowed to butt with their heads!

Duck Waddle Relay Race

Divide the class into three or four equal groups and line them up by group. Tell students that they will race like ducks. When you signal, have the first student in each group waddle to a marked point and return to his team and tag the next student in line. After the second student is tagged, he waddles as the first child did. The first team to finish wins.

Allergy and Food Preference Note

Before completing any food activity, ask parental permission and inquire about children's food allergies. Common food allergies include peanuts and other nuts, dairy, eggs, berries, etc. Parents may have religious or other preferences that will prevent children from eating certain foods.

Pigs in a Blanket

Have students wash their hands and then have each place an instant biscuit on a cookie sheet. Have the student place half of a hot dog in the middle of the biscuit and instruct him to fold the sides of the biscuit up around the hot dog. When all students have finished, bake according to the directions on the biscuit package. While the "Pigs in a Blanket" are cooking, discuss with students what the biscuits looked like before you put them in the oven. Ask students to predict what they will look like when done. If possible, allow students to peek at them as they cook. When they have cooled, enjoy as a snack.

Personalized Yogurt

Explain that yogurt is a food product made from cow's milk. Bring in a large container of frozen vanilla yogurt. Ask for parent volunteers to send in various toppings for the yogurt such as chocolate syrup, cookie crumbles, fruit topping, whipped cream, etc. Give each child a scoop of the frozen yogurt in a bowl and allow her to "personalize" her yogurt using the toppings. Encourage students to compare their creations with classmates to see what is the same or different. Ask children to describe differences in the taste of the vanilla yogurt and vanilla ice cream and tell which they like better.

Making Butter

Give pairs of students a small sealable container, preferably clear (baby food jars work well). Pour heavy cream into each container and seal. Explain that cream comes from cow's milk and butter is made by churning cream. Tell students to take turns shaking the containers. Have them observe the changes in the cream as they shake it. After several minutes of shaking, the cream should thicken into butter. Have students pour the mixture into a strainer to drain unchurned cream. Enjoy the butter on crackers at snack time.

Animal Cookies

Have students wash their hands and put on smocks. Give trays with flour and wax paper on them to groups of three or four students. You may want to do this activity with one or two students at a time instead of as a group. Place balls of pre-made sugar cookie dough on the students' trays. Allow them to roll out the cookie dough and use farm-animal cookie cutters to make their cookies. When all students are finished, place the cookies on a cookie sheet and allow students to paint the cookies with a mixture of food coloring and egg yolk. Follow the baking instructions on the dough package and eat later for a snack. As students eat, encourage them to name the animals they are eating. When they finish, have them imitate the animals' sounds.

Halloween

Contents

Pumpkin Seed Names

Provide construction paper, glue, and pumpkin seeds at an activity table for children to use. During center time, invite a few children to the table. Have a child say each letter in his name as you use glue to write the name on a piece of construction paper. When you finish writing the name, have child use dried pumpkin seeds to cover the glue. More advanced students can write their names in big letters with a pencil and then squeeze glue on the letter lines themselves. Encourage children to say the letters as they cover them. After the pictures are finished, place them in a designated area to dry.

Halloween Stories

Gather children and explain that the group will write a story about Halloween. They should first decide on a theme for the Halloween story. A few examples are a bat's Halloween flight, trick-or-treating, or a friendly ghost. After the theme is chosen, write down what children dictate, sentence by sentence, on poster board or chart paper. When the story is complete, allow each child to illustrate his choice of scenes from the story. Display the words and art together for the parents to enjoy.

Rhyming Halloween Words

Explain to children that they should name words that rhyme with Halloween words. Begin by reminding children that rhyming words are words that sound alike at the end. Then give children a Halloween word and ask them to think of any words that rhymes with it. Write the words on the chalkboard or chart paper to review later. Some Halloween words that work well for rhyming include: cat, ghost, trick, treat, fall, candy, mask, and night.

Button Jack-o'-Lantern

Cut a pumpkin from orange felt. Cut a jack-o'-lantern face from black felt using the Jack-o'-Lantern Face patterns (page 202). Sew buttons on the pumpkin where the eyes, nose, and mouth go. Cut slits for buttonholes in the black felt eyes, nose, and mouth. Allow children to button the facial features onto the buttons to create the jack-o'-lantern face.

Halloween Patterns
Jack-o'-Lantern Face

CD-0817 *Terrific Themes for Year-Round Fun*

Geometric Shape Masks

Gather tempera paint, paper grocery bags, paintbrushes, scissors, glue, and an assortment of geometric shapes cut from colorful construction paper. Allow children to choose a color of tempera paint and paint their paper bags. When the bags are dry, have children cut eye, nose, and mouth holes in them so that the bags can be placed over their heads and used as masks. (You may want to mark these areas on the bags so children will know where to cut.) Children can then decorate the masks using the geometric shapes. Have them say the names of the shapes as they glue them onto the bags. When the bags are dry, have each child show the class her mask and describe the colors and shapes she chose for her mask.

One or Many? More or Less?

Obtain six baby food jars. Put one candy corn or pumpkin seed in each of three jars and a handful of candy corn or pumpkin seeds into each of the other three jars. Place the jars on a table. Ask children to describe the words "one" and "many." Show the jars one at a time and ask the group to tell you whether the jar contains one or many. Once the group has answered several times, continue as before while calling on one child at a time for a response. Then, discuss the meanings of the words "more" and "less." Hold up two jars at a time and call on children to identify which contains more and which contains less than the other.

Graphing Halloween Candy

Purchase several kinds of Halloween candy and mix them together in a bag. Explain that the class will make a graph. Prepare a graph on the chalkboard or chart paper with each column representing a different candy. At the top of each column, attach a different type of candy. For each child, cut out three circles that fit in the boxes on the graph, write the child's name on the circles, and attach tape to the backs of the circles. Allow each child to reach in the bag (without looking) and pull out three pieces of candy. Have student place his circles on the graph under the types of candy he has. When all children have taped their circles on the graph, ask children to tell you which type of candy was chosen the most and which was chosen the least. Also have the class compare two columns to see which has more, how many more, which has less, and how many less. Have children tell you if there are any columns with equal amounts.

Halloween Feely Box

Prepare a feely box by cutting a hole in the side of a box. Tape or staple a piece of cloth above the hole so that it hangs over the hole and children cannot see in the box. When children are not looking, place Halloween-themed items inside the box. Some ideas for the feely box include: plastic false teeth, rubber spider or snake, rubber bat, pumpkin seed, popcorn, candy, etc. Call on one child at a time to reach into the feely box, choose an item in the box (without pulling it out), describe what the item feels like, and then guess what the item is.

What's in a Pumpkin?

Before students arrive, carve the top of a pumpkin and place the top back on the pumpkin. Show children the pumpkin and ask them to predict what is inside. Ask them if they think the inside is solid, liquid, air, etc. Take the top off the pumpkin and allow children to look at, smell, and touch the insides. Have them describe what they see, smell, and feel. Use the pumpkin and seeds for other activities in this section and the pumpkin shell as a decoration for your classroom.

Spooky Wind Socks

Give each child a large piece of construction paper and have him decorate his paper with a Halloween scenes. When the child has finished decorating, show him how to roll the paper to make the left and right edges of the paper meet, with the decoration showing. Tape or staple the paper where the two ends meet to create the body of the wind sock. Punch a hole on both sides of the top end of the wind sock. Tie the ends of an 8-10" piece of yarn through the holes to create a hanger. Provide strips (about 8" long) of orange, purple, and black crepe paper for students to attach to the bottom ends of their wind socks. Hang the wind socks outside and watch as the wind blows. Talk about what makes the wind socks move and why they move in different directions or stop moving.

Pumpkin Patch Field Trip

If possible, arrange for students to take a field trip to a local pumpkin patch. After the trip, have students illustrate what they saw. If possible, bring back a pumpkin and carve it with the class. If you are unable to visit a pumpkin patch, you might want to arrange a visit to a farmer's market or pumpkin sale area at a grocery store so students can view various types of pumpkins and other fall crops.

Adapted Songs

Nine Little Pumpkins

(to the tune of "Ten Little Indians")
One little, two little, three little pumpkins,
Four little, five little, six little pumpkins,
Seven little, eight little, nine little pumpkins,
On this Halloween night!

Three Little Witches

(to the tune of "Ten Little Indians")
One little, two little, three little witches;
Flying over haystacks, flying over ditches;
Sliding down moonbeams without any hitches;
Heigh-ho Halloween's here!

On Halloween

(to the tune of "She'll be Comin' Round the Mountain")
On Halloween we dress up and pretend.
On Halloween we dress up and pretend.
On Halloween we dress up,
On Halloween we dress up,
On Halloween we dress up and pretend!

Other verses:
The witches will be riding their brooms . . .
The ghosts will say, "Boo," to everyone . . .
The jack-o'-lanterns will wear big smiles . . .
All the children shout, "Trick-or-treat!" . . .

Movement Activities

Monster Mashing

Find the song "The Monster Mash" (sung by Bobby Pickett, Parrot Records, 1962). Play it for children and allow them to dance. Ask them to show you how a ghost, a silly monster, or a witch might dance.

Ghost Dancing

Play a spooky recording. Ask children to move around the room as if they were "haunting" a house. If children become frightened, remind them that ghosts are only pretend and then play silly music for children to be "silly ghosts."

Monster Emotions

Copy, color, and cut out the Monster Emotions activity cards (below). Hold up the pictures one at a time and ask children to describe the emotion the monster shows. Ask students to describe what may have made the monster feel that way. Encourage children to imitate the expressions seen on the cards. Allow each child to describe a time he or she felt one of the emotions on the cards. As an extension, allow each child to draw a picture of something that has made him feel one of the emotions described. Write a caption across the bottom as the child dictates what made him feel that way.

happy

surprised

sad

embarrassed

angry

scared

Egg Carton Spiders

Gather several paper egg cartons and cut the sections apart. For each section, use a hole puncher to make four holes along the edge of each side. Place the sections, along with crayons, markers, and 3" to 4" lengths of black chenille craft sticks on a table. Invite children over to the table and have them create spiders using the materials. Direct each child to push the chenille craft sticks through the holes for eight spider legs and draw a spider face with crayons and markers.

Pumpkin Vines

Give each child a white piece of construction paper. Explain that you will drop diluted green tempera paint near the bottom of their papers and they should blow the paint around the paper with straws. Encourage children to blow the paint toward the sides of the paper to create vine-like forms. Give each child five or six small orange pumpkin shapes and a black crayon. Allow children to draw faces on the pumpkins while the paint dries, then have them glue the pumpkins on the vines.

Classroom Halloween Wreath

Cut a large wreath shape from poster board. Have each child make four or five orange pumpkins for the wreath. Use the Pumpkin patterns (page 209) for children to color and cut out. Or, allow students to trace a pumpkin stencil onto orange construction paper, cut out the pumpkin, and then draw a face on it with a black crayon. Have each child cut or tear orange, purple, and black tissue paper into small pieces. Then, have students take turns gluing their tissue paper and pumpkins onto the wreath. When the wreath is complete, display on the door. If desired, use small paper plates and allow each child to create her own Halloween wreath to take home.

Orange Finger Painting

Give each child a piece of finger paint paper and drop red and yellow finger paint on it. Allow children to explore with the finger paint on the paper. Have the group discuss what happens when the two colors mix. Also discuss the differences in shades of orange made by mixing a small amount of red with more yellow or vice versa.

Ghost Footprints

Pour a thin layer of white tempera paint onto an old cookie sheet or into a tub. Have each child step in the paint (in bare feet) and then onto black construction paper with his toes near the bottom edge of the paper. Ask children to describe how the paint and paper feel on their bare feet. When the paint dries, allow children to draw ghosts' faces on the prints and spooky Halloween backgrounds on the black paper.

Jack-o'-Lantern Bags

Have paper lunch bags, small bowls of orange and green tempera paint, two brushes per paint, newspaper scraps, and short pieces of black yarn available on an art table:. Allow each child to paint a bag with his choice of tempera paint and then paint a face on the bag. When the bags are dry, instruct the children to stuff them with the newspaper scraps. Tie the tops closed with the pieces of black yarn.

Tissue Ghosts

Place the following materials on an art table: a box of white facial tissues; 8" strands of white, orange, and black yarn; cotton balls; and black fine-point markers. Instruct each child to place two or three cotton balls in the center of an unfolded white tissue. Allow her to use her choice of colored yarn to tie around the cotton balls so that a ghost head is formed. Have children to use black markers to carefully draw ghost faces as desired. Hang the ghosts from the ceiling of the classroom.

Glowing Jack-o'-Lantern Bags

Allow children to draw jack-o'-lantern faces on orange lunch bags (white bags *may* be painted with orange tempera paint if necessary). Help children cut out the facial features . Allow them to glue green paper "stems" to the tops of the bags. When the glue is dry, allow children to stuff yellow tissue paper in the bags to give the appearance of candlelight burning inside of the jack-o'-lantern.

Halloween Patterns
Pumpkin Patterns

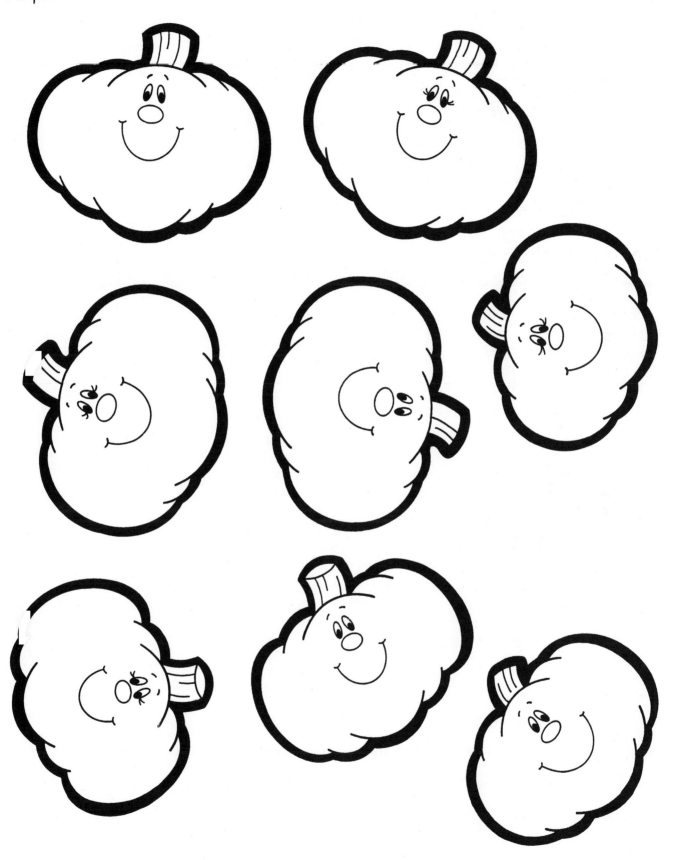

Pin the Nose on the Jack-o'-Lantern

Paint a large pumpkin on poster board or butcher paper. Draw or paint eyes and a mouth on the pumpkin. Laminate or cover the pumpkin with clear contact paper and tape it on a wall. Make a nose from construction paper and add tape to the back. Invite children to look at the pumpkin. Ask them to tell you what is missing. Allow every child to touch where the nose should be. Give each child a turn to play "pin the nose on the jack-o'-lantern." Children can be blindfolded or close their eyes if they prefer.

Jack-o'-Lantern Beanbag Toss

Paint a jack-o'-lantern on the side of a large box and cut out the mouth, nose, and eyes (large enough for a beanbag to fit through.) Gather a few children and show them how to toss beanbags through the openings. Once children have mastered tossing the bags through the openings, challenge them by asking them to throw the beanbags through the openings in a particular order (for example, eye, eye, nose, mouth).

Ghost, Ghost, Goblin

Play "Duck, Duck, Goose," but have children say, "ghost, ghost, goblin," as they choose someone to chase them. Encourage children to make spooky ghost and goblin noises as they run around the circle.

Don't Wake the Goblin

Play this game in an obstacle-free area. Choose one child to be the goblin. Instruct the goblin to curl up on the ground and pretend to be asleep. Have the other children approach the goblin by tiptoeing up to him and asking, "Are you asleep?" If he says, "Yes," the children continue to approach. When he says, "No," the children run from the goblin as he chases them. When a child is tagged, he sits down and pretends to sleep. The last player tagged becomes the new goblin.

Halloween Parade

Have the children choose their favorite Halloween costumes, either made in school or brought from home. Coordinate a Halloween parade with other teachers. You may wish to do this on the playground, or walk from classroom to classroom so children can show off their Halloween costumes.

Allergy and Food Preference Note

Before completing any food activity, ask parental permission and inquire about children's food allergies. Common food allergies include peanuts and other nuts, dairy, eggs, berries, etc. Parents may have religious or other preferences that will prevent children from eating certain foods.

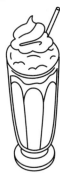

Pumpkin Milk Shakes

Have children help you mix $1/2$ gallon of vanilla ice cream, a small can of pumpkin pie filling, $1/2$ cup of milk, and one teaspoon of cinnamon in a blender. Allow children to squirt whipped cream on top and enjoy the pumpkin shakes for a snack.

Roasted Pumpkin Seeds

Purchase pumpkin seeds or scoop them out of a carved pumpkin. Show children the seeds and allow them each to taste one raw. Then, soak the pumpkin seeds in salty water (use approximately one teaspoon of salt per cup of water). Bake for about 20 minutes at 325°F. Allow children to eat the seeds while they are still warm.

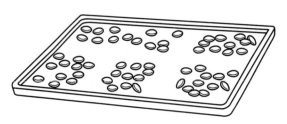

Pumpkin Faces

Give children toasted English muffin halves, round crackers, or rice cakes. Allow them to use spreadable cheese (or cream cheese mixed with orange food coloring) to cover their muffins, crackers, or rice cakes. Encourage children to make pumpkin faces with any of the following toppings: olives, raisins, carrot sticks, celery slices, candy pieces, etc.

Pumpkin Cupcakes

Have children help you measure and mix a pumpkin bread recipe. Pour the mix into cupcake papers in a cupcake tin and bake. While the pumpkin cupcakes are baking, give each child a small bowl of cream cheese and a few drops of orange food coloring to mix together with a spoon. Allow each child to frost a pumpkin cupcake and make a pumpkin face with seasonal black candies (during Halloween you can find black cinnamon candies, black gumdrops, black candy corn, etc.). Allow children to enjoy the cupcakes for a snack.

Nutrition

Contents

Food Grouping

Copy the food cards (pages 215-224). Color, cut apart, laminate, and show the cards to a small group of students. Explain that you will lay out several food cards for them to look at, and they should decide which food item does not belong with the others. Place out three cards which are similar in food group category, color, etc. One additional card should be different. Allow children to work together to decide which food item does not belong. Play for a few minutes with the group, then invite a new group to play. Continue until all children have had a chance to play. Students may also put the cards in alphabetical order according to the names of the foods on the cards.

Spelling with Food

Provide alphabet-shaped cereal or pasta, construction paper, crayons, and glue for children. Have students spell their names, simple words, or simple phrases with the letters and glue them to the construction paper. Allow students to decorate around their words with crayons.

Can-Label Matching

Ask parents to send in pairs of identical can wrappers. Glue each wrapper to a piece of tagboard or an index card and allow children to manipulate the cards. They may make pairs, sort by food classification, or sort by preferred foods. The children may also play Concentration or Go Fish with the cards. Challenge students to find words on the wrappers that they can read.

Recipe Book

Provide index cards and have students write the recipes for their favorite foods.. Younger students can dictate the recipes. Students should include all of the ingredients and each step to making the food. When the recipes are complete, have each student illustrate the recipe she wrote or dictated, then combine the recipes into a class book. You may also want to type the recipes, attach the illustrations, and reproduce a copy of the recipe book for each child to take home.

Food Adjectives

Explain to students that words which describe things are called adjectives, and give examples. When students are comfortable identifying adjectives, name a food or hold up a picture of a food for them to describe. Have children list as many words as they can think of to describe the food. Write the list on chart paper and count how many adjectives they named. Repeat the activity, letting students take turns choosing the food to be described.

Alphabet Food List

Tell children that they will go through the alphabet naming all of the foods they can think of for each letter. Write the letters of the alphabet on chart paper and record all the foods students can think of that begin with each letter. When finished, have children see which letter has the most food words listed beneath it. As an extension, share the book *Eating the Alphabet*, by Lois Ehlert (Harcourt, Brace, Jovanovich, 1989), with the class.

A	B	C	D	E	F
apple	beet bean	carrot	dates	eggs	
G	H	I	J	K	L
grape	ham		jam	kale	
M	N	O	P	Q	R
milk		orange			
S	T	U	V	W	X
squash					
Y	Z				

GREEN

peas

cabbage

beans

lettuce

Food Colors

Gather one piece of each color construction paper. Tape each piece to the wall or chalkboard. Have children focus on one color at a time and brainstorm all of the foods they can think of that are that color. Write each food on the construction paper as the children dictate. Allow children to add to any of the lists if they think of more foods. When the lists are complete, allow children to help you count to see which color has the most foods listed and which has the fewest.

From Seeds to Salads

Gather children and tell them they should think about how salads are made. Explain that the class will work as a group to create a detailed list of the steps that occur in the creation of a salad. Encourage children to begin the list with a step that includes the planting or growing of the ingredients. Their steps should detail how the ingredients reach the food preparer. The last step of the list should be the making of the salad. As children dictate the steps, write them on chart paper.

Nutrition Patterns

Fats, Oils, and Sweets Group

CD-0817 *Terrific Themes for Year-Round Fun*

Nutrition Patterns

Milk, Yogurt, and Cheese Group

Nutrition Patterns
Milk, Yogurt, and Cheese Group

COTTAGE CHEESE

American Cheese

CREAM CHEESE

Shredded Cheese

 CD-0817 *Terrific Themes for Year-Round Fun*

Nutrition Patterns
Meat, Poultry, Fish, Dry Beans, Eggs, and Nuts Group

Nutrition Patterns
Vegetable Group

219

Nutrition Patterns
Vegetable Group

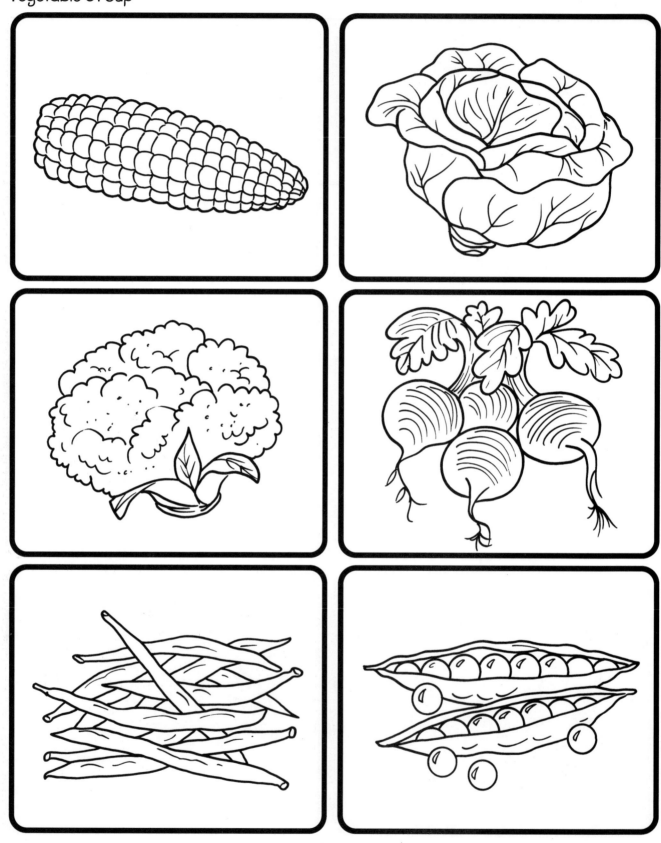

Nutrition Patterns
Fruit Group

Nutrition Patterns
Fruit Group

Nutrition Patterns
Bread, Cereal, Rice, and Pasta Group

Nutrition Patterns
Bread, Cereal, Rice, and Pasta Group

Food Matching

Copy, cut apart, and laminate the food card patterns (pages 215-224). Share the cards with students, naming each food as you show its picture. Have children match cards with pictures of foods that begin with the same letter.

Pancake Number Concentration

Cut 20 three-inch circles from cardboard. Make the circles into playing cards by drawing one dot on two of the "pancakes," two dots on the next two, three dots on two more, and so on until there are ten dots on the last two. (You may want to use a blue marker to draw on the pancakes so that the dots will resemble blueberries.) Have children place the pancakes dot-sides down and use them to play a game of Concentration. (Directions for playing Concentration can be found on page 166.) Make the game more fun by allowing players to use a spatula to flip the pancakes.

Pasta Sorting

Gather a variety of pasta shapes. Soak some of each type in vinegar colored with a different color of food coloring. Spread on a towel and allow to dry overnight. Mix the dried pasta together in a large bowl. Place the bowl and a few muffin tins on a table. Allow children to sort the pasta shapes into the muffin tins by color, size, or shape. As they sort each piece, have them name the shape, color, and size of the piece.

Watermelon Seed Count

Make five to ten copies of the Watermelon pattern (page 226). Write the number "1" on the first one, "2" on the second one, and so on, and color each pattern. Cut out watermelon seeds from black construction paper or gather and wash real ones. Challenge children to read the numeral on each watermelon and count out and place the appropriate number of seeds on each watermelon.

Favorite Ice Cream Graph

Make enough copies of the Ice Cream patterns (page 227) so that each student will get one pattern. Explain to children that they will graph their favorite flavors of ice cream. Use a chalkboard or poster board to create a graph on which each column represents a different flavor of ice cream. Ask children to help you label the columns with names of ice cream flavors. Each child should record his name on his pattern, choose his favorite ice cream flavor, and tape his pattern in the appropriate column of the graph. Allow children to count the patterns in each column to see which flavor is the favorite of most children in the class.

Nutrition Patterns
Watermelon

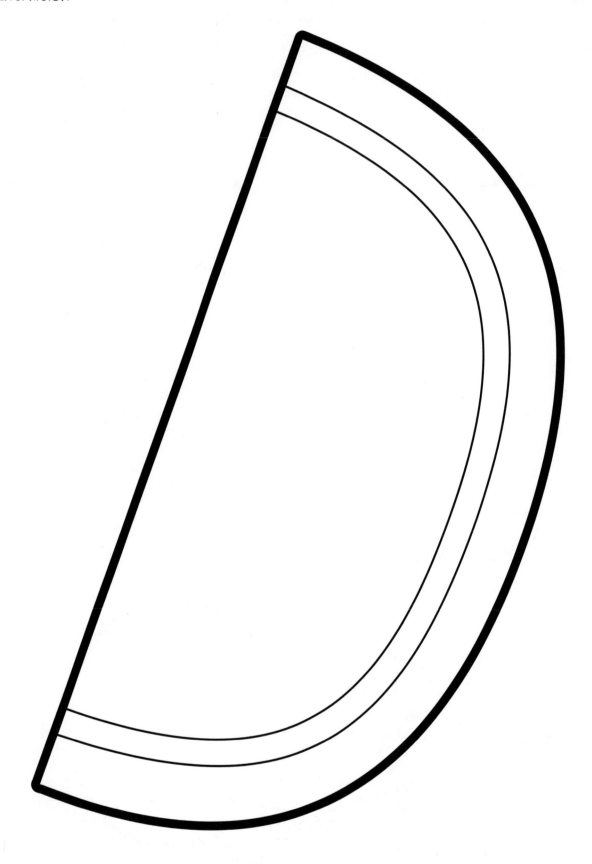

CD-0817 *Terrific Themes for Year-Round Fun*

Nutrition Patterns
Ice Cream

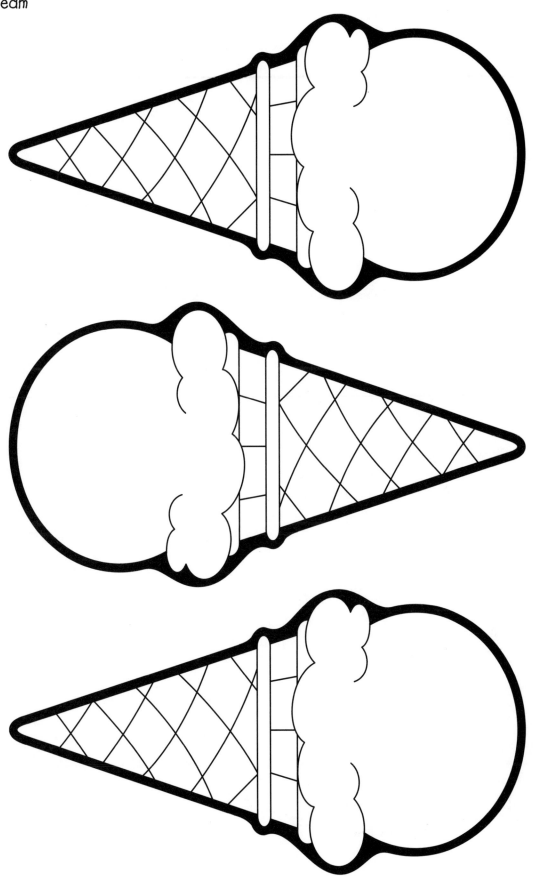

Meal Planning

Gather several old magazines and blunt scissors. Allow children to look through the magazines and cut out pictures of foods. Have them sort the pictures they have cut out into foods that are healthy and foods that are not healthy. Have students discuss their reasons for classifying each food as healthy or unhealthy. Have each child glue some of his healthy pictures to a paper plate to represent a well-rounded meal. Let students display their plates on a bulletin board or wall and talk about the meals that they created.

Frozen Grapes

Gather two different colors of grapes. Wash the grapes and place half of each color in the freezer and the other half of each in the refrigerator overnight. Serve both the refrigerated and frozen grapes for snack and have children compare and describe the two types of grapes. Encourage students to describe the texture, temperature, taste, and color of each type of grape.

Grapes to Raisins

First thing in the morning, allow children to help you gather and wash a few bunches of grapes. Have each child draw a picture of what the grapes look like and label the picture before. Place the grapes on a cookie sheet and bake on low heat all day. Discuss the fact that dehydrated fruits are made similar to the way you are making the grapes into raisins. Have children predict and discuss the changes that will occur in the grapes. At the end of the day, let the raisins cool and have children describe what changes occurred. On the back of their before pictures of the grapes, have them illustrate the raisins and label these pictures after. Enjoy the raisins for an afternoon snack.

Parts of Plants

Discuss the different parts of plants. Explain that foods we eat come from different parts of plants. For example, carrots and beets are *roots*; celery and asparagus are *stems*; cabbage, spinach, and brussels sprouts are *leaves*; artichoke and broccoli are *flowers*; and apples, corn, and peanuts are *fruits*. (You may want to discuss the term "fruit" with the class and explain that, since the fruit is the part of the plant that contains the seeds, peanuts and corn are considered fruits.) Allow children to name other foods we eat that come from plants, and have them decide which part of the plant each food represents. Have them tell you which they enjoy eating. Copy and cut out the Plant Parts Cards (pages 229–230) and the Plants Parts Sorting pattern (page 231). Allow children to take turns sorting the cards onto the sorting page.

Nutrition Patterns
Plant Parts Cards

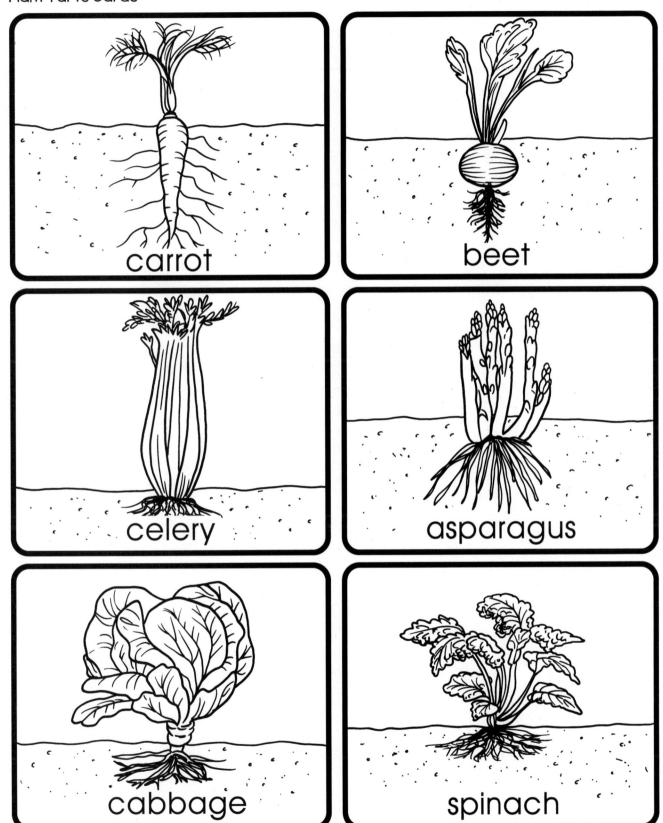

carrot

beet

celery

asparagus

cabbage

spinach

CD-0817 *Terrific Themes for Year-Round Fun*

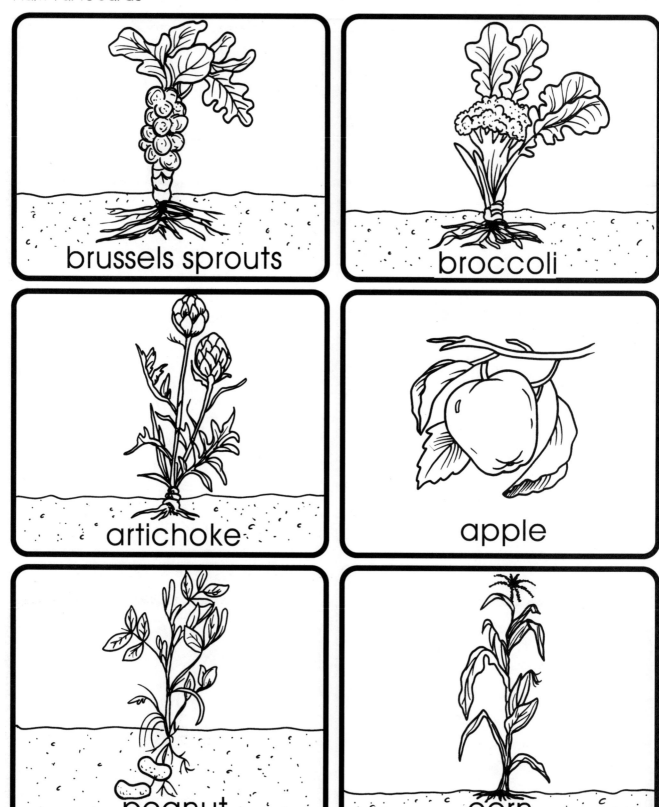

brussels sprouts

broccoli

artichoke

apple

peanut

corn

flowers

fruit
(and seeds)

leaves

roots

stems

Adapted Songs

We're Going to the Grocery Store
(to the tune of "Mary Had a Little Lamb")
We're going to the grocery store,
Grocery store, grocery store.
We'll buy our favorite food there,
(Child's name), what will you buy?
(Allow each child a turn naming a food
he would like to buy.)

Ten Bottles of Milk in the Fridge
(to the tune of "Ninety-Nine Bottles of Pop
on the Wall")
Ten bottles of milk in the fridge,
Ten bottles of milk.
Take one out and drink it all up,
Nine bottles of milk in the fridge.
(Continue singing and counting backwards to one.)

Traditional Rhymes

The Candy Store
I met some friends at the candy store.
We bought candy,
We bought cake,
We went home with a bellyache.
Mama, Mama, we feel sick.
Call the doctor, quick, quick, quick!
Doctor, Doctor, will we live?
Close your eyes and count to five.
One, two, three, four, five.
Hooray, we're alive!

The Grapefruit
I wish I were a grapefruit,
And here's the reason why:
When you come to eat me,
I'll squirt you in the eye!

Related Nursery Rhymes
"Georgie Porgie"
"Hot Cross Buns"
"Humpty Dumpty"
"I'm a Little Teapot"
"Jack Sprat"
"Little Jack Horner"
"Little Miss Muffet"
"Little Tommy Tucker"
"Pat-a-Cake"
"Pease Porridge Hot"
"Peter Piper"
"Polly Put the Kettle On"
"The Queen of Hearts"
"Simple Simon"
"Sing a Song of Sixpence"
"This Little Piggy Went to Market"
"To Market, To Market"

Finger Plays

Two Little Apples
Way up high on the apple tree,
   (Point as if pointing to top of a tree.)
Two little apples smiled at me.
   (Hold up two fingers, then point to smile.)
I shook that tree as hard as I could,
   (Pretend to shake tree.)
Down came the apples. Mmm, mmm, good!
   (Rub tummy.)

Five Shiny Oranges
Five shiny oranges hanging in a tree,
   (Hold up five fingers.)
The juiciest oranges you ever did see.
   (Point to your eyes.)
The wind came by and gave an angry frown,
   (Make a frown face.)
And one shiny orange came tumbling down.
   (Hold up one finger then roll hands.)

Where are They Grown?

Copy, color, cut out, and laminate the Food Group patterns (pages 215-224). Select the cards of foods that traditionally come from a specific location. Good choices are oranges (Florida and California), apples (Washington), potatoes (Idaho), etc. Gather children and explain that the foods we eat come from across the country. Show them the food cards you have selected and find their places of origin on a map. Compare these places to where you live and discuss how far or near they are.

Sharing Foods

Gather several used magazines and allow children to cut out pictures of food. Tell students that they should cut out only pictures of foods that they have never eaten. After each student has cut out several food pictures, encourage him to "trade" with other students to obtain foods that he has tried or with which he is familiar. After students have finished trading food pictures with their classmates, allow them to discuss the foods. Some students may require help from classmates in naming or describing their foods.

People Who Work with Foods

Copy the People Who Work with Foods patterns (pages 234-235). Review the cards with children and talk with them about all of the things that happen to foods from the time they are grown to the time they are eaten. Discuss the people involved, including the farmers who grow the food, delivery truck drivers who pick it up and take it where it needs to go, grocery store workers who stock and sell the foods, people who purchase the foods, and chefs and servers in restaurants who prepare and server the food. Let students review the cards and identify the people who work with food.

Food Likes and Dislikes

Make and cut out several copies of the Food Group patterns (pages 215-224). Allow each child to select a few cards showing foods he likes and have him glue the cards to green construction paper. Let student repeat the steps with foods he doesn't like, this time gluing the cards to red construction paper. Allow children to compare their papers to the papers of other students. Students can identify classmates that have similar likes and dislikes with sentences such as, "I am like Phillip because we both like ice cream," or, "I am like Anita because we both dislike peas."

Nutrition Patterns

People Who Work with Foods

CD-0817 *Terrific Themes for Year-Round Fun*

Nutrition Patterns
People Who Work with Foods

Food Collages

Place construction paper and bottles of white glue at the art center. Allow children to use the materials and the following foods to make collages as described below.

Rice Collage

Provide a variety of types of rice in small bowls. Allow children to use any of the different types of rice to make a collage.

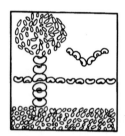

Bean Collage

Obtain a package of mixed dried beans. Allow children to use the beans to make a collage or mural.

Seed Collage

Allow the children to save seeds from fresh fruit they have had at snack time. Each day have children wash the seeds and place them in a cup. After several days of seed collecting, allow each child to glue the seeds he has saved onto construction paper to make a collage.

Cereal Box Collage

Have students bring empty cereal boxes to class. Provide them with scissors, construction paper, and glue. Let students cut the box panels into a variety of simple shapes. Allow each child to take a turn gluing some of the box-panel shapes onto a piece of construction paper to create a cereal box collage. Challenge students to read words on the cereal boxes.

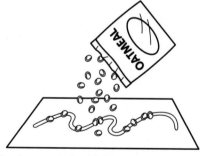

Oatmeal Art

Obtain a package of uncooked oatmeal. (Powdered tempera could be mixed with the oatmeal to color it.) Allow each child to squirt glue all over a piece of construction paper and sprinkle the oatmeal on the paper to make a fancy design.

Colored Salt Designs

Mix tempera powder and salt and put the mixture into a salt shaker. Allow each child to shake the colored mixture onto a glue design he has squeezed onto construction paper.

Food Printing

Provide children with sheets of construction paper and allow them to do any or all of the following food printing activities. Before students begin making prints, you may want to set aside some of each food for students to eat after they have made their prints.

Oranges

Gather several oranges and shallow bowls of orange tempera paint. Cut the oranges in half and allow children to print with the paint.

Cucumber/Pickle Prints

Gather several cucumbers and cut them into 2" to 3" sections. Place them on an art table along with shallow bowls of green tempera paint, and allow children to make prints.

Colorful Peppers

Gather red, yellow, and green peppers. Cut some of the peppers in half horizontally and others vertically. Place each near a bowl of tempera paint of the same color. Allow children to print with the peppers on dark pieces of construction paper.

Other Food Items for Printing:

Pears
Apples cut both vertically and horizontally
Raisins
Carrots
Potatoes (halved or carved)
Celery

Berry Basket Printing

Gather several green plastic berry baskets, a shallow bowl of green tempera paint, and construction paper. Have each child dip a berry basket in the paint and press the basket on a sheet of construction paper to make a print. When the paint dries, let students use several different colors of crayon or marker to draw berries inside the basket prints on their papers.

Favorite-Food Drawings

Give each child a paper plate and crayons. Ask children to draw pictures of their favorite foods on the paper plates. As children work, circulate among them to write the names of the foods on the pictures. Let students compare their pictures to their classmates' and then display them on a bulletin board or wall.

Food Pyramid Beanbag Toss

Use chalk to draw a Food Pyramid (page 239) on the pavement outside. For very young children, draw a few items from each category in the appropriate section to help them recognize the food group. If a paved area is not available for drawing, use a marker to draw the pyramid on a large piece of poster board. Gather a few beanbags and explain to children that they will take turns tossing a beanbag onto the pyramid. The tosser is to look at the section where the beanbag landed, then name the food category and one food that belongs in the category. If a beanbag lands outside the pyramid, allow the child additional tosses until his beanbag lands on a section of the pyramid.

Food Pyramid Relay Race

Copy three sets the Food Group patterns (pages 215-224). Color, cut apart, and laminate each set of cards. Label each of six boxes (shoe boxes work well) with a Food Pyramid (page 239) category picture and category name. Divide children into three teams. Line up the teams on one side of the playground and the boxes on the other. Place a set of the food cards in front of each team. The person in the front of each team's line should take a card from the top of his team's pile, name the food, run to the other end of the playground and place the card in the box that shows the correct food pyramid category. The child then runs and tags the next person in his team's line. The next child follows the same steps as his teammate. The first team to sort all of its cards wins. Position yourself near the boxes to be sure the children place the food items in the correct places and provide assistance if necessary.

Jump Rope

Take a few *jump* ropes outside and allow children to play and recite the following traditional jump rope rhyme:

A B C's and vegetable goop,
What will I find in the alphabet soup?
A, B, C, D, ..., etc.

When a child stops jump roping, have her name a food that begins with the letter she stopped on.

Nutrition Patterns
Food Pyramid

Allergy and Food Preference Note

Before completing any food activity, ask parental permission and inquire about children's food allergies. Common food allergies include peanuts and other nuts, dairy, eggs, berries, etc. Parents may have religious or other preferences that will prevent children from eating certain foods.

Lunch Meat Tasting Party

Gather several different types of lunch meat. Give each child a piece of each meat and allow him to taste and describe it. Let students tell you which ones they like and which ones they do not. You might want to let them roll up their slices around cream cheese, bread sticks, or other types of food to create interesting snack combinations.

Cucumber Chips

Wash and slice a few cucumbers. Allow children to eat the slices as a snack along with dips such as dill dip, spinach dip, french onion dip, ranch dressing, etc. Have children describe the taste and texture. You might want to allow them to try the cucumbers with small amount salt, too. Have them compare the way cucumbers taste with the way pickles taste.

Fruity Ice Cream

Gather $2\frac{1}{2}$ cups sugar, $1\frac{1}{2}$ cups crushed pineapple, 2 lemons, 1 orange, 5 bananas, 1 quart milk, 1 pint whipping cream, and 1 can condensed milk. Allow children to help you measure the ingredients, juice the orange and lemons, and mash the bananas. Mix the fruit, juice, and sugar together, then let stand at room temperature for two hours. Add both types of milk and the cream, mix well, and freeze. Give each student a portion of the ice cream to enjoy at snack time.

Healthy Milk Shake

Put students into groups of four and gather the following ingredients for each group: 1 cup milk, 1 banana, 2 tablespoons canned pumpkin, and a pinch of cinnamon. You will also need a blender, plastic knives, and plastic cups. Work with the groups one at a time to help students make their healthy milk shakes. Allow children to help you slice the bananas with the plastic knives, measure out the other ingredients, and place them all in the blender. Blend and serve chilled.

Apple Coleslaw

Gather one apple, one small head of cabbage, $\frac{1}{4}$ cup mayonnaise, $\frac{1}{4}$ cup milk, and 1 teaspoon lemon juice. Grate the apple and shred the cabbage. Let children mix the mayonnaise, milk, and lemon juice together. Pour the mixture over the apples and cabbage and toss. Serve as a snack or with lunch.

Sweetened, Chilled Carrot Sticks

Gather a few packages of fresh carrot sticks and a can of pineapple juice. Place the carrot sticks in a large bowl. Pour the pineapple juice into the bowl with the carrots until they are completely covered. Refrigerate the carrots in the pineapple juice for a minimum of one to two hours and serve as a snack.

Ocean

Contents

Ocean

Language Arts

Ocean Animal Arrangement

Gather several ocean animal toys or make copies of some of the animal patterns (pages 243-254). While children are busy with other tasks, invite one child at a time to come over and look at three of the animals you have placed in a row. Have the child turn his back while you rearrange the animals. Ask the child to turn around and return the animals to their original order.

Hidden Ocean Animals

Copy the Hidden Ocean Animals worksheet (page 255) for each child. Explain that there are two of each ocean animal hidden on the page. Have each child look closely to find the animals and then draw circles around those he sees. As he finds all of the animals in each group, have him cross out that group's name on the key at the top of the page.

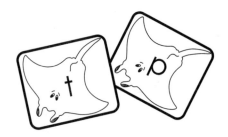

Manta Ray Letter Sorting

Make nine copies of the Manta Ray Letter Sorting Cards (page 256). Cut the cards apart. Write the uppercase letters of the alphabet on one half of the cards and the lowercase letters on the other half. Show the cards to children and explain that they should sort the uppercase letters from the lowercase letters. Allow them to complete this activity first as a class and then in small groups. Use the cards during center time to have children sequence the letters in ABC order.

Manta Ray Letter Matching

Gather the Manta Ray Letter Sorting cards (see above). Explain to the class that they should match each uppercase letter to the correct lowercase letter. As an extension activity, choose a letter and display it for the class to see. Encourage children to locate the letter on posters, wall hangings, signs, etc., found in the classroom. Be sure to have them identify it as an uppercase or lowercase letter.

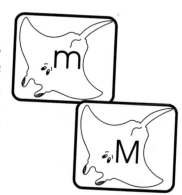

Dolphin Adventures

Gather children and explain that they will work together as a group to write a story. Explain that the story will be about a dolphin's adventures. Have children work together to decide on a name for the dolphin and the adventure it will have. When they have decided on a storyline, allow each child to dictate a sentence to you as you write it on chart paper or poster board. Remind each child that, when she contributes a sentence to the story, her sentence should continue the thought of the sentence before it. Have each child illustrate her sentence. Combine the sentences with the pictures into a book for children to read in small groups.

Ocean Patterns
Angelfish, Parrotfish

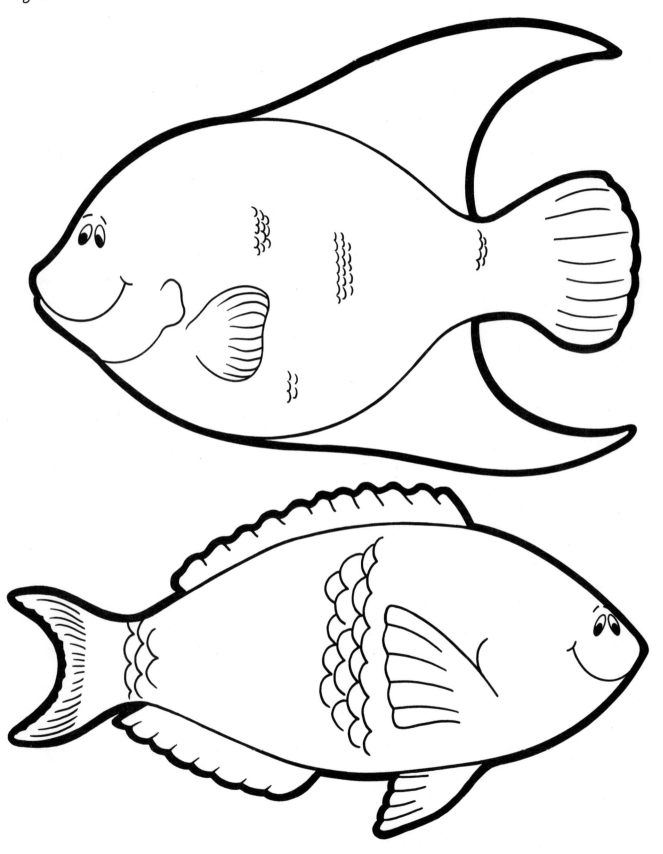

CD-0817 *Terrific Themes for Year-Round Fun*

Ocean Patterns
Dolphin, Manatee

CD-0817 *Terrific Themes for Year-Round Fun*

Ocean Patterns
Clam, Oyster, Starfish

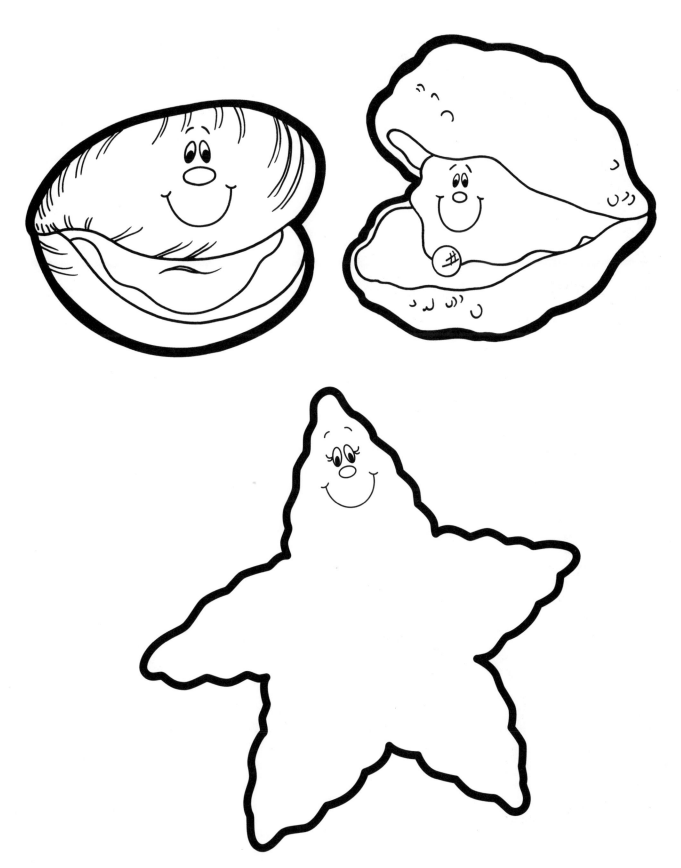

Ocean Patterns
Clownfish, Jellyfish, Sea Anemone

CD-0817 *Terrific Themes for Year-Round Fun*

Ocean Patterns
Killer Whale, Humpback Whale

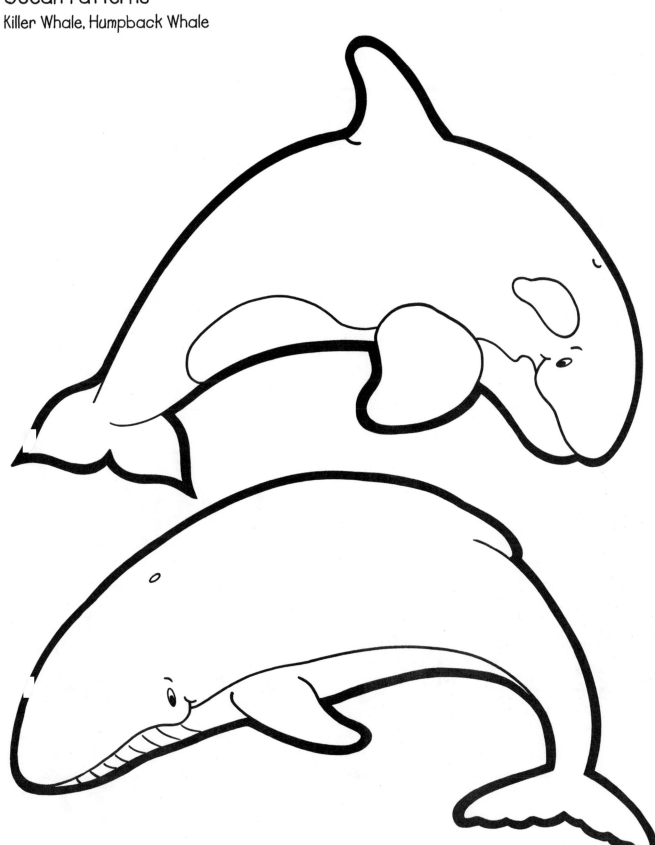

 CD-0817 *Terrific Themes for Year-Round Fun*

Ocean Patterns
Shark, Octopus, Squid

Ocean Patterns
Flamingo, Sea Gull, Pelican

CD-0817 *Terrific Themes for Year-Round Fun*

Ocean Patterns
Sea Horse, Shrimp, Lobster

CD-0817 *Terrific Themes for Year-Round Fun*

Ocean Patterns
Sand Crab, Hermit Cra, Horseshoe Crab

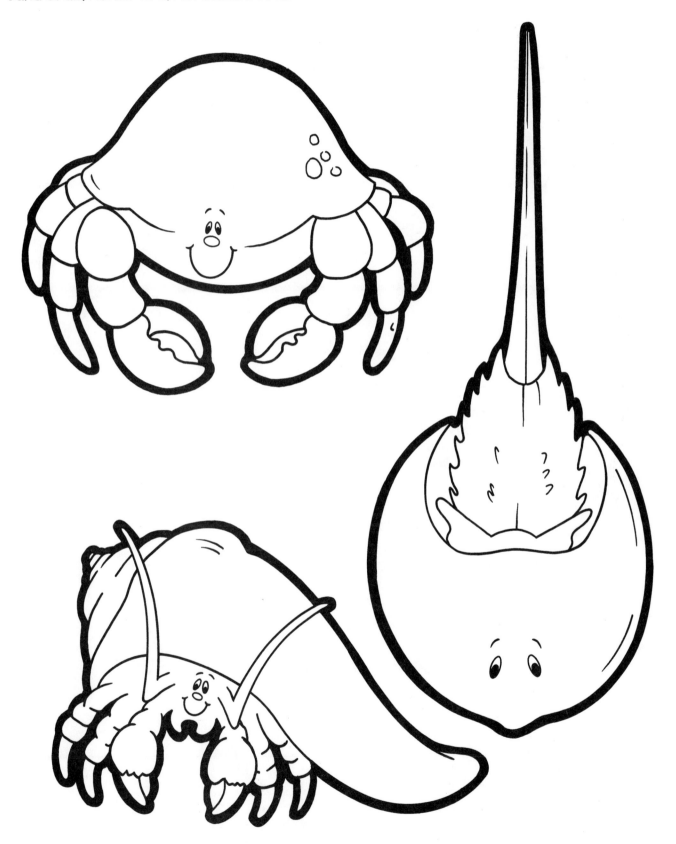

Ocean Patterns
Seal, Sea Lion, Sea Otter

CD-0817 *Terrific Themes for Year-Round Fun*

Ocean Patterns
Moray Eel, Manta Ray

 CD-0817 *Terrific Themes for Year-Round Fun*

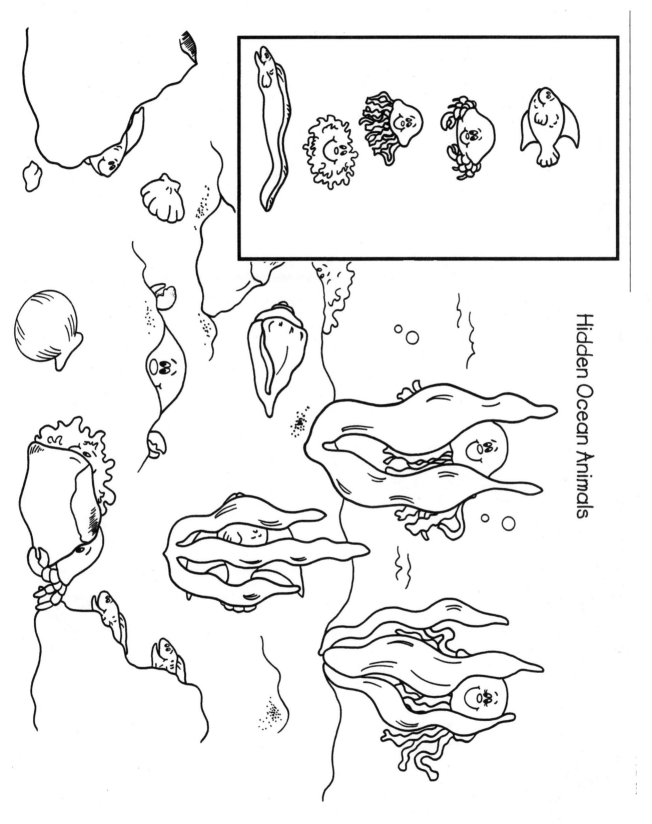

Hidden Ocean Animals

Ocean Patterns
Manta Ray Letter Sorting Cards

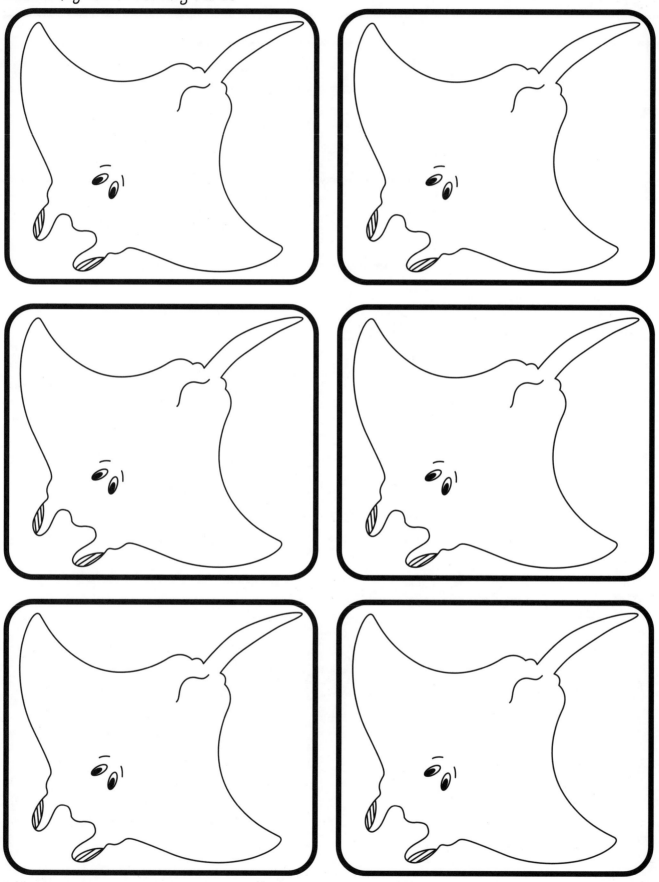

Octopus Counting

Copy the Octopus pattern (page 248). Show the pattern to children and have them count the number of legs on the octopus. Challenge them to find groups of eight objects. Allow them to work in pairs to gather sets of eight small items, such as buttons, crayons, erasers, etc.

Ocean Scene Counting and Coloring

Make one copy of the Ocean Scene Counting and Coloring worksheet (page 258) for each child in the class. Give each child a worksheet and crayons. Begin by naming a specific ocean animal and asking the class to count how many of that animal they find on their worksheets. (There are 4 jellyfish, 5 angelfish, 2 clams, 2 crabs, and 1 dolphin.) Assign a different color to each set of animals and instruct children to color their worksheets accordingly. Allow them to finish coloring the ocean scene.

Fishy Number Match

Gather an egg carton, six wooden craft sticks, construction paper, scissors, markers, and glue. Make the base for this counting game by cutting one row of six cups from the egg carton. Cut a small slot in the bottom of each cup large enough to slide the craft stick through. Turn the row of cups upside down and write a number from 1 to 6 on the side of each cup. Cut six fish from construction paper and draw a group of one to six dots on each fish. Glue the fish to the tops of the craft sticks. When the glue has dried, allow children to play a matching game by counting the number of dots on each fish, then placing the stick in the corresponding slot in the egg carton.

Shell Shapes

Gather a large bowl of seashells. Have students work in pairs to create shapes (circles, rectangles, squares, triangles, etc.) by placing the shells next to each other on a table. Begin by having one child create a shape while the other child identifies it. After completing a turn, have the children switch roles. If children have difficulty creating shapes, draw shape outlines on construction paper for students to place shells on.

Close Up and Far Away

Copy the Close Up and Far Away Cards (pages 259-260). Cut the cards apart. Color and laminate if desired. Talk with children about the visual differences between objects that are close up and those that are far away. Show a card to the class and have a volunteer tell whether the animal is close up or far away. Continue until all children have had a turn.

Ocean Scene Counting and Coloring

Ocean Patterns
Close Up and Far Away Cards

259

Ocean Patterns
Close Up and Far Away Cards

Whales in a Bottle

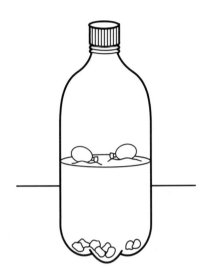

Fill a two-liter bottle halfway with water. Add a few drops of blue food coloring to the water. Inflate two small blue balloons with a small amount of air, tie a knot in the end of each, and squeeze them into the bottle. Drop a few pebbles into the water and then securely tighten the lid on the bottle. Place the bottle on a table and allow children to observe. Ask them to describe what they see in the bottle. Tell them that you will turn the bottle over and ask them what they think will happen to the balloon "whales" and the pebbles. Allow children to describe what they see as you turn the bottle over. Encourage them to use the words "floating" and "sinking." Make the bottle accessible to children during center time for further explorations.

How Do They Get Food?

Gather several books about ocean animals and their eating habits. Have children listen as you read about how certain ocean animals get their food. The eating habits of the jellyfish, sea anemone, and sting plankton are especially interesting. Discuss how electric rays shock their prey or how anglerfish have lures on their heads to trick small fish. After you have shared these facts with children, ask the class questions about each animal. Challenge children by asking them to recall the information they have heard.

"Jellyfish get their food by ..."

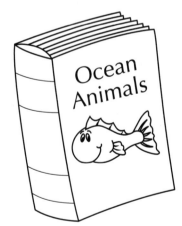

Herbivore, Carnivore, or Omnivore?

Gather several books about ocean animals and their eating habits. Explain to the class that a herbivore is an animal that eats plants, a carnivore eats meat, and an omnivore eats both plants and meat. Look through the books with children and have them talk about what each animal eats. Copy the Ocean Animal patterns (pages 243–254) and have the class sort them into herbivore, carnivore, or omnivore categories.

Shell Examinations

Gather a variety of seashells and place them on a table along with several magnifying glasses. Allow children to use the magnifying glasses to examine the shells. Have them describe the colors, shapes, and other details they see. Encourage them to describe the texture of each shell and compare similarities and differences among the shells.

Traditional Songs

"Once I Caught a Fish Alive"
"Over in the Meadow in an Itty Bitty Pond"
"My Bonny Lies Over the Ocean"

Related Commercial Songs

Raffi's "Baby Beluga," from the album *Baby Beluga*
Disney's "Under the Sea" from *The Little Mermaid*
Barney's "If I Lived Under the Sea"
    from *Barney* series

Finger Plays

Five Little Fish

Five little fish, swimming in a school.
    (Hold up five fingers, then swim with hands.)
The first one said, "This water's cool."
    (Hold up one finger, then shiver.)
The second one said, "There's a shark over there!"
    (Hold up two fingers, then point excitedly.)
The third one said, "We'd better beware."
    (Hold up three fingers, then look scared.)
The fourth one said, "Where can we hide?"
    (Hold up four fingers, then hold out hands
    questioningly.)
The fifth one said, "There's a cave! Go inside."
    (Hold up five fingers, then point.)
Then in went the fish, and the shark went away,
And the five little fish swam out to play.

Eight Little Tentacles

(to the tune of "Ten Little Indians")
One little, two little, three little tentacles,
Four little, five little, six little tentacles,
Seven little, eight, yes, eight little tentacles,
On an octopus.

Have children hold up the correct number of fingers
as they recite the finger play.

Adapted Songs

A-Fishing We Will Go

(to the tune of "The Farmer in the Dell")
A-fishing we will go, a-fishing we will go,
We'll have some fun playing in the sun,
A-fishing we will go.

A-fishing we will go, a-fishing we will go,
Oh, how I wish to catch a fish,
A-fishing we will go.

When the Fish Go Swimming By

(to the tune of "When the Saints Go Marching In")
Oh, when the fish go swimming by,
Oh, when the fish go swimming by,
I'll be on the shore watching closely,
When the fish go swimming by.

Repeat, replacing "fish" with other ocean animal
names.

Movement Activities

Swimming Whales

Play a recording of whale songs for the children. After
they have listened for a few minutes, allow them to
move gracefully to the rhythms and sounds.

Moving to Ocean Sounds

Play a recording of a variety of ocean sounds. If
possible, include such sounds as dolphins, sea gulls,
waves crashing on the beach, etc. Have children listen
to the sounds, then move their bodies to express how
they feel when they hear the sounds.

Sea Gull Flying

Encourage children to pretend they are flying like sea
gulls. As they fly, direct them to pretend to do the
following: look out over the ocean, fly up higher,
swoop down to catch a fish, etc.

Field Trips

The Beach

If you live in a coastal area, arrange for your class (along with several chaperones) to visit the beach. Check with the local parks and recreation department to find out if there are specific areas or times when you and your students could go to observe ocean animals.

Aquarium, Ocean Life Park, or Science Center

If you are within traveling distance of any type of aquarium or ocean life park, make plans for your class to visit. Also check to see if a science center located in or near your hometown has any displays on ocean life that the class can visit.

Pet Store

If you do not live near a beach or aquarium, a good alternative field trip can be made to a local pet store. Arrange a visit to a local pet shop to see the fish, preferably one with a variety of saltwater fish. Ask if a store worker could speak to children about care given to the fish.

Animals Working Together

Locate several books about the relationship between the sea anemone and the clownfish. Explain how the clownfish uses the sea anemone for shelter and how the anemone relies on the clownfish for protection. Read the stories to children and have them comment on the unique relationship between these two animals. Ask them to think of other relationships that require the participants to work together. Encourage children to think of situations where they need to cooperate with others. Make a list as the children dictate the benefits of cooperation and helping others.

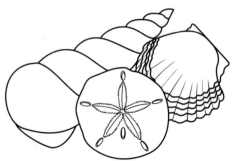

Sharing Ocean Experiences

Send a note to parents requesting that their child bring an object to class relating to the ocean. The child may bring in shells collected during a trip to the beach; a stuffed ocean animal, such as a dolphin or whale; pictures or souvenirs from a trip to the beach or aquarium; pictures cut from a magazine; etc. Allow children to take turns telling the class about their items.

Cellophane Ocean Mural

Purchase several rolls of blue cellophane. Cut a 12" square section of the cellophane for each child. Gather several different colors of tempera paint and paintbrushes. Allow children to work one at a time, taping their pieces of cellophane to a window or on top of white paper at the easel. Allow each child to use the paint to create an underwater ocean scene with ocean animals on the cellophane.

Starfish Printmaking

Gather several sponges and cut them into starfish shapes using the pattern (page 245). Place the sponges, along with construction paper and small bowls of tempera paint, on a table. Allow children to use the sponges and paint to make starfish prints on their papers.

Starfish Rubbings

Purchase a package of sandpaper and cut it into several different-sized starfish shapes. Place these "starfish," along with newsprint paper and crayons, on a table. Show children how to make a starfish rubbing by placing the starfish pattern under the paper and rubbing the surface with the side of a peeled crayon. Allow children to make as many starfish rubbings on their papers as they desire.

Sand Starfish

Make starfish templates from tagboard or poster board. Fill several salt shakers with sand. Place these items, along with pencils, craft sticks, glue, and paper, on a table. Allow two to three children to work at the table. Instruct children to use the starfish patterns and pencils to trace several starfish on their papers. Then, they should cover the starfish with glue and use craft sticks to spread it into thin, even layers. Have them shake the sand on the glue. Have children shake off the excess sand, then set their papers aside to dry.

Fish with Scales

If you are working with very young children, pre-cut a large fish from colored construction paper for each student. You may want to use a Fish pattern (page 243). For older children, draw or reproduce a fish shape on construction paper and allow each child to cut out her own fish. Purchase a package of cellophane tissue paper and cut it into several oval-shaped pieces. First, have each child use crayons to draw details such as eyes, fins, etc., on her fish. Then, allow each child to glue the shiny scales on her fish.

Ocean

Art

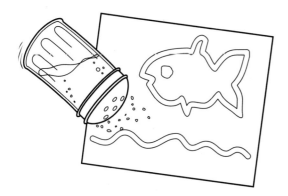

Colored Sand and Salt Shakers

Gather several salt shakers and fill each with a mixture of equal parts of clean sand and powdered tempera paint. Place the salt shakers, along with construction paper and glue, on a table. Allow children to use the glue to make ocean animal designs on their papers and then cover them with different salt shaker mixtures. After the glue has dried, shake excess sand/salt off of the papers to reveal their beautiful creations.

Sea Anemone with Clownfish

Give each student a copy of the Clownfish pattern (page 246), several brightly-colored chenille craft sticks, a sheet of blue construction paper, glue, and scissors. Let him color, cut out, and glue the clownfish in the top center of the construction paper. Then, have him create a sea anemone by gluing the chenille craft sticks under the clownfish.

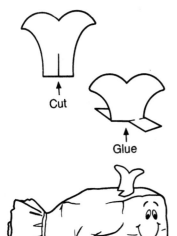

Cut

Glue

Paper Bag Whales

Provide one white paper bag for each child in your class. Place string, glue, construction paper, scissors, and crayons on a table. Make a model whale by drawing details, such as a mouth and eyes, on the bottom of the bag. Then, blow air into the bag until it is partially full. Use the string to tie the open end of the bag closed. To make a spout, cut a 3" x 4$^1/_2$" spout shape from blue construction paper. From the bottom of the spout, make a 1$^1/_2$" cut up the center to form two tabs. Fold one tab backwards and one tab forward. Secure the spout on top of the whale by gluing the tabs to the bag.

Hand-Covered Stuffed Fish

Before you begin, cut two identical fish shapes from a large piece of white poster board. Stack the two fish shapes so the edges are lined up. Draw a side view of a fish face on both sides of the fish. Gather a stapler, newspaper, 9" x 12" sheets of construction paper in a variety of colors, pencils, and scissors. Begin by giving each child construction paper in several colors, a pencil, and scissors. Explain to children that each student should trace both of his hands onto the construction paper, then cut them out. As they finish working, allow them to come up and glue their paper hands on the sides of the fish. Set the fish aside to dry. When the glue is dry, allow children to help you staple edges of the two fish together, leaving about an 8" opening. Have them ball up single sheets of newspaper and stuff them inside the fish. After each fish has been stuffed with newspaper, staple the opening shut and hang it from the ceiling with string.

Fishing with Magnets

Gather a large box or tub. Cut out several fish shapes from colored construction paper. Attach a paper clip to each fish. Place the fish in the box or tub. To make a fishing pole, tie one end of a string to a stick. Tie the other end of the string to a magnet. To catch a fish, have a child hold the magnet end of the fishing pole over the box or tub. Adjust the level of difficulty of this game for the developmental level of your children. For very young children, have them simply try to catch the fish. To increase the difficulty slightly, ask children to catch a certain color fish. You may have children catch one fish, then try to catch another fish of the same color. Challenge children by drawing shapes, letters, or numbers on the fish and asking them to try to catch matching fish.

Go Fish

Make two copies of each of the Go Fish Cards (pages 267-268). Color, cut out, and laminate the cards. Gather a small group of two to four children and teach them to play the traditional game of "Go Fish" with the ocean animal cards. Allow one child to pass out five cards to each player. Place the rest of the deck facedown on the table. Each child takes a turn asking a player for a card to match one of those he is holding. If the player makes a match, he places both cards on the table. If he does not, he draws a card and the next player takes a turn. The game ends when all of the cards have been matched. If you wish to have children keep score, the child with the most matches wins. Teach a different group of children how to play each day until all students have learned the game.

Follow the Leader Fish

Gather children on the playground and explain that they will be playing a version of the game "Follow the Leader." Tell them that you will be selecting a child to be the "leader fish" and the others should pretend to be a school of fish. Explain that schools of fish move in the same direction together when swimming. Allow students to take turns being the "leader fish" and leading the other swimming fish around the playground.

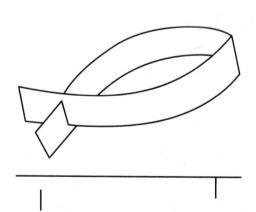

Paper Flying Fish

Cut several 1" x 8" strips of colored construction paper for each child in the class. Make a $1/2$" cut $1 1/2$" from each end as shown. Place the cuts on opposite sides of the strips. Give each child a strip of paper and show her how to make a flying fish by carefully folding and fitting the slots together. Explain that when the fish is tossed into the air, it will glide and twirl down to the ground. Remind children to be careful not to step on the fish that land near their feet.

Ocean Patterns
Go Fish Cards

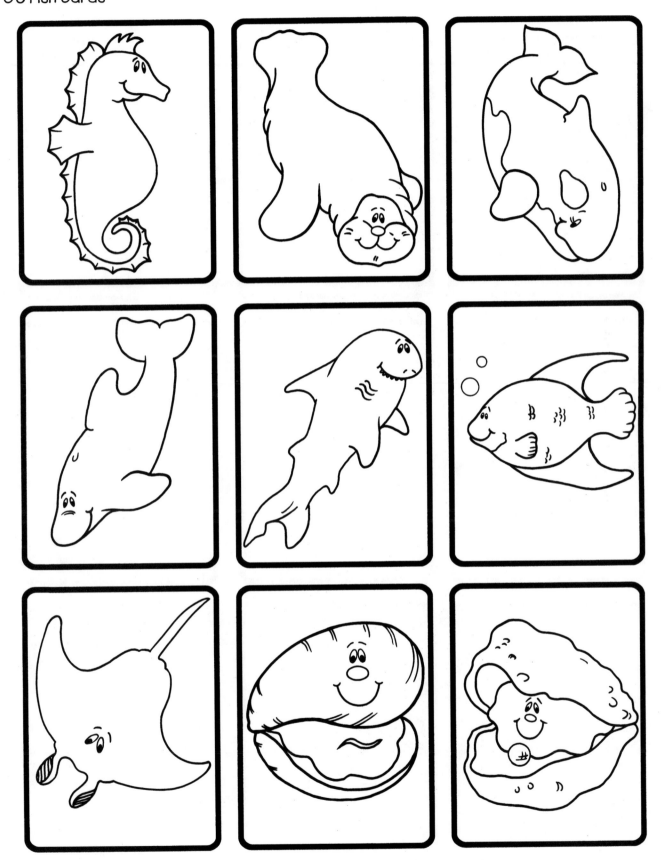

Ocean Patterns
Go Fish Cards

Allergy and Food Preference Note

Before completing any food activity, ask parental permission and inquire about children's food allergies. Common food allergies include peanuts and other nuts, dairy, eggs, berries, etc. Parents may have religious or other preferences that will prevent children from eating certain foods.

Shell Salad

Gather precooked shell-shaped pasta, mayonnaise, celery, olives, diced tomatoes, and a variety of shredded cheeses. Pre-cut the celery and olives into small pieces. Give each child a small bowl of pasta and allow him to spoon selected toppings on the shells. Let students mix and enjoy the shell salad.

Starfish Finger Gelatin

Purchase a package of gelatin mix and follow the directions on the box to make finger gelatin. When cooled, allow children to cut their gelatin into starfish shapes using star-shaped cookie cutters.

Marshmallow Octopuses

Purchase a package of large marshmallows, cotton swabs, dark food coloring, and string licorice. Have each child paint a face on the "octopus" (marshmallow) using a cotton swab and food coloring. Let her cut several pieces of licorice into eight equal lengths, about two inches long. Have her place the eight lengths of licorice into the bottom of the marshmallow to represent the octopus's legs.

Ocean Animal Lunch

If possible, ask the cafeteria staff to prepare fish sticks, popcorn shrimp, or clam strips for lunch one day during your ocean animal unit. Encourage children to discuss the look, taste, and texture of the foods. Allow them to also talk about any other ocean animals they have tasted. Be sure to check with parents for food allergies before introducing new foods.

Clam Chowder

Bring in several cans of white (New England) or red (Manhattan) clam chowder. Heat the chowder in the microwave or on the stove according to the directions on the can. After soup has cooled, serve the chowder to children as a snack. You may also wish to provide oyster crackers for them to eat with the chowder. As they are eating, ask them to identify some of the ingredients. Encourage them to describe the taste and texture of the chowder. If possible, provide both types of clam chowder and have the children compare and contrast the ingredients and flavors.

Thanksgiving

Contents

Thanksgiving Storytelling

Copy, color, and cut out the Thanksgiving Storytelling Cards found (pages 272-273). Tell children that they will make a class story. Show one of the pictures to the class. Talk about what they see in the picture. Ask them to think about what the people are doing, or how they are feeling. Tell children that they are each going to make up one sentence for the class story. Give each child a turn to say a sentence while you write it on chart paper. Encourage children to make the sentences flow together. You may wish to later write the story down on the bottom half of blank paper, copy it, and allow each child to illustrate the story to take home. Use the other storytelling cards in the same way. You can also place the storytelling cards at a writing center to allow children to independently write Thanksgiving stories.

Thankful List

Put up a piece of chart paper with a picture of a big smiley face in the center. Talk with children about what the word "thankful" means. Then, ask each child to tell you one or two things for which he is very thankful. Write these on the chart paper. Have each child try to think of something that has not been mentioned before. You may need to help children think of things that they do think of, such as rain to make plants grow, cars and planes to take us to visit loved ones, etc. When the list is finished, ask children if they are thankful for some of the things others named. Point out that we all have many things for which to be thankful.

Thanksgiving Word Sequence

Explain to children that you will say a list of Thanksgiving words, and you would like them to repeat them to you in the same sequence. Begin with two words such as *turkey, Pilgrim.* Have the group repeat them back to you three or four times, making sure you say them again between the repeats. Then, add another word. Continue adding a word each time until your list reaches five or six words.

Thanksgiving Beginning Sounds

Tell the class that you will say a Thanksgiving word and you would like them to try to name other words that start with the same sound. For example, you might say "turkey." The children might then say, "time, turnip, tank," etc. List the sets of words to display during the Thanksgiving unit.

Thanksgiving Patterns
Thanksgiving Storytelling Cards

CD-0817 *Terrific Themes for Year-Round Fun*

Thanksgiving Patterns
Thanksgiving Storytelling Cards

 CD-0817 *Terrific Themes for Year-Round Fun*

Turkey Feather Pattern Matching

Copy 12 Turkey Feather patterns (page 275) onto tagboard and cut out. Draw the same shape or color pattern on two feathers. Continue until you have six pairs of matching patterns. Have children look at the feathers and describe the pattern they see on each. Explain that each feather has a matching feather with the same pattern. Allow children to match the feathers that show the same patterns.

Turkey Tail Shape and Color Matching

Cut out several Turkey and Turkey Tail patterns (page 276). Make matching sets by drawing a shape on the body of each turkey and the same shape on the tail. Make several sets with the same shape, but with different colors. Laminate the pieces for durability. As a group, have children match each tail to the turkey with the same color and shape on it. Allow children to do the activity in small groups or individually during center time.

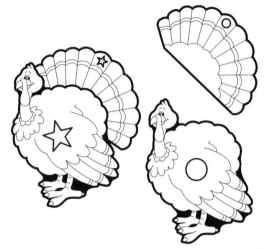

Thanksgiving Outline Match

Trace the outlines of several Thanksgiving objects, such as a turkey cookie cutter, a small cornucopia, a rolling pin, etc., on a large piece of poster board. Show children the items and explain that each item has been traced to show its outline. Allow each child to take a turn matching each item to its outline.

Countdown to Thanksgiving

A few weeks before Thanksgiving Day, show children a calendar for the month of November. Point to the date for Thanksgiving, as well as the current day's date. Have children count how many days until Thanksgiving Day arrives. Write this number on the board. Each day, revisit the calendar and ask students to tell you what number is one less than the number written on the board. Tell them this is now how many days are left until Thanksgiving. Continue counting down until Thanksgiving Day finally arrives.

Thanksgiving Patterns
Turkey Feather

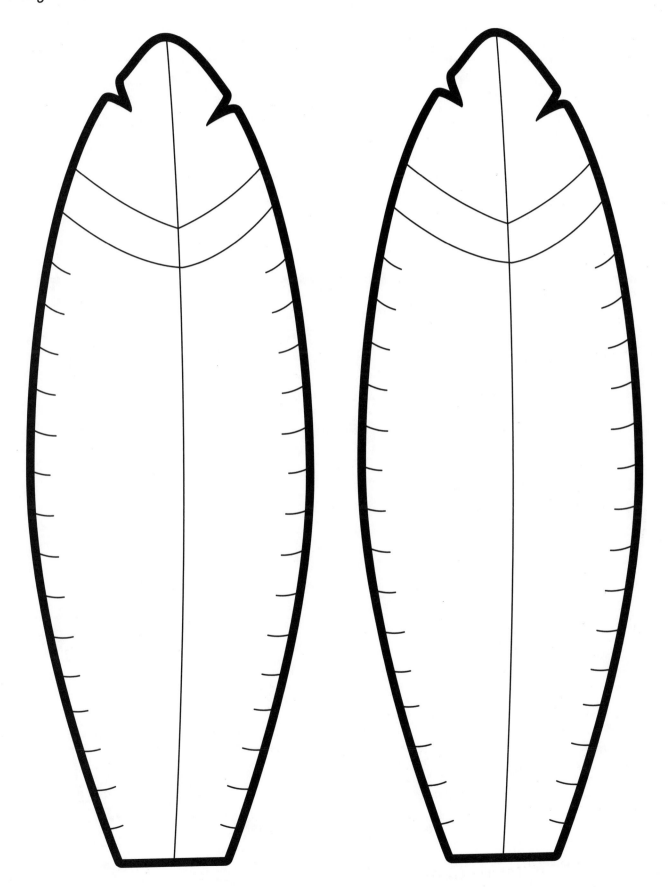

CD-0817 *Terrific Themes for Year-Round Fun*

Thanksgiving Patterns
Turkey and Turkey Tail

CD-0817 *Terrific Themes for Year-Round Fun*

Thanksgiving

Corn Cob Painting

Gather several dried corn cobs, some with the corn still intact, some without. Also gather a few trays of tempera paint and construction paper. Show children the corn cobs and ask them to describe what the cobs look like. Explain to them that they will paint with the corn cobs by rolling the cobs in trays of paint and then rolling the cobs on construction paper. When the paintings are dry, talk about how the two different types of corn cobs made the paintings look.

Thanksgiving Taste Test

Check with parents about food allergies prior to completing this activity. Prepare any combination of the typical Thanksgiving dishes, such as cranberry sauce, pumpkin pie, dumplings, stuffing, etc. Encourage children to taste the items. As each child tastes a dish, ask him to describe how it tastes and feels in his mouth. Ask him to tell you if it is sweet, salty, sour, etc., or if it is smooth, crunchy, etc. Another idea is to have children close their eyes and see if they can guess what food(s) they are eating by using only their senses of taste and smell.

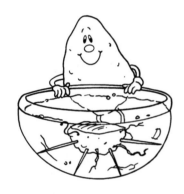

Sweet Potato Garden

Show the class a raw sweet potato and have them describe what it looks like and where it came from. Cut an inch off of one end of the potato and put it in a clear bowl of water, supporting it with toothpicks so it does not touch the bottom of the bowl. Ask children to guess what will happen. Each day, have children observe and describe the changes they see taking place.

Music and Movement

Traditional Songs

"Over the River and Through the Woods"
"She'll be Comin' Round the Mountain"
"Turkey in the Straw"

Adapted Song
Did You Ever See a Turkey?

(to the tune of "Did You Ever See a Lassie?")
Did you ever see a turkey, a turkey, a turkey,
Did you ever see a turkey gobble this way and that?
Gobble this way and that way, and this way and that way,
Did you ever see a turkey gobble this way and that?

Movement Activity
Native American Dance

Play a recording of Native American music and allow children to dance and play drums made from decorated oatmeal boxes, butter bowls, or coffee cans.

Thanksgiving

Field Trips/Visitors

Turkey Farm
Visit a local turkey farm. Allow children to see where the turkeys live, what they eat, etc.

Library
Visit the local library and arrange for the librarian to read a story about the first Thanksgiving. If you are not able to visit the library, a librarian might be able to visit your class.

Pilgrim
Arrange for a visitor to come to class dressed up like a Pilgrim. Have the visitor talk about what life was like as a Pilgrim and explain that Pilgrims did not have many of the things we now feel are necessities (microwaves, telephones, television, etc.). You may wish to have him tell the story of the first Thanksgiving.

Our Time vs. Pilgrim Time
Brainstorm with students a list of things that we have now that were not developed during the time of the Pilgrims (around 1620). Make a list on a chalkboard or chart paper that lists the modern-day appliances on the left and what the Pilgrims may have used on the right. Encourage students to think of what Pilgrims did for fun, how they cooked their meals and washed their clothes, and how the Pilgrims performed other tasks without the modern-day inventions that are available today.

Rules to Live By
Explain that after the *Mayflower* landed in Plymouth, the Pilgrims realized they needed to work together in order to survive. The *Mayflower Compact* was the Pilgrims' promise to live by fair laws in the New World. The men who signed the *Mayflower Compact* agreed to stay together and follow any laws that were made. Have children brainstorm a classroom compact where students agree to treat each other fairly and follow classroom rules. Copy the classroom compact onto a large piece of chart paper and have each student sign it. Post the compact as a reminder to students to treat each other fairly.

Native American Necklace

Talk with children about Native Americans and their ways of life. Explain that many Native Americans make articles of clothing and jewelry by hand. Tell children that, during colonial days, Native Americans took the items they made to trading posts to trade for goods they needed. Allow children to string round cereal, straw pieces, and macaroni on heavy string to make their own handmade necklaces.

Tissue-Paper Turkey

Copy the Turkey pattern (page 280) onto construction paper for each child. Have each child color and cut out the turkey pattern. Cut pieces of colored tissue paper into squares. Allow children to roll the tissue paper into balls and glue onto the turkey.

Thanksgiving Wreath

Cut a wreath shape from yellow poster board (approximately 12" x 12") for each child. Copy the Turkeys, Cornucopia, and Log Cabin patterns (page 281) onto different colors of construction paper so that each student will have two turkeys, two cornucopias, and two pilgrim hats in various colors. For younger students, cut out the patterns. Older students can cut the patterns out themselves. Allow children to glue uncooked macaroni; yellow, orange, and brown tissue paper; and the Thanksgiving patterns onto their wreaths.

Turkey Handprints

Give each child two sheets of construction paper in fall colors, scissors, crayons, glue, and a copy of the Turkey Body, Feet, and Wings patterns (page 282). Direct each child to make two outlines of his hand on the sheets of construction paper and cut them out. He should glue one handprint on top of the other so that the fingers look like fanned turkey feathers. Then, he should color and cut out the Turkey Body, Feet, and Wings patterns (page 282). Assist children as they glue the turkey "feathers," body, feet, and wings together.

Thanksgiving Patterns
Turkey

CD-0817 *Terrific Themes for Year-Round Fun*

Thanksgiving Patterns
Turkeys, Cornucopia, Log Cabin

CD-0817 *Terrific Themes for Year-Round Fun*

Thanksgiving Patterns
Turkey Body, Feet, and Wings

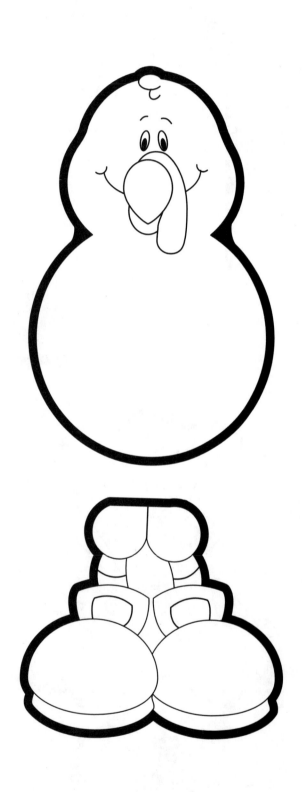

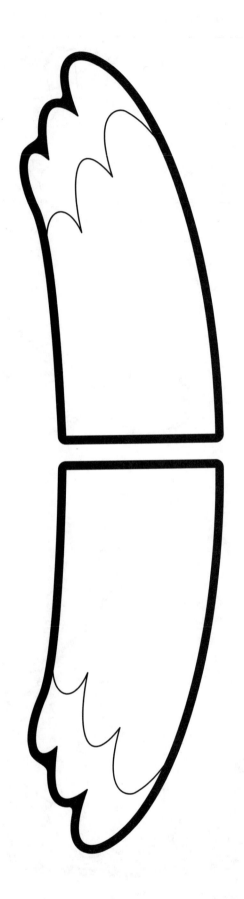

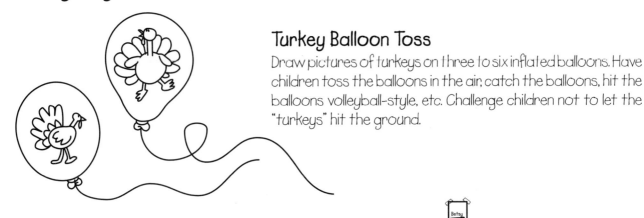

Turkey Balloon Toss

Draw pictures of turkeys on three to six inflated balloons. Have children toss the balloons in the air; catch the balloons, hit the balloons volleyball-style, etc. Challenge children not to let the "turkeys" hit the ground.

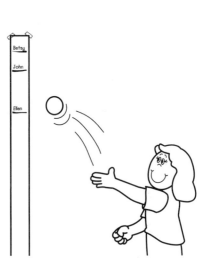

Ball Game

Many Native American tribes celebrate the corn crop before harvest work is done. A Green Corn Festival is held when the corn becomes ripe to thank the spirits for the corn harvest. Several Native American tribes play a game with a pole and a ball during the Green Corn Festival. The object of the game is to throw a small ball at a pole and hit it at the highest point. Display a strip of paper vertically on a wall. Allow students to take turns throwing a small bean bag ball at the "pole" and marking where the ball hit with their names. See who can throw the ball highest on the "pole."

Who Am I?

Choose one child to be "it." Have "it" sit with his back to the class. Point to another child to make turkey noises. "It" tries to guess which classmate is making the noises. Give "it" three chances to guess the correct classmate. Choose a new "it" every few minutes.

Thanksgiving Feast Tag

Choose one child to be "it." Explain to children that they are safe from being tagged if they stop right before "it" catches them and name a dish they like to eat on Thanksgiving. They will remain safe until they move again. "It" must turn his attention to another child when a child has become "safe." Also explain that a child may not use the same Thanksgiving dish twice in a row. Name a new "it" every few minutes.

Allergy and Food Preference Note

Before completing any food activity, ask parental permission and inquire about children's food allergies. Common food allergies include peanuts and other nuts, dairy, eggs, berries, etc. Parents may have religious or other preferences that will prevent children from eating certain foods.

Vegetable Soup

This is a yummy cooking project for a cool fall day. Bring in a slow cooker and begin this activity early in the morning. Allow children to help you wash and prepare a variety of vegetables for your soup. Good vegetables for this mix are canned corn, fresh mushrooms, garbanzo beans, fresh okra, whole stewed tomatoes, celery, peas, green beans, canned carrots, onions, etc. Place all of the vegetables in the pot and add enough water to cover them. Add a small amount of salt and pepper. Place the slow cooker on a medium setting and allow it to simmer all morning. Stir occasionally and add water if needed. Arrange the classroom tables for a Thanksgiving feast and allow children to pretend it's the first Thanksgiving as they eat their vegetable soup.

Thanksgiving Recipes

Thanksgiving is a time that lends itself to cooking activities. Ask parents to send in their favorite recipes for Thanksgiving dishes such as corn bread, sweet potato pie, pumpkin pie, homemade stuffing, etc. Write the recipes on poster board using pictures and symbols and allow children to compare the differences or similarities in ingredients. Choose a few simple recipes to make with the group. If possible, invite the parents and grandparents in for a special luncheon and spend the morning with children preparing some of the recipes. Make sure to put a title card by each dish (for example, "Made from Bobby's Mom's Pumpkin Pie Recipe").

Corn Bread Biscuits

The Pilgrims used the corn that Squanto taught them to plant to make small cornmeal cakes. These cornmeal cakes were a substitute for the wheat cakes they ate in England. Make these corn bread biscuits, similar to the cornmeal cakes eaten at the First Thanksgiving in Plymouth. Preheat oven to 350°F Bring 4 cups water and 1 cup cornmeal to a boil. Reduce heat and simmer for $^1/_2$ hour, stirring occasionally. Mix $1^1/_2$ cups whole wheat flour and 1 teaspoon salt thoroughly into the cornmeal. Drop biscuits (approximately $^1/_2$ cup of dough each) onto an ungreased cookie sheet and press down lightly. Bake for 15 minutes, turn biscuits over and bake for 10 more minutes. Yields about 20 biscuits.

Transportation

Contents

Transportation

Transportation Stories

Enlarge and reproduce the Transportation patterns (pages 287-292). Have students brainstorm a list of transportation-themed story starters, such as "I rode a space shuttle to Mars ..." or "One day I saw a purple taxi..." Place the patterns at a center with white paper, pencils, and crayons. Allow students who finish early to trace patterns on pieces of paper, choose story starters from the list, and write transportation stories on their traced patterns.

Transportation Sounds

Purchase or make a recording of several transportation sounds. The recording should include sounds such as a train on railroad tracks, a train whistle, a fog horn, an airplane flying, a helicopter flying, a car horn, etc. Gather students and have them listen to the tape and try to guess the sounds that they hear. Allow children to name each vehicle they hear on the tape. Write the names of vehicles on the chart paper and display the list throughout the transportation unit of study.

Luggage Tags

Copy the Luggage with Tag pattern (page 293) for each child. Explain to children that when they travel, they should put a luggage tag on each suitcase to help them and others identify the suitcase. Write each child's name on a luggage tag using a highlighting marker. Have her use a pencil to trace the letters. Encourage her to say the name of each letter as she traces it. Allow children to draw some of the things they would take on a trip on the patterns.

Radio Repeat

Gather several real or play portable radios or walkie-talkies. Explain to children that they will pretend to be transportation dispatchers or air traffic controllers. Share information about these two jobs and why they are important for travel safety. Allow children to work in pairs. Have one child say a sentence into his radio, and have his partner repeat it just as she heard it. Have children continue taking turns repeating each other's sentences.

Transportation Analogies

Gather children and tell them that you will play a word game. Explain that you will say a sentence, leaving out one word, and they should figure out the missing transportation word. Read the following sentences to children and have them say the missing word in each: "A street is to a car as water is to a (boat.) A station is to a bus as an airport is to a/an (airplane or helicopter)." Work with the children to create their own transportation analogies.

Transportation Patterns
Train Engine, Cars

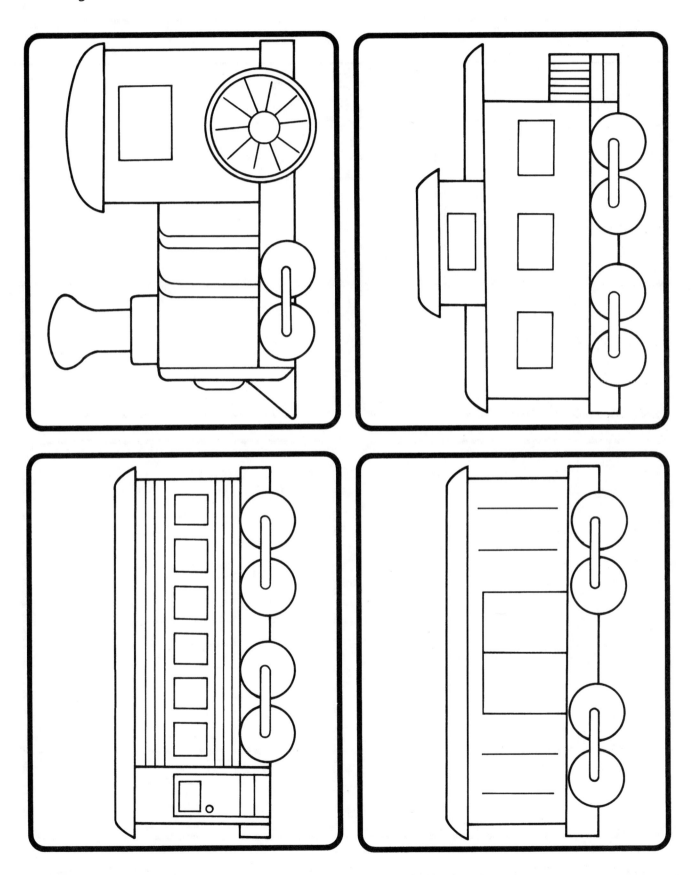

Transportation Patterns
Van, Car, Trucks

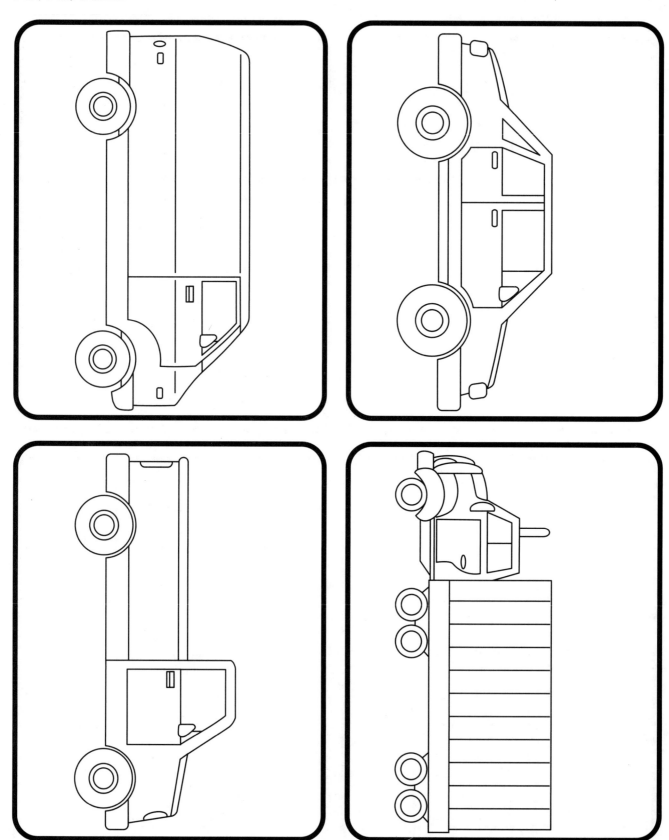

CD-0817 *Terrific Themes for Year-Round Fun*

Transportation Patterns
Sea Plane, Helicopter, Blimp, Jet

CD-0817 *Terrific Themes for Year-Round Fun*

Transportation Patterns
Rowboat, Submarine, Sailboat, Cruise Ship

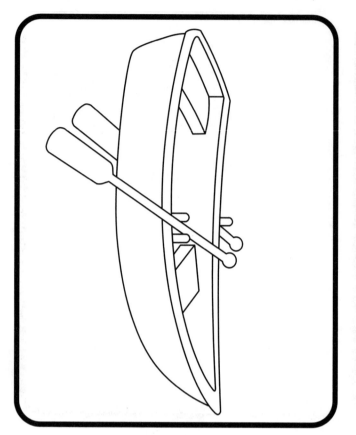

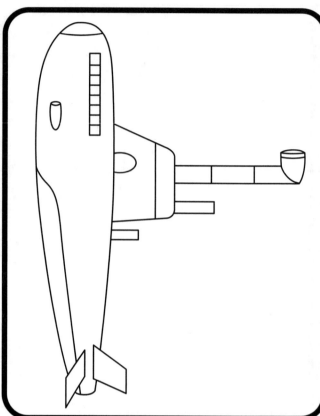

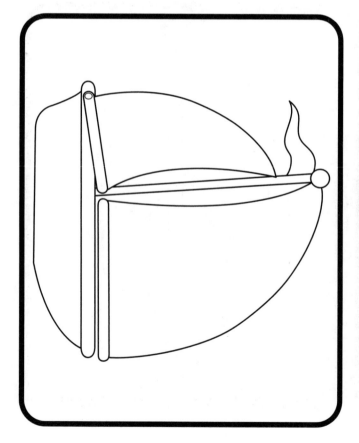

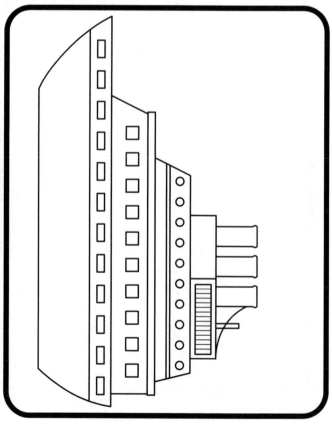

Transportation Patterns
Space Shuttle, Taxi, Rocket, Ambulance

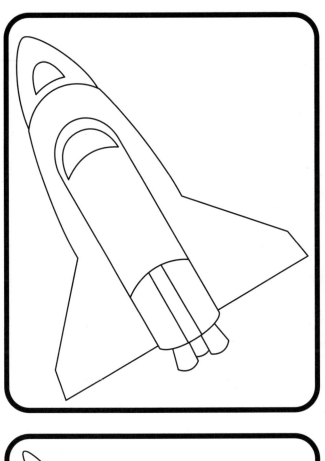

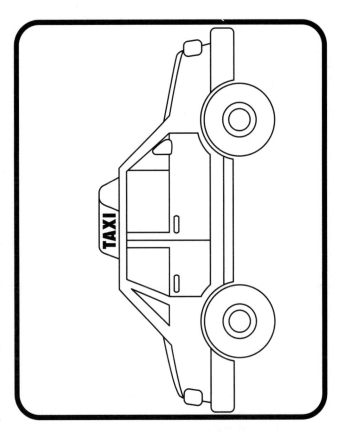

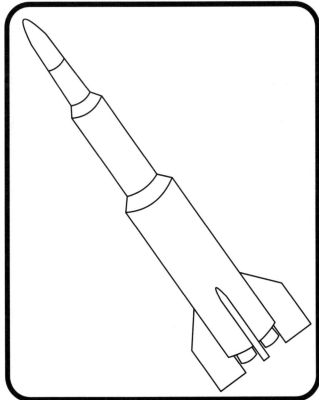

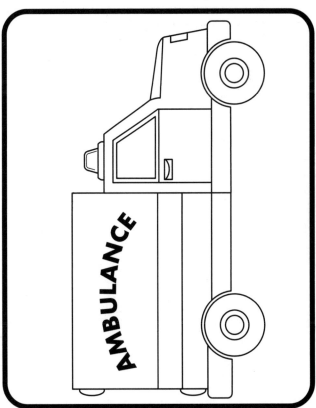

Transportation Patterns
Fire Truck, Police Car, Mail Truck, Cement Truck

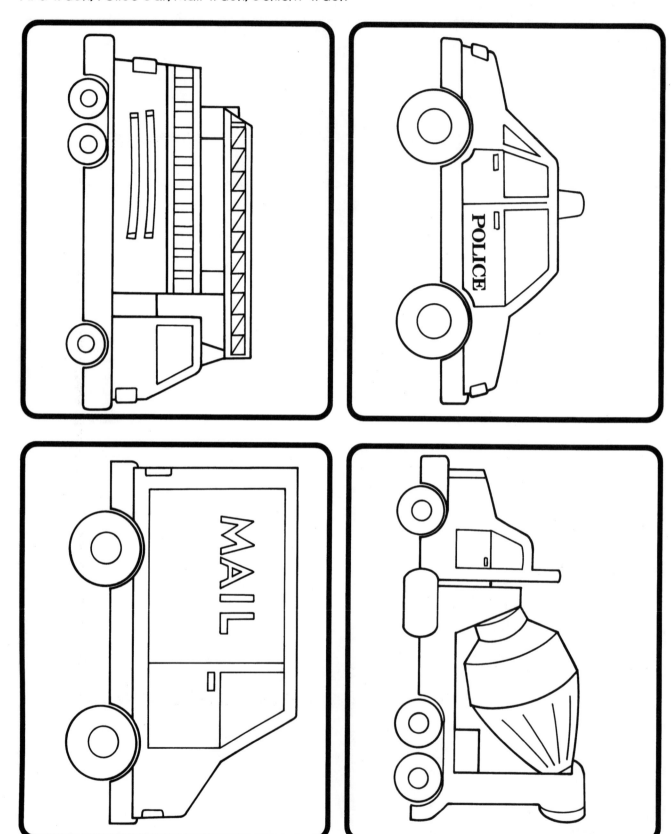

Transportation Patterns
Luggage with Tag

Fare and Toll Play

Make several copies of the Fare and Toll Play Money (page 295). Have children brainstorm the types of transportation that require tolls or fares to be paid. You may also have them think of other expenses for these vehicles such as buying gas for a car, buying new tires, etc. Allow children to use the play money to role-play paying tolls and fares for different vehicles. Have them take turns pretending to be the toll- and fare-takers and the travelers. The toll- and fare-takers should choose an amount to charge ($10 or under) and the travelers should count out the money and pay the appropriate toll or fare. Also allow children to role-play gas station attendants or other persons requiring payment from travelers.

Transportation Classification

Enlarge and cut apart the Transportation Classification cards (page 296). Display each scene. Using copies of the Transportation patterns (pages 287-292), ask children to sort the modes of transportation and place them on the appropriate scenes by determining where each vehicle travels. Challenge students to explain how they chose where to sort the cards.

Car and Truck Sort

Ask children to describe differences between cars and trucks. Have them look through old magazines and cut or tear out pictures of cars and trucks. Cut a large piece of poster board in half. Write the word *Cars* at the top of one half, and the word *Trucks* at the top of the other half. Allow children to sort the pictures and glue them on the appropriate piece of poster board.

Freight Sorting

Make a large train with the Train patterns (pages 297-298) enlarged onto construction paper. Cut out pictures of different items that trains may transport, such as foods, toys, clothes, animals, etc., from magazines. Label each train car with a category and draw a small picture or place a sticker to represent each word. Allow children to sort the pictures and glue them in the appropriate train car. When they have finished sorting the items, have the group count how many items are in each train car.

Transportation Patterns
Fare and Toll Play Money

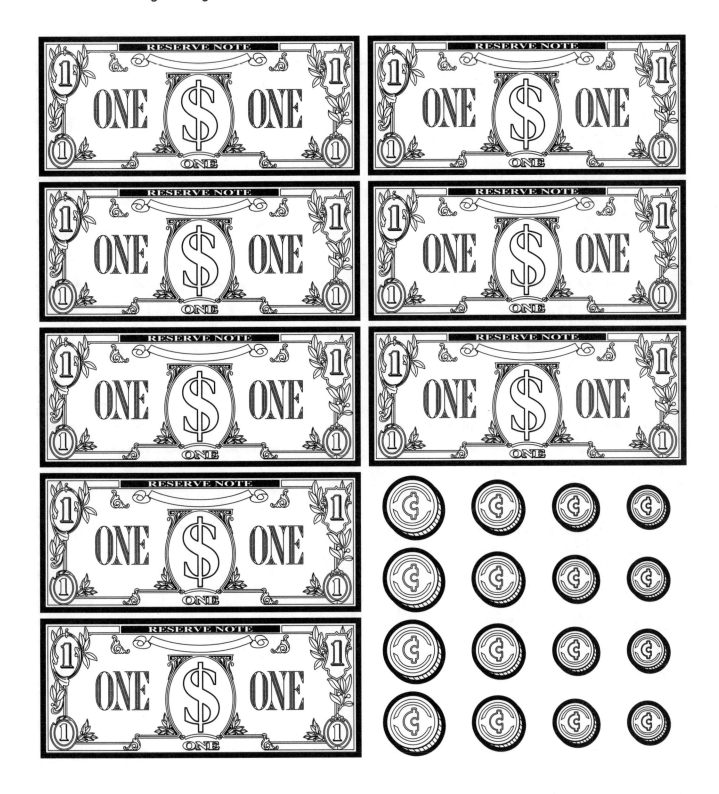

Transportation Patterns
Transportation Classification Cards

Transportation Patterns
Train Engine, Caboose, and Cargo Cars

Transportation Patterns
Train Car Cards

CD-0817 *Terrific Themes for Year-Round Fun*

How Does it Move?

Copy the Transportation patterns (pages 287-292). Have children look at each vehicle closely. Ask them to describe how each vehicle moves. Explain that some vehicles have wheels (cars, buses, trains), some have wings (airplanes), some have sails (sailboats), and some have propellers (helicopters, sea planes). Explain that propellers can move vehicles through both air and water. Challenge students to name other things that various modes of transportation require in order to move (gas, water, air, etc.) Explain to them that some vehicles require people power to help them move (bicycle, tricycle, unicycle). Challenge children by asking them to identify how each vehicle moves and whether it requires work from a person.

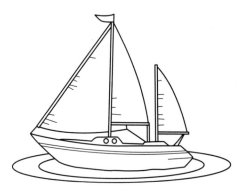

Moving Sailboats

Gather several miniature or paper sailboats and an infant bathtub. Float the sailboats in the water and allow children to describe how the sailboats move across the water. Have children help move them by blowing into the sails. Ask them to describe the speeds at which the boats moved with both the natural and the child-made wind. Ask them to tell you which type of wind helped the boats move faster. Have them compare the two speeds.

Which Can Defy Gravity?

Talk with children about gravity. Explain that gravity is the force that keeps us on the ground and pulls objects toward the ground. Ask children to think of the types of transportation that can break free from, or defy, gravity. Allow them to look at the Transportation patterns (pages 287-292) and have them point out the vehicles that are able to fly. Remind children that these aircraft need help, such as engines or helium, to defy gravity. Explain that some vehicles, such as rockets and space shuttles, actually leave the atmosphere. Allow children to sort the transportation cards into two piles: vehicles that can defy gravity or fly, and vehicles that cannot fly.

Working Axles

Gather several small boxes; wooden dowels, pencils or straws; spools or other objects that will work as wheels; and glue. Allow children to use these materials to create box vehicles with actual working axles. They may make any type of vehicle with wheels. Encourage them to be creative when making their vehicles. Have children observe and describe how their vehicles look and move. If desired, have children decorate them. Allow them to use their vehicles to role-play transportation situations.

Traditional Song

The Wheels on the Bus

The wheels on the bus go round and round,
Round and round, round and round.
The wheels on the bus go round and round,
All through the town.

Other bus verses:

People . . . go up and down; Wipers . . . go swish, swish, swish; Money . . . goes clink, clink, clink; Mommies . . . say, "Shh! Shh! Shh!"; Babies . . . cry, "Waa! Waa! Waa!"; Driver . . . says, "Move on back"; Doors . . . go open and shut; Horn . . . goes beep, beep, beep.

Additional adapted verses to sing to the tune of "The Wheels on the Bus":

The wheels on the train go clickety clack,
Clickety clack, clickety clack.
The wheels on the train go clickety clack,
All along the track.

Additional train verses:

Whistle . . . goes Whoo! Whoo! Whoo!; Conductor . . . says, "All aboard!"; People . . . go bumpety bump; Brakes . . . go Chhhh! Chhhh! Chhhh!

The anchor on the ship goes up and down.
Up and down, up and down.
The anchor on the ship goes up and down.
Across the big blue ocean.

Additional ship verses:

People . . . have lots of fun; Captain . . . says, "Full steam ahead!"; Engine . . . goes Rrrr! Rrrr! Rrrr!

Other Traditional Songs

"Anchors Aweigh"
"Bicycle Built for Two"
"Bumpin' Up and Down in My Little Red Wagon"
"Camptown Ladies"
"Down by the Station"
"I Love to Go A-Wandering"
"I've Been Working on the Railroad"
"Off We Go into the Wild Blue Yonder"
"Old Brass Wagon"
"Row, Row, Row Your Boat"
"Sailing, Sailing"
"Three Jolly Fishermen"
"Tinga Layo"

Traditional Finger Plays

"Hurry, Hurry, Drive the Fire Truck"
"She'll be Comin' Round the Mountain"
"Skip to My Lou"

Related Nursery Rhymes

"The Noble Duke of York"
"Rub-a-Dub-Dub"
"This is the Way a Lady Rides"

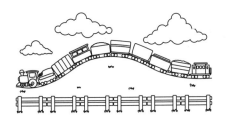

Field Trips

Arrange for your class to visit some of the following places: airport, bus depot, train station, helipad, etc. While there, allow children to look at the transportation provided, where tickets are bought (if necessary), where luggage is checked in, and any amenities, such as a restaurant, snack bar, gift shop, etc. Have a class discussion about what children observed on their trip.

How Would You Get There?

Copy the Transportation patterns (pages 287-292). Color, cut apart, and laminate the cards. Tape them to a chalkboard or wall where the class can see them. Tell children that you will name several different destinations and you would like them to decide which mode of transportation they could use to get there. Allow for all reasonable answers. Give destinations such as a store a few miles away, a friend's house in the next state, the moon, a tropical island, etc.

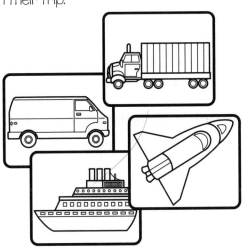

Pretending to Pack

Discuss with children that one of the great things about modes of transportation is that these vehicles can take us to different places. Prompt children to share what one has to do to prepare to go on a trip. Collect several overnight bags and suitcases and place them in an area of the classroom. Provide a supply of different types of clothes, shoes, empty toiletry bottles, discarded tickets, Fare and Toll Play Money (page 295), toy cameras, etc. Encourage children to tell about a place or person they would like to visit and have them pretend to pack their bags for the trip. Have children draw pictures to illustrate where they are pretending to visit.

Transportation Around Us

Take children to the playground and encourage them to observe and describe any type of transportation they see or hear. If possible, make arrangements to have the class watch as delivery trucks come to the school to deliver goods. You may also wish to have children watch for mail trucks, taxi cabs, city buses, ambulances, or other specific modes of transportation.

Egg Carton Trains

Place several egg cartons cut lengthwise into six-section pieces, colored construction paper, buttons, beads, chenille craft sticks, scissors, yarn, construction paper scraps, crayons, and glue at an art table. Allow each child to use these materials to create his own unique egg carton train.

Shoe- and Appliance-Box Transportation

Gather a collection of several shoe boxes and appliance boxes in various shapes and sizes. Encourage children to think of ways in which they can make the boxes resemble different vehicles. Provide the class with a variety of materials that they can use to decorate the boxes. Allow children to glue or tape the boxes together to resemble the vehicles. Provide scissors and construction paper scraps for children to use to add details to their vehicles.

Craft Stick Airplanes

Gather craft sticks, glue, markers, crayons, and small stickers. Have each child make an airplane by gluing craft sticks together. To make the body of the airplane, have him stack and glue approximately three craft sticks together. To make the wings, have him use crayons, markers, or stickers to decorate one craft stick. Glue this craft stick perpendicular across the top of the airplane body. To make the tail of the airplane, have him decorate and break one of the craft sticks in half. Stand each stick half up on one end and glue it against the body of the airplane. When the airplanes are dry, display them by suspending them from the ceiling using pieces of string.

Boat Sponge Prints

Cut several half-circle shapes out of sponges to represent boats. Place blue construction paper and several shallow pie tins of colored tempera paint at an art table. Allow children to gently press the sponges in the paint and carefully press them onto the paper to make boat prints. Have them glue paper triangles to the tops of each boat to represent the sails.

Colored Plane Match

Select an attribute such as color or size and make several pairs of matching airplanes from construction paper. You may wish to use different colors of paper for color matching, reduced and enlarged copies of the Jet pattern (page 289) for size matching, or a combination of the two. Glue one airplane from each pair to a file folder or a piece of poster board. Laminate or cover with clear contact paper if possible. Laminate the remaining planes and place them in a storage bag or basket. Show the playing board to children and explain that each plane in the basket (or plastic bag) has an identical match on the board. Allow children to take turns matching the planes.

Vrrrooooom

Gather children and have them sit in a circle. Explain that they will pretend to be automobiles. Tell them that you will make a sound, then the child next to you will imitate the sound, then the next child, and so on until the last child in the circle imitates the sound. Have all of the children continue making the first sound until a new sound is "passed" along to them. Include such sounds as an engine "vrooming," brakes "squealing," windshield wipers "swishing," horns "honking," etc. You will have quite a traffic-jam on your hands!

Playing with Blimps

Purchase one helium-filled balloon for each child in the class. Explain to children that they will pretend that the balloons are blimps. Give each child a balloon and allow him to pretend to "motor" it around the room. Encourage children to describe the movements of the balloons and their positions. Do not to release the balloons outside as this can be an environmental hazard.

I Spy

While on the playground, encourage children to look for the different vehicles they may see passing by the school or pulling into the parking lot. Have them call out the names of the vehicles as they see them. For example, if a school bus were to pass by, the children would call out, "I spy a yellow school bus!" Encourage children to count the number of wheels and to discuss the colors, shapes, and sizes of the vehicles. Challenge children by asking them to listen and look for vehicles in the air as well.

Allergy and Food Preference Note

Before completing any food activity, ask parental permission and inquire about children's food allergies. Common food allergies include peanuts and other nuts, dairy, eggs, berries, etc. Parents may have religious or other preferences that will prevent children from eating certain foods.

Hard-Boiled Egg Transports

Hard-boil enough eggs for each child in your class to have one. Provide children with cheese cut into triangle shapes, black and green olives cut in half lengthwise, celery sticks, carrot sticks, cucumber slices, and toothpicks. Place these items on a table for children to use. Slice the eggs in half lengthwise and give each child both halves on a paper plate. Allow children to use the toothpicks and other foods to make their eggs into cars, trains, airplanes, or boats. Be sure to check for food allergies before completing this activity.

Celery Vehicles

Provide children with celery sticks and peanut butter, egg salad, or spreadable cheese. Also, provide sliced black or green olives, cucumber slices, carrot sticks, and toothpicks. Allow each child to fill his celery stick with one of the toppings listed above. Have him make the celery stick into the vehicle of his choice. He may use the other foods to add details to the vehicle.

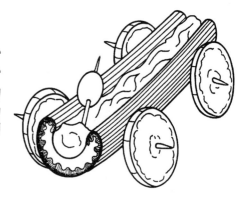

Banana Boats

Provide one banana for every two children in the class. Slice each banana in half lengthwise and spread a thin layer of peanut butter across the top of each one. Place small cups of miniature marshmallows, peanuts, and raisins at each table. Have children place marshmallows, raisins, and peanuts on top of the peanut butter to represent "passengers" on the banana boats.

Axle Snacks

Gather an assortment of circle-shaped foods such as cucumber slices, cheese wheels, grapes, banana slices, etc. Provide children with pretzel sticks and/or toothpicks. Show them how to make axles using the pretzels/toothpicks and "wheel" snacks. Make an axle by gently placing both ends of the toothpick or pretzel through the center of the snacks listed above. Allow children to make their own axles. Have a class discussion about the different vehicles that have wheels.

Winter

Contents

Winter Scenarios

Early in December, ask parents to save holiday cards for students to bring to class. Choose different scenes from the cards for students to view. Have students use descriptive language to explain what they see. Encourage students to look for similarities and differences between two scenes. For individual writing, allow each student to choose one scene. Have the student write one or two sentences to describe her scene or write a story about what is happening in her scene.

Winter Senses

Discuss the five senses: sight, taste, smell, touch, and hearing. Have students think about things they might sense in winter. Then, have each student dictate a sentence about one of the senses, such as "In winter, I can see snow on the ground," or "In winter, I can taste hot chocolate." Have students illustrate their sentences. Ask older students to write and illustrate one page for each of the five senses.

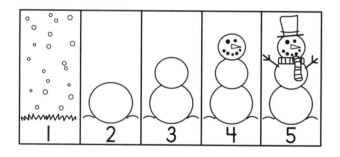

Snowman Sequencing

Have students think about what must happen before a snowman can be built. (First, it snows!) Then, have them name what should be done second, etc., to build a snowman. Give each child a piece of paper with five columns drawn on it. Assist children as they number the columns from 1 to 5. Have children illustrate a sequenced step for building a snowman in each column.

Winter Word Building

Use a pocket chart to display winter vocabulary words, such as snow, mitten, coat, hat, cold, ice, etc. Have children name beginning and ending sounds of the words. Then, have children brainstorm words that rhyme with each winter word. Write (or illustrate for younger children) rhyming words on index cards and place them under the appropriate winter words. Ask older children to identify the endings of the words. For reinforcement, use the pocket chart and words for a literacy center activity on sorting rhyming words.

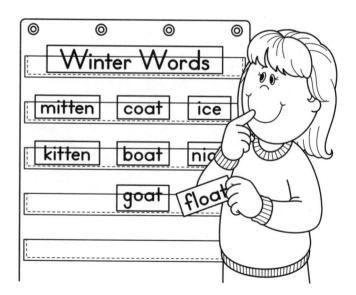

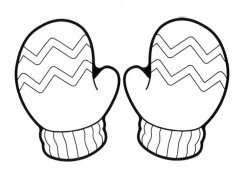

Mitten Match-Up

Copy the Mitten patterns (page 309) onto different colored paper. Use the mitten patterns to make matching games that reinforce language skills. Cut out each mitten pattern and have students match left and right mittens that are the same color. Other language arts skills that can be practiced by matching mittens include uppercase/lowercase letters, pictures/beginning sounds, pictures/words, colors/color words, and rhyming words. Laminate the cards for durability and mark matching mittens with identical symbols on the backs of the mittens so students can self-check their matches.

Snow Person Glyphs

A glyph (short for hieroglyphics) is a form of picture writing that conveys information about the person that created it. Use the directions below for children to complete a "Snow Person Glyph." Remind children that listening skills are very important as they work to create their personalized snow people. After the snow people glyphs are created, have each student share her creation with the class. Display all of the glyphs for children to compare and contrast. Challenge children to guess who created each snow person by thinking about their classmates' attributes and how the snow people were designed.

Snow Person Glyph Directions

Step 1:   If you are a boy, draw a blue hat on your snow person. If you are a girl, draw a pink hat on your snow person.

Step 2:   Add two eyes and a mouth to your snow person.

Step 3:   If you are the oldest child in your family, draw an orange carrot nose.
If you are a middle child in your family, draw a black coal nose.
If you are the youngest child in your family, draw a red apple nose.
If you are the only child in your family, draw a yellow banana nose.

Step 4:   Draw a number of buttons on your snow person that matches your age.

Step 5:   If you ride the bus or subway to school, draw a scarf on your snow person.
If you ride in a car to school, draw mittens.
If you walk to school, draw earmuffs.

Step 6:   Draw twig arms on your snow person.

Speaking about Winter

Have students think of things they like and dislike about winter. Give each child a plain piece of paper to draw an illustration of what he likes about winter on one side and what he doesn't like about winter on the other side. Invite students to talk about their likes and dislikes and share their pictures. Encourage students to express what emotions they feel when their liked (or disliked) characteristic of winter occurs.

I like cold weather.

winter Things

Winter Collage

Provide magazines and catalogs for children to look through for pictures of items that relate to winter. Items could include winter clothing (coats, mittens, hats, sweaters, etc.), winter sports equipment (skis, sleds, ice skates, etc.), or winter holiday items (Christmas, Hanukkah, etc. items) Direct children to cut out pictures and glue onto pieces of construction paper to make "Winter Things" collages. Pictures could include bathing suits, swimming pools, etc. Ask children why certain seasonal items would not be appropriate during another season. If desired, have students label their pictures with words.

Winter Word Fun

Play a game using winter vocabulary words and a snowman. Begin with a complete snowman drawn on a write-on/wipe-away board and blanks to represent letters in a winter word. Call on individual students to guess letters in the word. If a letter is guessed correctly, write the letter on the correct word blank(s). If an incorrect letter is guessed, erase part of the snowman. The object of the game is for students to guess the winter word before the snowman is completely melted (erased).

Temperature Graph

Below 15°	15°–30°	30°–40°	40°–50°

Winter Predictions

Winter is a great time to introduce or reinforce the reading skill of making predictions. Explain that when someone makes a prediction, it is like making a smart guess about something. Give some examples of smart guesses (and not-so-smart guesses) to help children understand this concept. Have the class compare the weather predictions from newspaper and TV to see if the predictions were accurate. Read aloud several winter-related storybooks. Have children make predictions about what will happen in the stories.

Winter Patterns
Mittens

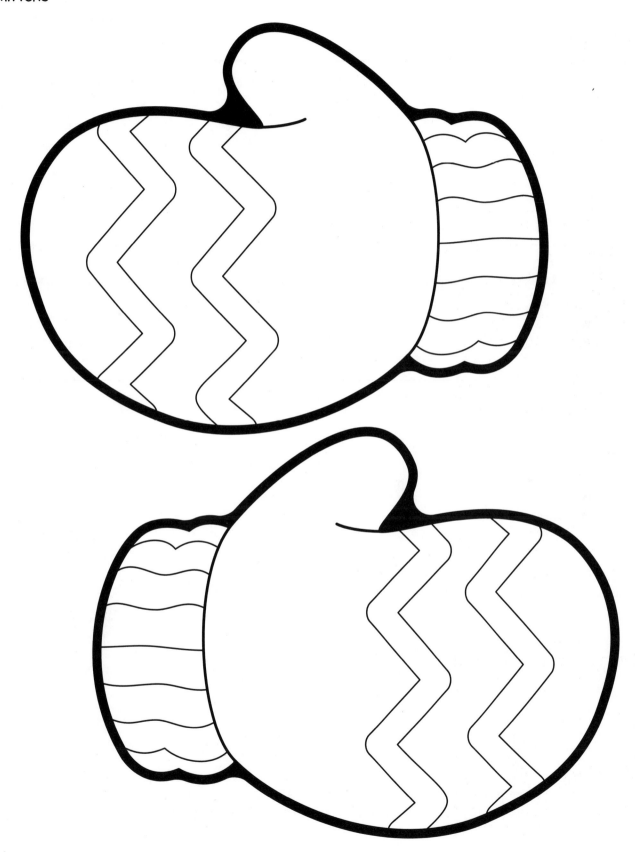

Left or Right?

Use mittens to reinforce the positions of left and right hands. Let each child wear a pair of mittens and have a partner trace the mitten outlines onto a piece of paper. Or, enlarge and copy the Mitten patterns (page 309) so that each child has one left and one right mitten. Direct children to color and glue the mitten patterns onto a piece of paper. Have student label their mitten outlines or patterns left and right.

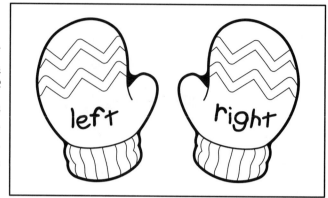

Line Up the Snowmen

Display different snowmen figures or pictures. Use ordinal position words to direct students to line up the snowmen in a specific order. After all of the snowmen are lined up, ask questions to reinforce the ordinal position words such as "Which snowman is third in line?", "What place in line is the snowman with the red hat?", etc.

Snowball Counting

Enlarge and copy a Mitten pattern (page 309) for each child. Provide each child with 20 cotton balls to represent 20 snowballs. Show children a numeral from 1 to 20 and call on an individual child to count out that many snowballs on his mitten. Let children compare their mittens to determine who has more or less snowballs. Older children can combine mittens for addition practice or remove snowballs from a mitten to practice subtraction. Have children group snowballs into groups of fives or tens to count how many snowballs are on multiple mittens.

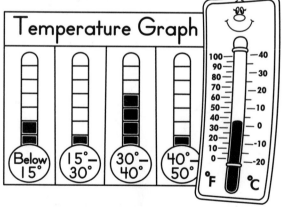

Winter Weather Measurement

Show students an outdoor thermometer and explain that it can be used to measure the temperature of the air outside. Let students look at the numbers on the thermometer and then place it outside in a safe place. Collect data over several weeks of the temperature at certain times of the day. Use the data to make a graph of the temperatures.

Winter Patterns

Gather winter-related stickers or stamps for children to use to make patterns on sentence strips. For younger children, allow them to finish a simple pattern that you start. Older children can create their own patterns using stickers or stamps. If desired, use the pattern strips as a bulletin board border or let children turn their pattern strips into fun winter headbands.

Winter

Math

Shapely Snowmen

Copy the Shapely Snowmen patterns (page 312) for each student. Have students identify the shapes and then cut out the patterns. Direct students to use the shapes to create snowman pictures by gluing the shapes onto construction paper. Have students draw smaller shapes for facial features and buttons.

Winter Estimation

Show a mitten and a set of objects, such as teddy bear counters. Have each student estimate how many of the objects will fit inside the mitten. (Remember, some mittens stretch out. You might want to use a mitten made from non-stretchable material!) After the mitten is full, have the class count out loud as you remove each object from the mitten. Let students discuss if their estimates were close to the actual number. Repeat the estimation activity several times with different types of objects or with a larger mitten.

Sort by Season

Bring in three boxes and various items that represent winter or summer. For example, include winter items such as gloves, an ice scraper, a holiday ornament, etc., and summer items such as a bathing suit, sunglasses, sand bucket, etc. Provide at least 10 items to represent each season. Label one box "winter" and another box "summer." Put all of the items into the remaining box. Pull out one item at a time and have students decide which box it belongs in. Encourage students to tell why they placed an item in a particular box.

Did You Wear a Hat to School?	
■	
■	
■	
■	■
■	■
YES	NO

Winter Graphs

Use winter months to practice graphing skills. Choose a winter-themed topic and poll students. Some topics might include: *Favorite Winter Holiday, Favorite Winter Activity, Do You Like Snow?, Did You Wear a Hat to School?, Favorite Winter Month,* and *Favorite Season of the Year.* Record students' answers on a graph. Discuss math vocabulary words such as *most, less, equal, fewer,* and *more.* Teach students the various types of graphs by creating a different graph for each winter topic.

Winter Patterns
Shapely Snowmen

Animals in Winter

Activate student knowledge for a discussion on animals in winter by asking, "What do we do differently in winter?" Prompt, if necessary, until students name changes in our behavior such as wearing heavier clothing, using heat to warm our houses, etc. Discuss how and why some animals hibernate in the winter. Then, discuss how and why some animals migrate in the winter. Gather pictures of animals that hibernate and animals that migrate. Let students use these for reference as they create posters about animals in winter. Direct students to divide large pieces of construction paper into three columns. Have students label the columns *Hibernators*, *Migrators*, and *Me*. Have students illustrate animals that are hibernators or migrators in the appropriate columns. Then, for the *Me* column, have each student draw a picture of herself that shows something she does in the winter months.

Water Experiment

Show children a foam cup filled with water and ask them to predict what will happen if the cup is put outside during a cold winter night. Record the children's predictions on chart paper. Put the cup of water outside on a night that is cold enough for the water to freeze. (If you live in warmer climates, put the cup of water in a freezer.) The next morning, show the class what happened to the water and have them check to see if their predictions were correct. Discuss how the water was a liquid and it became a solid when it froze. If desired, also have children predict what would happen if the frozen water is placed in an electric frying pan. Melt the ice in the pan and have students observe the ice melting back into liquid. When the water begins to develop steam, point out that the water has taken a new form. Introduce children to the term evaporation as they observe the water "disappearing."

Polar Regions

Show the students a globe and point out the polar regions (north pole and south pole). Explain the climates of these regions and discuss how the climates affect the types of animals that live in polar regions. Using the Venn Diagram pattern (page 316), have students make Venn diagrams to compare living in their city and living in a polar region.

Adapted Songs

Hooray for Winter!

(to the tune of "London Bridge")
Fall has ended, winter is here, winter is here, winter is here.
Fall has ended, winter is here.
Hooray for Winter!

Other verses:
Get your coats and mittens, too…
Bundle up, the weather is cold…
Snowy days, we want them soon…
Let's drink hot cocoa to warm us up…

Movement Activities

Snowman Dance

Play classical music and let students dance like falling snow. Then, have them "grow" into snowmen. After a few moments of standing like snowmen, have the students slowly "melt" to the ground.

Migration Formation

Share information about how geese fly together in a "V" when migrating to warmer climates. Take students outside to a large open area. Place them in a "V" formation and tell the student at the point of the V that he will be leading the other "geese" south. Tell the class that you will give a signal when the leader should move to the back of the flock and a new leader should take over. Have the students "honk" (or give them party horns) to encourage the other "geese" to stay in formation!

Finger Play

Bundle Up!

Zip up your coat; put a hat on your head.
(Pretend to zip up coat and on a hat.)
Pull on your boots if you want to sled!
(Pretend to put snow boots on.)
Mittens on hands, wrap your scarf on tight.
(Pretend to put mittens on and wrap a scarf around neck.)
Better bundle up or the snow will bite!
(Hug self and then snap hands together like alligator jaws.)

Winter Round Robin

Give students an opportunity to work together to create an imaginative winter story. Have students sit in a circle and explain the rules for cooperation: listen to the speaker, respect others' contributions, and wait for your turn to speak. Show students a winter hat (or other winter object) and tell them that whoever has the hat is the speaker, and everyone else should quietly listen. Begin an imaginative winter story such as "One morning I woke up and there was 10 feet of snow on the ground!" or "Once, I went sledding down a really steep hill." Then, pass the hat around the circle and allow each child to contribute to the story. If desired, record the story with a tape recorder so that you can transcribe it later for students.

Community Service Project

During the holiday season, discuss with your class the difference between things we want and things we need. Explain that there are some people who have a hard time getting things that they need, such as food and warm clothing, and that winter can be difficult without these necessities. Provide a large cardboard box for students to decorate. Send home a letter to parents requesting donations of canned goods and old clothing (or other items). Have the class set a goal of how many items they would like to collect for the donation box. As children bring in donations, have them place the items in the decorated box. After the class has reached its donation goal, arrange for pickup or delivery of the donated items to a local service agency. Students will gain an understanding of helping others less fortunate and the importance of teamwork!

Wintertime Venn

Pair each student and have the two discuss among themselves the things they like to do in winter. Point out that there are some things that one person may like to do that another person does not. Encourage students to celebrate their differences. Give each pair of students a copy of the Venn Diagram pattern (page 316). Explain that there are two circles on a Venn diagram, one circle for each student. On the outer section of a circle, have each student write his name in the blank and draw a picture of something he likes to do in winter, but his partner does not like to do. The two circles overlap to create a space where a winter activity that they both like to do should be drawn. Allow the pairs to share their Venn diagrams with the rest of the class.

Winter Patterns
Venn Diagram

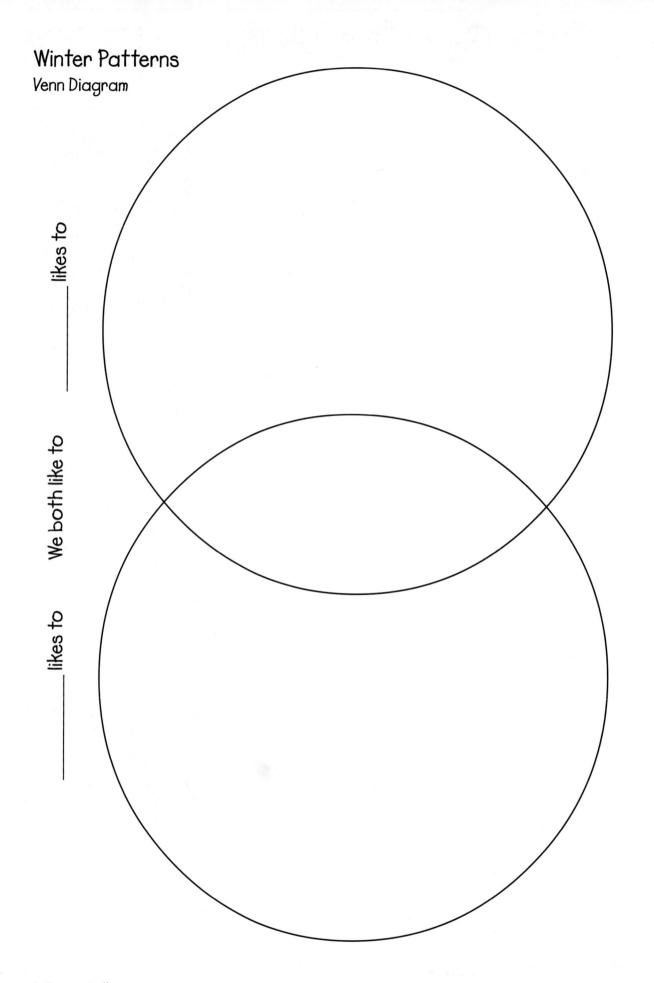

_____ likes to

We both like to

_____ likes to

CD-0817 _Terrific Themes for Year-Round Fun_

Winter

Art

Snowman Mosaics

Provide a piece of dark blue or black construction paper for each child. Have each child use white chalk to draw three circles to represent a snowman's body. (You may want to provide a circular object for children to trace.) Provide small cut pieces of white paper or white rice for children to glue inside of the circles to create mosaics. Be sure to have children put some pieces of the cut paper or rice on the "ground" to look like fallen snow. After the glue has dried, have children glue facial features, hats, scarves, arms, etc. using construction paper or fabric cutouts.

Glittery Snowflakes

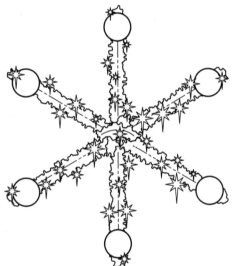

Gather white chenille craft sticks, glue, silver glitter, and clear, white, or silver beads. (Make sure the threading holes in the beads are large enough for a chenille craft stick to go through.) Demonstrate how to twist three chenille craft sticks together to create a six-pointed snowflake. Give each child three chenille craft sticks and assist as students twist their craft sticks into snowflakes. Once everyone has a snowflake, provide each child with six beads. Show students how to slide one bead on the end of each snowflake point, and then twist the ends into knots to make the beads stay in place. Allow students to squeeze glue on top of the snowflakes and sprinkle glitter on top of the glue. After the glue has dried, shake off excess glitter and tie a string to one end of each snowflake. Hang these around the classroom or on windows to create a winter wonderland!

Snow Globes

Let students create a snowy winter scene that they can look at all year long by making snow globes. Collect a baby food jar and lid for each student. Wash the jars thoroughly before using. Gather small, inexpensive plastic holiday ornaments or cake decorations that represent winter. Allow each student to select a decoration and use waterproof glue to securely glue the decoration onto the inside of the lid. After the glue has dried, let each child fill his baby food jar 3/4 full with water and add one teaspoon of white or silver glitter. Add a teaspoon of cooking oil to each jar. Have students squeeze waterproof glue around the inside edges of the lids and screw the lids onto the jars. Have students leave jars in upside-down positions (lids on bottom) and allow glue to dry overnight with jars in upside-down positions. The next day, let students turn their globes over and shake to see their snow globes in action.

Easy Snowflake Stampers

Bring in uncooked wagon-wheeled shaped pasta for students to use as snowflake stampers. Provide white tempera paint or a white ink stamp pad and blue or black construction paper. Allow students to explore with the materials on their own and create individualized snowflake art.

Build-a-Snowman Center

Reproduce several copies of the Shapely Snowmen pattern (page 312). Cut out and laminate these pieces and place them in a "Build-a-Snowman" learning center with write-on/wipe-away markers, buttons, hats and scarves cut from a variety of material, beans, and any other materials that students could use to build a snowman. Allow students visiting the center to build several different snowmen designs.

Bagel Bird Feeders

This art project will create a wintertime snack for your feathered friends. Bring in miniature-sized bagels, peanut butter, and bird seed. Lightly toast the bagels. Have students spread peanut butter onto bagel halves and then sprinkle with bird seed. Loop a piece of yarn through each bagel hole and tie a knot. Hang bagels on a tree, preferably near a classroom window. Let students observe the birds enjoying their snack gifts!

Hibernation Stations

After students have developed an understanding of hibernation, allow each to create "hibernation stations." Have each student bring a shoe box from home. Let students glue raffia, straw, or craft moss on the insides and outsides of their boxes. Provide each student with a copy of one Hibernating Animal patterns (page 319). Have students color their animals and place them inside their boxes. Display these "hibernation stations" around the room. (When the class is getting too noisy, remind students that there are "sleeping" animals in the room!)

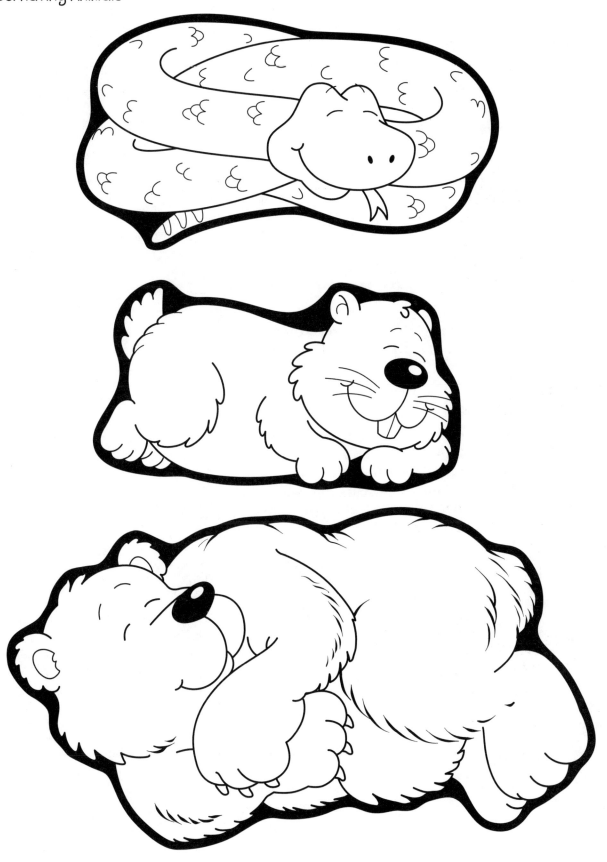

CD-0817 *Terrific Themes for Year-Round Fun*

Sleeping Bears

Have children lie down and pretend to be bears sleeping in winter. They should lie on their backs, keeping as still as possible, but with their eyes open. Choose someone to be "it." The child who is "it" should walk around and try to make the sleeping bears laugh by making funny faces, but not touching them. Anyone who giggles is out. The last bear left becomes the next "it."

Mitten Memory

Bring in several pairs of mittens or gloves. Show all of the pairs before putting them into a large paper bag. Divide the class into two teams. Call on one person at a time to come to the bag and, with eyes closed, pull out two items. If the two items are a matching pair, have the student place them beside the bag and award that person's team one point. If the two items do not match, instruct the student to put them back into the bag. Encourage students to use their sense of touch to find matching pairs. After all of the pairs have been matched, count up each team's points to determine a winner.

Winter Charades

Have students act out scenes from winter activities. Use the suggestions listed below or come up with your own. Call on one student at a time to come to the front of the class. Whisper into his ear which winter activity you want him to dramatize. Ask other students to watch and guess what winter activity he is pretending to do.

Have students pretend to . . .
- build a snowman.
- ice skate.
- snow ski.
- put on winter clothes.
- shovel snow from a sidewalk.
- hibernate.
- migrate.
- catch snowflakes on their tongues.
- make snow angels.
- have a snowball fight.

Crispy Snowballs

Melt $^1/_2$ stick of margarine in a microwave. While the margarine is still hot, add one bag of miniature marshmallows and stir until completely melted. Add six cups of rice cereal and stir until well coated. Provide students with a piece of wax paper. When the mixture has cooled, spoon out some of it onto each student's wax paper. Allow students to form the mixture into snowball shapes and eat their creations.

Snow Cones

Bring in an ice shaver or ice crusher, ice, cherry juice, and disposable cups and spoons. Shave or crush ice and use an ice-cream scoop to fill each child's cup with ice pieces. Slowly pour cherry (or any flavor) juice on top of each ice scoop until covered. Do not to pour too much juice or the snow cones will become watery.

Edible Snowmen

Bring in several cans of refrigerated biscuits. Give each child about $^1/_2$ cup of the biscuit dough, a handful of raisins or candy-covered chocolates, and a piece of wax paper. Have each student form her dough into the shape of a snowman. Direct students to place raisins or candy pieces on the dough for eyes, noses, mouths, and buttons. Use a spatula to pick up and place each student's snowman on a cookie sheet. (You may want to make a diagram of the cookie sheet and write down the locations of students' snowmen.) Follow the package directions to bake the snowmen. When the snowmen are finished baking, provide honey for students to spread on their snacks and eat.

Hot Chocolate

On a cold school day, bring in an electric slow cooker to heat up hot chocolate for students to enjoy during the day. For each student in the class, you will need: 2 tablespoons unsweetened cocoa, $^1/_2$ cup of water, 2 teaspoons of sugar, and 1 cup of milk. You might want to include a math extension by allowing each child to measure out her own ingredients to put in the slow cooker. After the ingredients have been added to the slow cooker for each student, heat on high long enough for the cocoa and sugar to dissolve. Then, turn the heat down to medium or low heat so that it does not become too hot. After an hour or so, test the hot chocolate to see if it is ready. Provide marshmallows to make the hot chocolate extra delicious!

Blueberry Cobbler

Enjoy this snack in honor of hibernating bears. Remind students that before a bear hibernates, he fills up his tummy so that he will not have to eat for several months. Wild berries are a favorite treat among bears, and for this treat you will use blueberries. Melt one stick of margarine in a 9" x 13" pan. Mix one cup of milk, one cup of sugar, and one cup of flour. Pour the mixture over the melted margarine. Add one quart of washed blueberries. Do not stir. Bake at 350°F for 30 -45 minutes.

Woodland Animals

Contents

Lacing Bears

Make copies of the Lacing Bear pattern (page 324). Color each bear pattern. Glue patterns onto tagboard, laminate, and rim around the patterns. Use a hole punch to make holes about $1/2$" away from the edge and about 1" apart around the borders of the bear patterns. Tie a 2' to 3' piece of yarn to one hole on each bear. Use masking tape or transparent tape to stiffen the ends of the yarn like shoestrings. Allow children to lace the bears during center time.

Turtle Buttoning

Copy the Turtle Buttoning patterns (pages 325-326). Gather at least three different colors of felt and create three turtles from the felt for buttoning practice. Before you sew on the buttons (sew on the X marks), you may wish to draw a design on the opposite side like the outside of a turtle shell. Mix all of the pieces, except the shells, together. Show the pieces to the children and explain that they should find the head, tail, and feet that are the same color as each shell. Allow children to match the colors and button the head, tail, and legs to each turtle's shell. When the turtles are buttoned, have the child turn the project over to reveal a felt turtle.

The Three Bears Q & A

Obtain a copy of Goldilocks and the Three Bears. Gather children and explain that you will read the story to them. Tell them to listen very carefully (even if they have heard the story many times) because you will ask questions about the story when you are finished reading. Read the story and after the story is finished, ask the children several questions requiring them to recall what happened first, last, etc. Also, have children think about how the three bears could have avoided their uninvited guest. If you have an advanced group, add details that are not traditional to the story such as naming characters, describing setting, identifying real or make-believe elements, and comparing plot and characters with other books the class has read. Use this activity with a variety of books about woodland animals.

Goldilocks and the Three Bears

Woodland Animals Pattern
Lacing Bear

CD-0817 *Terrific Themes for Year-Round Fun*

Woodland Animal Pattern
Turtle Buttoning

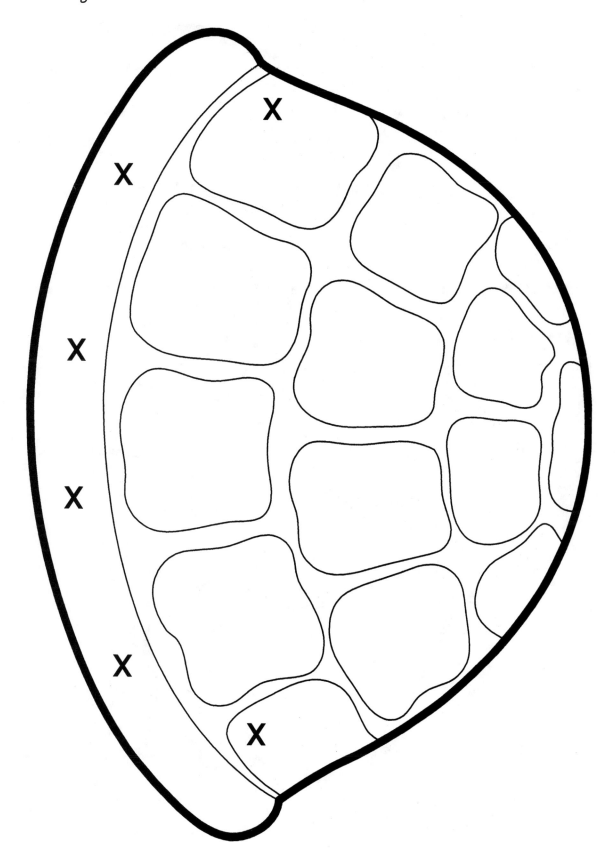

Woodland Animals Patterns
Turtle Buttoning

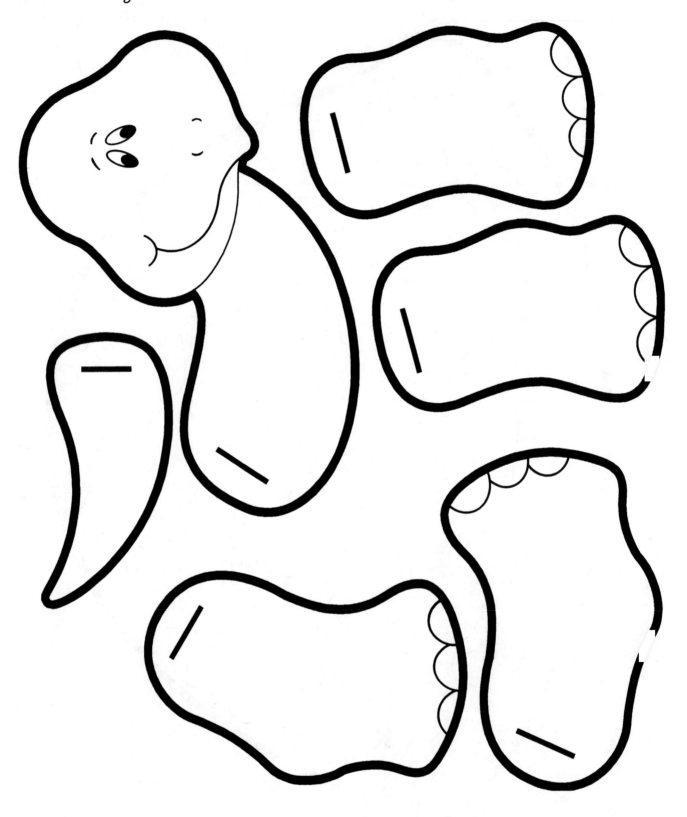

CD-0817 *Terrific Themes for Year-Round Fun*

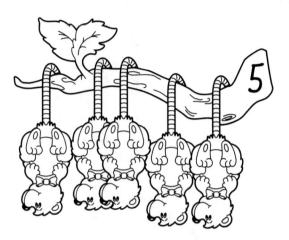

Opossum Count

Make 10 copies of the Opossum Count patterns (page 328) onto tagboard. Cut out the patterns and write a numeral from 1 to 10 on each branch. Invite over a pair of children and explain that they should take turns picking a branch. The child who chooses a branch should read the numeral written on it. She should then count out that number of opossums. Next, she should hang the opossums from the branch and have her partner check her work. It is then partner's turn, and so on. After each child has had a turn, place the activity as a selection during center time.

Five Little Ducks By Size

Copy on yellow construction paper the Five Little Ducks By Size patterns (pages 329-330). Cut out the ducks and decorate. Show the ducks to children and ask them to describe them to you. Children should realize that the ducks are different sizes. Have children place the ducks from smallest to largest or largest to smallest. This may be done on a table, on the wall or chalkboard with tape, or on a flannel board by attaching felt or hook-and-loop fastener to the back of each duck.

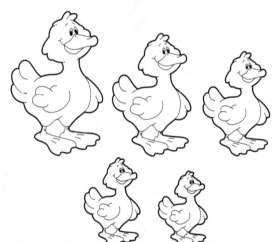

Woodland Animal Patterning

Make one copy of the Woodland Animal Patterning worksheet (page 331) for each child. Talk with children about patterns. Draw a few simple patterns using circles, squares, and triangles on the chalkboard or chart paper. Have children continue the patterns by saying aloud which shapes should come next. Tell them that you will give them a worksheet with patterns of woodland animals. Tell them that they should look at each pattern. At the end of each pattern will be two smaller animals. Explain that they should circle the animal that should be next in the pattern. As children work, walk around the room and have children "read" the patterns and explain how they made their choices.

Woodland Animals Patterns
Opossum Count

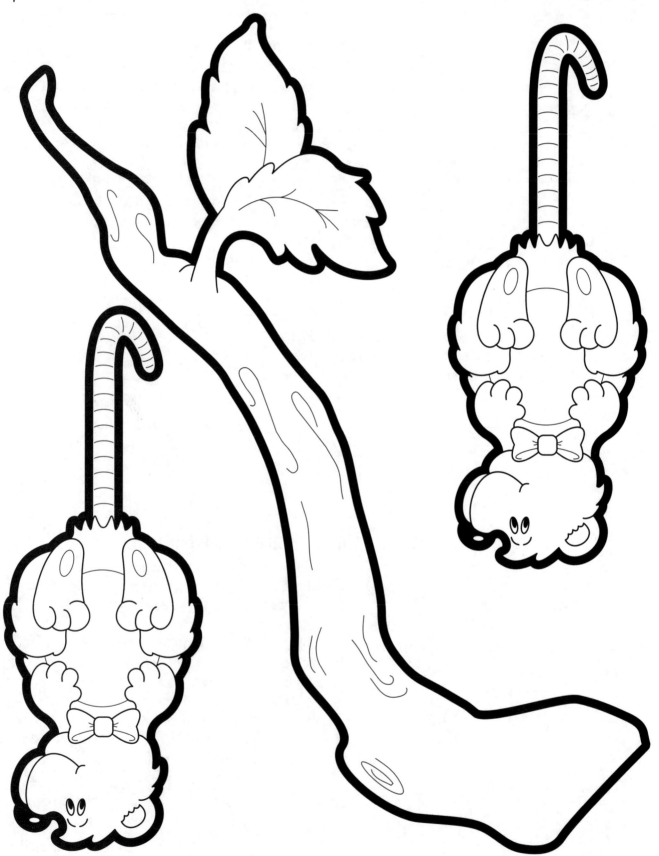

CD-0817 *Terrific Themes for Year-Round Fun*

Woodland Animals Patterns
Five Little Ducks By Size

CD-0817 *Terrific Themes for Year-Round Fun*

Woodland Animals Patterns
Five Little Ducks By Size

Name _____

Woodland Animal Patterning

Circle the animal in the box that best completes each pattern.

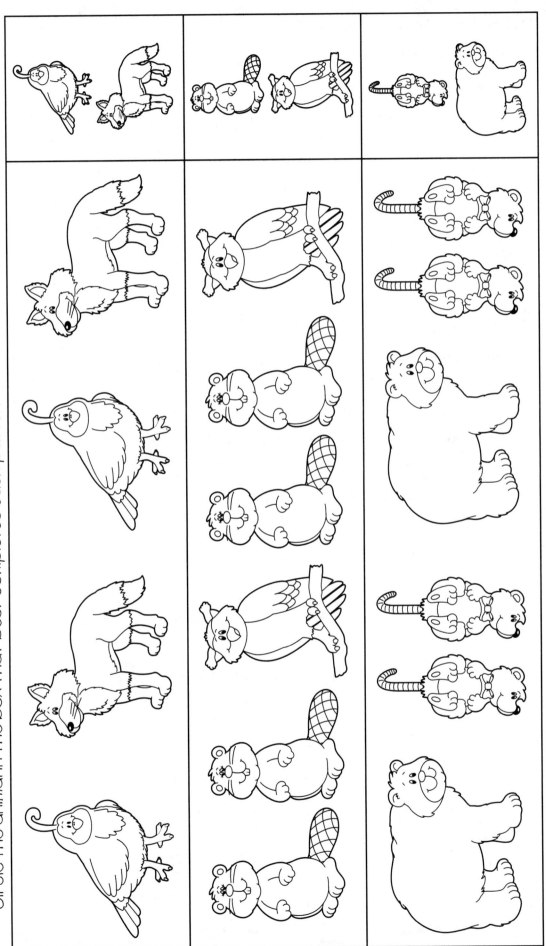

Growing Carrots

Have your class grow carrots (a favorite snack of rabbits) by allowing each child to fill a shallow dish with water (paper or plastic bowls work well). Cut the top off a carrot for each child. Help each child suspend the top of the carrot in the water by inserting a few toothpicks horizontally into the carrot and resting the toothpicks on the edge of the bowl. (Make sure to have the bottom of the carrot in the water.) In a few days, the carrots will begin to sprout. When they have sprouted, allow children to move their carrots to soil. You may do this outside in the ground or have children plant their carrots in soil in paper cups to take home. If you plant the carrots at school, allow children to water, observe, and record the growth daily.

Foods Animals Eat

Copy the Foods Animals Eat Sorting Cards (page 333). Gather children have them name as many foods as they can that woodland animals eat. Show children the cards and explain that as you show them each card, you would like them to say "yes" if it is a food a woodland animal would eat, or "no" if it is a food a woodland animal would not eat. After the group has sorted the cards one time, mix up the cards and have volunteers sort the cards into the two piles again. You may also wish to have the cards available for small group exploration during center time.

Feeding Station

Set out a feeding station of any sort for a bird or a squirrel. Place the feeding station in a location that can be seen from a classroom window if possible. Give children several opportunities daily to observe and describe what they see happening at the feeding station. Have children make note of any feeding patterns they may observe.

Flies, Walks, or Swims?

Copy the Flies, Walks, or Swims? sheet (page 334). Also copy the Woodland Animals patterns (pages 335-343), and cut them out. Gather children and talk with them about the way the various woodland animals move. For example, ask children how a bluebird gets from one place to another. Repeat with a squirrel, beaver, etc. Remind children that beavers both walk and swim, but walking is their main mode of transportation. Ask children to name other animals that move in more than one way and have them name the animal's primary way of movement. After the discussion, show children the Flies, Walks, or Swims? sheet and have them sort the animal cards into appropriate categories.

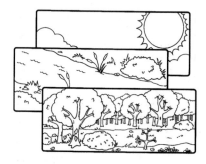

Woodland Animals Patterns
Foods Animals Eat Sorting Cards

French Fries

Peanuts

Seeds

Woodland Animals Patterns
Flies, Walks, or Swims?

Woodland Animals Patterns
Deer, Rabbit

Woodland Animals Patterns
Bear, Raccoon

CD-0817 Terrific Themes for Year-Round Fun

Woodland Animals Patterns
Woodpecker, Duck, Robin

Woodland Animals Patterns
Bluebird, Squirrel, Fish, Frog

CD-0817 *Terrific Themes for Year-Round Fun*

Woodland Animals Patterns
Skunk, Fox

Woodland Animals Patterns
Mouse, Beaver

CD-0817 *Terrific Themes for Year-Round Fun*

Woodland Animals Patterns
Snake, Gopher

Woodland Animals Patterns
Chipmunk, Porcupine

CD-0817 *Terrific Themes for Year-Round Fun*

Woodland Animals Patterns
Opossum, Turtle

Traditional Songs

"The Bear Went Over the Mountain"
"Do Re Mi"
"Five Green and Speckled Frogs"
"Five Little Ducks"
"Hickory Dickory Dock"
"In a Cabin in the Wood"
"Little Bunny Foo Foo"
"Over in the Meadow"
"There Once Was a Green Little Frog"
"Two Little Blackbirds"

Finger Plays

My Turtle (Traditional)

This is my turtle, (Make a fist with thumb extended.)
He lives in a shell. (Tuck thumb inside fist.)
He likes his home very well.
He pokes his head out
When he wants to eat, (Extend thumb from fist.)
And pulls it back again
When he wants to sleep (Tuck thumb in fist.)

The Wise Old Owl (Traditional)

A wise old owl sat in an oak. (Make a fist and set on other forearm.)
The more he heard, the less he spoke. (Cup hand around ear, then cover lips.)
The less he spoke, the more he heard. (Cover lips, then cup hand around ear.)
Why aren't we all like that wise old bird? (Hold hands out questioningly.)

Adapted Song

I'm a Little Gopher
(to the tune of "I'm a Little Teapot")

I'm a little gopher, furry and brown.
I play in the sun and sleep underground.
Sometimes you will see me playing outside,
But when I'm scared, in my burrow I hide.

Movement Activities

Scarf Wings

Let children use scarves or scrap material to flutter like wings. Play music and allow children to move around the room moving the fabric up and down like birds' wings. Encourage children to role-play what it is like to be a bird in different types of weather: calm, windy, stormy, etc.

Froggy Hop

Select an upbeat piece of music and allow children to hop around the room like frogs.

Fast Bunnies and Slow Turtles

Choose a piece of music that has both quick and slow tempos. Allow children to move to the music. Encourage them to move quickly like bunnies when the tempo is fast, and slowly like turtles when the music is slow. A record player with variable speeds is handy for this activity so that you can regulate the speed yourself.

Nocturnal vs. Diurnal

Copy each Woodland Animal pattern (pages 335-343). Ask children if they have ever heard the word "nocturnal." If no one has, explain to them that nocturnal means active at night. Explain that "diurnal" means active during the day. Ask children if they have ever seen any woodland animals out at night. Discuss some animals that are nocturnal: owls, skunks, raccoons, foxes, opossums, and porcupines. Have the group sort the animal pattern cards into two categories: nocturnal woodland animals and diurnal woodland animals. Allow children to do this activity in small groups during center time.

Where Do Animals Live?

Begin a discussion with children about where woodland animals live. See how many of the homes the children can name. Point out that some of the animals, such as skunks, may live in a variety of homes; most skunks live in dens, but some live in trees. Have the children discuss the positive and negative aspects of each animal home. Let children tell you which animal home they think would be the best to live in.

Animals That Hibernate

Talk with children about the word "hibernation." Ask them if they have ever heard the word, then ask if they can define it. Explain that when animals hibernate, they spend the winter in a warm, safe place in a type of deep sleep. Talk about how the animals often eat a lot of food during fall to build up fat in their bodies to keep them fed during the winter. Ask children if they know which woodland animals hibernate. The following animals hibernate (some varieties in warmer climates may not need to): bears, bats, ground squirrels, and chipmunks. Allow children to discuss the various aspects of hibernation. (An interesting note: Beavers spend the entire winter in their lodges, but do not hibernate. They gather food and store it.)

Woodland Animals

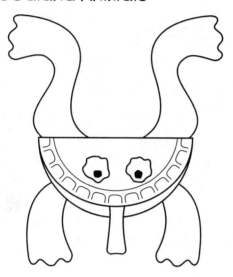

Funny Frog

Gather two cotton balls, one small strip of red or pink felt, and one paper plate for each child. Also, gather green tempera paint; paintbrushes; red, green, and black construction paper; scissors; and glue. Each child should fold his paper plate in half, then paint it green on the outside. While the paint is drying, he should cut out frog feet, tongue, and eyes from the construction paper as shown in the example. When the paint has dried, allow each child to cut out and add a felt tongue and glue on cotton-ball eyes to complete his funny frog.

Hand Bunny

Have each child place his hand on a piece of construction paper (with fingers together and thumb extended) and trace. He is then to turn the paper sideways and decorate the hand outline as a bunny using crayons and cotton balls.

Brown Bear

Copy the Brown Bear pattern (page 347) for each child. Gather brown materials such as sawdust, coffee grounds, etc. You may offer one material, or allow children to choose the material they would like to use for their brown bears. Set the brown material(s), along with glue, on the art table. Allow children to spread a thin layer of glue over their bear pictures, then sprinkle the sawdust or coffee grounds over the glue to make a picture of a brown bear. Children should let their pictures dry thoroughly, then shake off excess material.

Twig Frames

If you have trees on the playground, take children outside to gather twigs. If you do not have access to twigs on or near your playground, have each child bring in a small bag of twigs. Place the twigs and glue on an art table. Allow children to illustrated and color their favorite woodland animals on construction paper, then "frame" them by gluing a selection of twigs around the edges of the pictures.

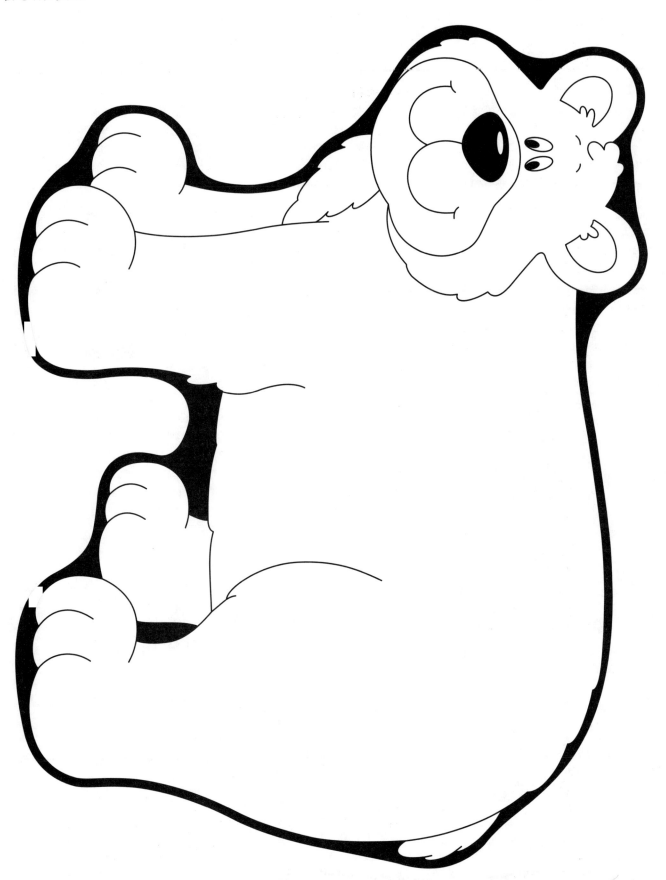

Whooo is Calling?

Gather children and have them sit in a circle. Place a chair in front of the group with its back to children. Choose one child to be the first to sit in the chair. Explain that you will point to a child in the group. That child is to say, "Whooo!" like an owl and the child sitting in the chair tries to guess who is making the sound. Allow each child to have a turn being the owl and the guesser.

Bunny Number Hop

Gather a few regular dice or, if possible, make a larger die from a small square box. Gather children and explain that they will play a counting and hopping game. Allow one child at a time to roll a die and count the number of dots. They are then to count aloud as they hop like a bunny that number of times. After children understand the game, divide them into small groups to shorten the wait time between turns.

Bear Mouth Box Toss

Gather a large box and make a Bear Mouth Toss Box. To create, cut a large hole in the box. Then, draw a bear face on construction paper and attach it to the box so the mouth is centered over the hole. To play, gather a few beanbags. Allow a few children at a time to take turns trying to toss the beanbags into the mouth of the bear. You may encourage children to keep note of their best record and try to improve on it each turn.

Frog Hop Races

Gather children and explain that they will participate in Frog Hop Races. Designate a starting line and a finish line. Line up children at the starting line and have them race in the following silly frog ways: fewest hops to the finish line, tiny frog hops, high frog hops, etc. Emphasize to children that the goal is to get to the finish line in the described manner.

Bear Cave Hunt

Gather at least one medium-sized to large box per child (boxes should be large enough for a child to fit in). Have children help you to spread the boxes out over the playground, with the opening facing to the side. Tell children that these are "bear caves." Explain that they are to walk or run around the playground until you whistle. When they hear the whistle, they are to run and hide in one of the bear caves.

Award Patterns

minutes of

FREE TIME

For _____

Signed _____

Date _____

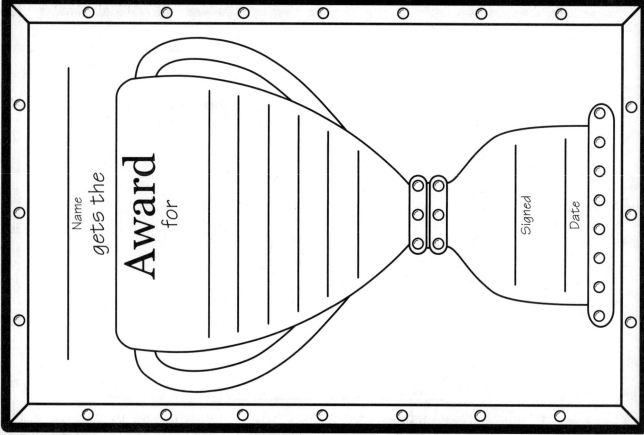

Name _____

gets the

Award

for _____

Signed _____

Date _____

 CD-0817 *Terrific Themes for Year-Round Fun*

YOU DID IT!

Name _____

For _____

_____

Signed _____

Date _____

_____ shows

Tremendous Teamwork!

Signed _____ **Date** _____

CD-0817 *Terrific Themes for Year-Round Fun*

_____ can

"Bee" Proud!

"Bee" cause _____

Signed _____

Date _____

_____ is a

SUPER CITIZEN!

Date _____

Signed _____

CD-0817 *Terrific Themes for Year-Round Fun*